“*Two Bow’s Length or Nearer*”

Discourses on the Inestimable Greatness of Sayyidinā Muhammad ﷺ

Shaykh Muhammad Hisham Kabbani

"Two Bow's Length or Nearer"

Discourses on the Inestimable Greatness of Sayyidinā Muhammad ﷺ

Shaykh Muhammad Hisham Kabbani

INSTITUTE FOR SPIRITUAL & CULTURAL ADVANCEMENT

Published and Distributed by:

Institute for Spiritual and Cultural Advancement (ISCA)
17195 Silver Parkway, #401
Fenton, MI 48430 USA
Tel: (810) 593-1222
Email: staff@naqshbandi.org
Web: http://www.naqshbandi.org

First Edition: September 2025

"TWO-BOW'S LENGTH OR NEARER"
ISBN: 978-1-938058-44-8

Library of Congress Cataloging-in-Publication Data

TBD

The late Mawlānā Shaykh Muhammad Hisham Kabbani in the renowned Naqshbandi *zawiya* in Fenton, Michigan where, since 1999, he established the Ramadan tradition of reciting the *adab* in congregation before sunrise, accompanied by an inspired spiritual discourse after the Dawn Prayer (Fajr). This book is a compiled sampling of some of these discourses over many years with a special focus on the greatness and spiritual reality of Prophet Muhammad ﷺ.

Contents

About the Author xiii
Preface xv
Publisher's Notes xvii
Transliteration xviii
Masters of the Naqshbandi-Haqqani Golden Chain xix
Recitation before Every Association xxiii
The Spiritual Significance of Isrā' and Mi'rāj 3
Spiritual Vehicles of the Prophet ﷺ 7
Ibrāhīm's ﷺ Vision; Sayyidina Muhammad's ﷺ Reality 8
The Reality of Prophet ﷺ in the Presence of Allah 15
The Immense Greatness of Prophet Muhammad ﷺ 27
We Can Never Give the Prophet ﷺ His Rights 33
'Alif is for "Allah" and *Mīm* is for "Muhammad ﷺ" 43
The Light of Muhammad ﷺ is the Fabric of All Creation 53
The Unique Station of Ḥabībullāh ﷺ 67
Allah's Possessiveness 75
Secrets of Isrā' and Mi'rāj 83
Secrets of Isrā' and Mi'rāj, Part2 89
Secrets of Isrā' and Mi'rāj, Part 3 99
Awliyā' take from the Secrets of the Prophet ﷺ 107
The Arrogance of Some 'Doctors' 107
Allah Created the Judgment to Show the Greatness of Prophet Muhammad ﷺ 121
Only Prophet ﷺ Can Carry the Greatness of Qur'ān 129
The Four Levels of *Dhikr* and the Heart of Sayyidinā 'Alī ﷺ 133
To Kiss the Holy Threshold of Prophet ﷺ 141
To Follow in the Prophet's Footsteps ﷺ 143
The Difference between an *'Alim* and a *Walī* 146
Passing of the World through the Eye of the Needle 159
Power of the Shaykh 159
The Last Seven Breaths 160
Earth, Moon and Sun 162
Islamic Calendar and Holy Days 165
Important Dates 165
Glossary 169

About the Author

World-renowned religious scholar, the late Shaykh Muhammad Hisham Kabbani has been featured many times in the ground-breaking annual compilation published by Georgetown University, *The 500 Most Influential Muslims in the World*. For decades he has promoted traditional Islamic principles of peace, tolerance, love, compassion and brotherhood, while rigorously opposing extremism in all its forms. He hails from a respected family of traditional Islamic scholars, which includes the former head of the Association of Muslim Scholars of Lebanon and the present grand mufti (highest Islamic religious authority) of Lebanon.

Shaykh Kabbani was highly trained, both as a western scientist and an Islamic scholar. He received a bachelor's degree in chemistry and later studied medicine. Under the instruction of Shaykh ʿAbdAllāh al-Fa'iz ad-Daghestani, upon whose personal notes this book is based, he holds a degree in Islamic Divine Law. Shaykh Muḥammad Nazim Adil al-Haqqani, world leader of the Naqshbandi-Haqqani Sufi Order, authorized him to guide students around the world in the ancient spiritual practices of Sufism.

In his long-standing endeavor to promote a better understanding of traditional Islam, in February 2010, Shaykh Kabbani hosted HRH Charles, the Prince of Wales at a cultural event at the revered Old Trafford Stadium in Manchester, U.K. He has hosted two international conferences in the U.S., and regional conferences on a host of issues, which attracted moderate Muslim scholars from Asia, the Far East, Middle East, Africa, U.K. and Eastern Europe. His counsel is sought by journalists, academics, policymakers and government leaders.

For forty years, Shaykh Kabbani consistently promoted peaceful cooperation among people of all beliefs. Since the early 1990s, he launched numerous endeavors to bring moderate Muslims into the mainstream. Often at great personal risk, he was instrumental in awakening Muslim social consciousness regarding the religious duty to stand firm against extremism and terrorism, for the benefit of all. Towards this goal, his bright, hopeful outlook and tireless campaign to spread the light of divine consciousness aided millions in understanding the difference between moderate mainstream Muslims and minority extremist sects.

In the United States, Shaykh Kabbani served as Chairman, Islamic Supreme Council of America; Founder, Naqshbandi Sufi Order of America; Advisor, World Organization for Resource Development and Education; Chairman, As-Sunnah Foundation of America; and Founder, *The Muslim Magazine*. In the United Kingdom, Shaykh Kabbani was advisor to Sufi Muslim Council, which consults to the British government on public policy and social and religious issues.

Among over 30 titles by Shaykh Kabbani are: At the Feet of My Master (2010, 2 vols.), The Nine-fold Ascent (2009), *Banquet for the Soul* (2008), *Illuminations* (2007), *Universe Rising* (2007), *Symphony of Remembrance* (2007), *A Spiritual Commentary on the Chapter of Sincerity* (2006), The *Sufi Science of Self-Realization* (Fons Vitae, 2005), *Keys to the Divine Kingdom* (2005), *Classical Islam and the Naqshbandi Sufi Order* (2004), *The Naqshbandi Sufi Tradition Guideboo /-09876 h5gf k* (2004), *The Approach of Armageddon? An Islamic Perspective* (2003), *Encyclopedia of Muḥammad's Women Companions and the Traditions They Related* (1998, with Dr. Laleh Bakhtiar), *Encyclopedia of Islamic Doctrine* (7 vols. 1998), *Angels Unveiled* (1996), *The Naqshbandi Sufi Way* (1995), *and Remembrance of God Liturgy of the Sufi Naqshbandi Masters* (1994).

Preface

This book is based on the divinely inspired spiritual discourses of the late Mawlānā Shaykh Hisham Kabbani, who spoke from the heart of his master the late global head of the Naqshbandi-Haqqani Sufi Order, Mawlānā Shaykh Nazim Adil al-Haqqani. It is a compilation of Shaykh Kabbani's *suḥbas* over many years in which he speaks of the immense status of our master Prophet Muhammad whom he defines as the ultimate goal of Divine Creation, for as the primordial and perfected devout servant, Muhammad ﷺ, represents the azimuth of creation and its quintessential purpose—servanthood to the Divine.

This comprehensive discourse delves deeply into the spiritual realities and exalted status of Sayyidinā Muhammad ﷺ, the Prophet of Islam, as understood through the rich Sufi teachings of the Naqshbandi-Haqqani tradition. It explores the profound knowledge, divine light, and unique spiritual hierarchy connected to the Prophet, emphasizing the transformative power of *Dhikr* (remembrance of Allah), the significance of the Prophet's ﷺ intercession—not just to his community, but to all human beings and even the invisible creations known as the Jinn--and the essential role of spiritual guides and saints in the believer's path toward divine proximity. At the heart of the discourse is the unparalleled status of the Prophet Muhammad ﷺ, who was created first as the primordial Light of Muhammad ﷺ, the first creation of Allah from which all other creation and prophets emanate. This reality is infinite and beyond human comprehension, reflecting his eternal closeness to Allah and his role as Ḥabībullāh —the Beloved of Allah—who receives from Allah without asking. The Prophet's ﷺ love and mercy are central to the spiritual journey of Muslims, with his intercession (*shafa'ah*) being indispensable for the salvation of the Ummah and even the jinn. His spiritual presence and breath hold immense power, surpassing the lifetimes of all other prophets combined.

The Prophet's ﷺ ascension is a pivotal event revealing his witnessing of Allah's presence with the "eyes of his head"—a unique occurrence in Islamic tradition. At each stage of the heavenly journey, he received vehicles and divine knowledge, culminating in profound spiritual realities including the knowledge granted to all the 124,000 prophets before him. His continuous observation of the Ummah's deeds and prayers for their forgiveness underscore his ongoing intercessory role

The Prophet Muhammad ﷺ was entrusted with immense divine knowledge during the Night Journey and Ascension (Laylat al-Isrā' wa'l-Mi'rāj), divided into accessible knowledge revealed through Archangel Gibril (Jibrīl) for the Community, and higher, esoteric knowledge reserved for the Prophet ﷺ, alone. This includes the manifestation of the 99 Names of Allah and the Greatest Divine Name, which only the Prophet ﷺ, fully comprehended. The Prophet's ﷺ heart acts as a receiver of divine realities, and the deeper meanings of the Holy Qur'ān, which are still to be unfolded from the heart of the Prophet ﷺ are prophesied to be unveiled in the time of Sayyidinā al-Mahdī ؑ. The knowledge granted to the Prophet ﷺ surpasses all human understanding and that of other prophets, and the Prophet has not stopped reaching further horizons of knowledge due to his passing from this world, rather he continues his ascension in the oceans of divine knowledge and power which have no end.

This title is recommended for anyone engaged in the study Sufism.

Publisher's Notes

This book is directed to those familiar with the Sufi Way. However, to accommodate lay readers unfamiliar with Sufi terminology and practices, we have provided English translations of Arabic texts and a comprehensive glossary. Where Arabic terms are crucial to the discussion, we have included transliteration and explanations. For readers familiar with Arabic and Islamic teachings, for further clarity please consult the cited sources.

The original material is based on transcripts of a series of holy gatherings known as *ṣuḥbah*, a divinely inspired talk given by the "shaykh," a highly trained spiritual guide. To present the authentic flavor of such rare teachings, great care was taken to preserve the speaking styles of both the author and the illustrious shaykhs upon whose notes this book is based.

Translations from Arabic to English pose unique challenges that we have tried our best to make understandable to Western readers. Please note our application of the common Arabic oral tradition of omitting definite articles such as "the Prophet" and "the Holy Qur'ān," as practiced by Muslims around the world as intimate references.

We apply contemporary American English publishing standards and therefore do not italicize commonly known foreign nouns (jihād, Qur'ān, shaykh).

Quotes from the Holy Qur'ān and Holy Traditions of Prophet Muḥammad are offset, italicized and cited.

The pronoun "they" is frequently used by Sufi guides to reference heavenly beings and holy souls who support them and give them orders, a usage that appears throughout this book. Where gender-specific pronouns such as "he" and "him" are applied in a general sense, no discrimination is intended towards women, upon whom The Almighty bestowed great honor.

The following universally recognized symbols have been respectfully included in this work. While they may seem tedious, they are deeply appreciated by a vast majority of our readers.

ﷻ *Subḥānahu wa ta'alā* (may His Glory be Exalted), recited after the name "Allāh" and any of the Islamic Names of God.

ﷺ *ṢallAllāhu 'alayhi wa sallam* (God's blessings and greetings of peace be upon him), recited after the holy name of Prophet Muḥammad.

عليه السلام *'Alayhi 's-salām* (peace be upon him/her), recited after holy names of other prophets, names of Prophet Muḥammad's relatives, the pure and virtuous women in Islam, and angels.

رضي الله عنها/رضي الله عنه *Raḍī Allāhu 'anh(um)* (may God be pleased with him/her), recited after the holy names of Companions of Prophet Muḥammad; plural: *raḍī Allāhu 'anhum.*

ق represents *Qaddas Allāhu sirrah* (may God sanctify his secret), recited after names of saints.

Transliteration

Transliteration from Arabic to English poses challenges. To show respect, Muslims often capitalize nouns that appear in English in lowercase.

To facilitate authentic pronunciation of names, places and terms, use the following key:

Symbol	Transliteration	Symbol	Transliteration	Vowels: Long	
ء	ʾ	ط	ṭ	آ ى	ā
ب	b	ظ	ẓ	و	ū
ت	t	ع	ʿ	ي	ī
ث	th	غ	gh	Short	
ج	j	ف	f	َ	a
ح	ḥ	ق	q	ُ	u
خ	kh	ك	k	ِ	i
د	d	ل	l		
ذ	dh	م	m		
ر	r	ن	n		
ز	z	هـ	h		
س	s	و	w		
ش	sh	ي	y		
ص	ṣ	ة	ah; at		
ض	ḍ	ال	al-/’l-		

Masters of the Naqshbandi-Haqqani Golden Chain

May Allāh ﷻ preserve their secrets.

1) Prophet Muḥammad ibn ʿAbdAllāh ﷺ

2) Abū Bakr aṣ-Ṣiddīq
3) Salmān al-Fārsī
4) Qāsim bin Muḥammad bin Abū Bakr
5) Jaʿfar aṣ-Ṣādiq
6) Ṭayfūr Abū Yazīd al-Bistāmī
7) Abūl-Ḥassan ʿAlī al-Kharqānī
8) Abū ʿAlī al-Farmadī
9) Abū Yāʿqūb Yūsuf al-Ḥamadānī
10) Abūl-ʿAbbās, al-Khiḍr
11) ʿAbdul-Khāliq al-Ghujdawānī
12) ʿArif ar-Riwakrī
13) Khwāja Maḥmūd al-Anjīr al-Faghnawī
14) ʿAlī ar-Ramitānī
15) Muḥammad Bābā as-Samāsī
16) As-Sayyid Amīr Kulāl
17) Muḥammad Bahāuddīn Shāh Naqshband
18) ʿAlāuddīn al-Bukhārī al-ʿAṭṭār
19) Yāʿqūb al-Charkhī
20) ʿUbaydullāh al-Ahrār
21) Muḥammad az-Zāhid
22) Darwish Muḥammad
23) Muḥammad Khwāja al-Amkanakī
24) Muḥammad al-Bāqī bilLāh
25) Aḥmad al-Fārūqī as-Sirhindī
26) Muḥammad al-Maʿṣūm
27) Muḥammad Sayfuddīn al-Fārūqī al-Mujaddidī
28) As-Sayyid Nūr Muḥammad al-Bayadūnī
29) Shamsuddīn Ḥabīb Allāh
30) ʿAbdAllāh ad-Dahlawī
31) Khālid al-Baghdādī
32) Ismaʿīl Muḥammad ash-Shirwānī
33) Khāṣ Muḥammad Shirwānī
34) Muḥammad Effendī al-Yarāghī
35) Jamāluddīn al-Ghumūqī al-Ḥusaynī
36) Abū Aḥmad aṣ-Ṣughūrī
37) Abū Muḥammad al-Madanī
38) Sharafuddīn ad-Dāghestānī
39) ʿAbdAllāh al-Fāʾiz ad-Dāghestānī

40) Muḥammad Nāẓim ʿAdil al-Ḥaqqānī

Recitation before Every Association

بسم الله الرحمن الرحيم

A'ūdhu billāhi min ash-shayṭānir-rajīm.
Bismillāhir-raḥmānir-raḥīm.
Nawaytu-l-arba'īn, nawaytu-l-'itikāf,
nawaytu-l-khalwah, nawaytu-l-'uzlah,
nawaytu-r-riyāḍah, nawaytu-s-sulūk,
lillāhi ta'ālā fī hādhā-l-masjid.
Aṭī'ullāha wa aṭī'ur-rasūla
wa ūli-l-amri minkum.

I seek refuge in Allāh from Satan, the rejected.
In the Name of Allāh, the Merciful,
the Compassionate.
I intend the forty (days of seclusion);
I intend seclusion in the mosque,
I intend seclusion, I intend isolation,
I intend discipline (of the ego); I intend to travel
in God's Path for the sake of God,
in this mosque.
Obey Allāh, obey the Prophet,
and obey those in authority among you.
Sūratu 'n-Nisā (The Women), 4:59

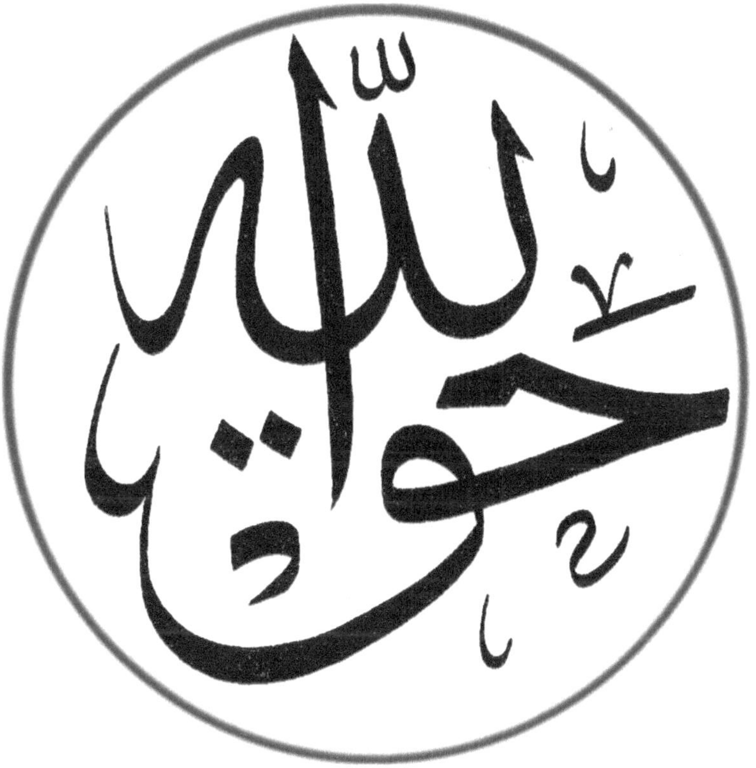

The Spiritual Significance of Isrā' and Mi'rāj

Bismillāhir-raḥmānir-raḥīm

سُبْحَانَ ٱلَّذِيٓ أَسْرَىٰ بِعَبْدِهِۦ لَيْلًا مِّنَ ٱلْمَسْجِدِ ٱلْحَرَامِ إِلَى ٱلْمَسْجِدِ ٱلْأَقْصَى ٱلَّذِي
بَٰرَكْنَا حَوْلَهُۥ لِنُرِيَهُۥ مِنْ ءَايَٰتِنَآ ۚ إِنَّهُۥ هُوَ ٱلسَّمِيعُ ٱلْبَصِيرُ

Subḥāna 'lladhī asrā bi-'abdihi laylan mina 'l-masjidi 'l-ḥarām ilā 'l-masjidi 'l-aqṣā alladhī bāraknā ḥawlahu li-nuriyahu min āyātinā innahu huwa 's-Samī'u 'l-Baṣīr

Glory be to He Who transported His servant by night from the Inviolable House of Worship (at Mecca) to the Remote House of Worship (at Jerusalem), the environs of which We had blessed so that We might show him some of Our signs. Verily, He Alone is All-Hearing, All-Seeing. (Sūrat al-Isrā', 17:1)

Allah ﷻ has revealed this as the first verse of Qur'ān's chapter al-Isrā', the Night Journey, which is also known as the chapter of the Children of Israel or the chapter of Glorification (*Subḥān*). In it Allah mentions the Night Journey (*Isrā'*) in which He called the Prophet ﷺ to His Divine Presence.

As Allah opened the Holy Qur'ān in the Opening chapter Sūrat al-Fatiha, with the words "*Al-ḥamdu Lillāh – Praise be to Allah,*" in this verse of Sūrat al-Isrā' (17:1), He ﷻ opens the chapter of the Night Journey with, *Subḥāna* – "*Glory be to Allah.*"

Allah is glorifying Himself saying, *Subḥāna 'lladhī asrā bi-'abdihi* which means "Glory to Me, the One who brought the Prophet on the Night Journey calling him to My Divine Presence." This is beyond the comprehension of the human mind. Allah is not just reminding us about this event, rather, He ﷻ is glorifying Himself on account of it. That is because the Night Journey, moving almost instantaneously from Mecca to Masjid al-Aqṣā and the Ascension, traversing in an incredibly short span of time the worldly domain of this universe and beyond, transcend the laws of physics governing movement. There is no way for any scientist's mind to comprehend how the Prophet ﷺ moved across the globe and was then carried to Allah's Divine Presence. Such a journey is beyond the scope of imagination. Therefore Allah ﷻ glorifies Himself saying, "Yes it happened! Glory to Me Who can do this! I am beyond these laws and systems. I am the Creator of all systems."

> Mālik bin Anas ؓ related that the Prophet ﷺ said, "I was lying in the *hijr* (of the Masjid al-Ḥarām of Mecca) when someone [the archangel Jibrīl ؑ] came to me and cut open my chest from throat to belly. He removed my heart and cleaned it with the water of the well of Zamzam before putting it

back in its place. Then he brought me a white creature called *al-Buraq* by whose means I was lifted."

Another narration relates that the two archangels:

Jibrīl ﷺ and Mika'il ﷺ came to the Prophet ﷺ when he was laying down in *al-Hijr* [of the Sacred Mosque in Mecca] and carried him to the well of Zamzam. They laid him down on his back and Jibrīl ﷺ opened his chest from top to bottom, despite which there was no bleeding. He said to Mikā'īl ﷺ, 'Get me water from Zamzam,' which he did. Jibrīl ﷺ took the Prophet's heart and washed it thrice before putting it back. He filled it with faith and wisdom. Then he closed his chest and they took him out from the door of the masjid to where the Burāq was waiting."

Archangel Jibrīl ﷺ could have removed the Prophet's heart miraculously by means of a small opening or without opening his chest at all. Yet we see in this Tradition of the Prophet ﷺ a hint of how to perform open heart surgery. This same technique of opening the entire chest cavity is used by heart surgeons today.

How did Allah describe the one whom He brought on the Night Journey? He describes him ﷺ as "His servant." Abū'l-Qāsim Salmān ibn Nāṣir al-Anṣārī al-Nīsābūrī said that when the Prophet ﷺ reached the highest levels and distinguished stations, Allah revealed to him, "With what shall I honor you?" The Prophet said, "By relating me to you through servanthood (*'ubūdiyya*)." This is why Allah revealed this verse of the Holy Qur'ān honoring the Prophet ﷺ by the title 'His servant' when describing the Night Journey. Allah did not grant such an honor to Moses. Rather He said, *"And when Moses came to Our appointed tryst..."* (Sūrat al-A'rāf, 7:143) referring to Moses ﷺ by his name. Instead of saying, "*Glory be to He Who transported His servant by night ...*" Allah honored the Prophet ﷺ by referring to him as *'abdihi*, "His servant.

Another subtle inference from Allah's use of the term *'abdihi* – a construct in the absent form or third person – is the meaning that, "He called the Prophet to a void where there was nothing except His Own Presence." Allah called the Prophet to a point where there is no place and there is no time, no 'where' and no 'when.' More miraculous than calling the Prophet ﷺ to His Presence was His bringing the Prophet's ﷺ body and soul, which exist in time and place, to where there is no time and no place. Allah brought His sincere servant, our master Muhammad ﷺ, from a physical form of this worldly life to the completely abstract Divine Presence which is beyond any of the laws of science and physics which govern the universe.

The verse goes on to describe the Prophet's movement through five stations. Allah's description of the Prophet ﷺ as servant *'abd,* precedes His mention of the two mosques: the Sacred Mosque (Masjid al-Ḥarām) and the Far Distant Mosque (Masjid al-Aqṣā). Having perfected his character through constant worship, *'ubūdiyya,* the Inviolable Mosque, or Holy Sanctuary, is here an indication of the Prophet's ﷺ having already been elevated beyond all sin. Allah did not say His Servant was taken "from Mecca," rather He said, "from the Sacred Mosque." "Sacred" means that no sin is permitted within its precincts, nor backbiting, cheating, or lying. There one must be ever mindful of Allah's ﷻ Presence. Masjid al-Ḥarām is a station where those sins which signify the animal life, can never be committed. *Aqṣā* in Arabic means 'the Farthest'. Thus Masjid al-Aqṣā here is named as the farthest mosque in relation to Masjid al-Ḥarām and symbolizes the spiritual realm. The literal meaning is, 'He brought His servant from Masjid al-Ḥarām to the mosque at the farthest end.' Symbolically, Allah brought the Prophet away from that which is forbidden, things of this earthly life, *ḥarām*, to the place furthest away from it – *al-aqṣā*. The furthermost point from the animalistic life is the spiritual dimension.

The contrast between these 'stations' is further demonstrated by the famous stone at each of these holy sites. In Masjid al-Ḥarām the Black Stone is a stone governed by physical constraints, held up in an encasement, having fallen from heaven and been darkened by the sins of humanity. At Masjid al-Aqṣā the holy stone marking where the Prophet ﷺ ascended to the heavens is miraculously suspended in the air, disregarding the physical law of gravity, seeking to leave the earthly pull of gravity to soar towards the Divine Presence.

The subtle meaning derived from the order of the words here is that Allah's one true servant, the Prophet ﷺ began from station of *'abdiyya*, servanthood, for which he was created, allowing him to begin from the station of perfected and flawless character (*'iṣmat*) and move from there to the farthest station, the highest rank of all creation, as indicated by the station of the farthest mosque.

Allah brought Prophet Muhammad ﷺ to Masjid al-Aqṣā in Palestine from which most of the prophets hail. There he found all of the prophets gathered there, and they prayed in congregation behind him ﷺ. From there Allah raised him to the heavens, as if saying, 'O My prophets! I did not raise anyone from Masjid al-Aqṣā as I am raising Muhammad ﷺ.' This was in order to demonstrate to them Prophet Muhammad's ﷺ ascendancy – unlike any one of them, he was not restricted by the laws of this universe.

Allah then moved him from Masjid al-Aqṣā by means of the Mi'rāj, lifting him up to His Divine Presence. Why did Allah use the words, *laylan* – by night'? Why didn't He say, *nahāran* – by day'? *Laylan* here illustrates the darkness of this world which becomes illumined only by the bright moon of the Prophet ﷺ who lights up every darkness.

"*Glorified be He Who carried His servant by night…*" Look at every word of this holy verse. First Allah praised Himself in the third person, in absence. Allah then miraculously moved the Prophet (*asrā'*) from Mecca to Masjid al-Aqṣā. Then He referred to the Prophet as *'abd,* 'servant', distinguishing him through that elevated title as being related to the spiritual life, not the animal life.

The message of Prophet Muhammad ﷺ completed and perfected both the physical discipline and jurisprudence (shari'ah) of Mūsā ؑ and the spirituality (*rawḥāniyya*) of 'Isa. The shari'ah of Mūsā ؑ relates to the worldly life and the spirituality of 'Isa relates to the heavenly life. By passing from the worldly life, represented by the Night Journey, to heavenly life, represented by the Ascension, the Prophet ﷺ was carried on these two wings. No prophet was carried on both except our master Muhammad ﷺ.

> The Dajjāl (Anti-Christ) would be prevented from entering four places: Masjid al-Ḥarām in Mecca, Masjid an-Nabawiyy in Madina, Masjid al-Aqṣā and al-Ṭūr, Mount Sinai where Moses used to speak to Allah. (<u>*Musnad Imām Aḥmad*</u>)
>
> The Mother of the Believers Maymūna ؓ said she asked the Prophet about Bayt al-Maqdis. He ﷺ said, "It is the place of Judgment Day where everyone will be called. Come to it and pray in it because one prayer in it is like 1,000 prayers anywhere else." (<u>*Musnad Imām Aḥmad*</u>)
>
> Prophet said that "One prayer in Masjid an-Nabawiyy is like 10,000 prayers elsewhere. One prayer in Masjid al-Ḥarām is like 100,000 prayers elsewhere."

In another narration of Aḥmad one of the Prophet's wives asked what one should do if they are not able to go to Masjid al-Aqṣā. He said, "If someone is not able to go let them send lamp oil there to give light in the mosque. If anyone sends lamp oil to light the mosque it is as if you went and prayed there."

According to this hadith one can send something to the mosque from far away attain the reward of one having reached the masjid despite not going there oneself, this though it is not a human being, but only four walls. This is one of many text proofs that intercession in Islam is accepted.

Allah mentioned in the Holy Qur'ān:

كُلَّمَا دَخَلَ عَلَيْهَا زَكَرِيَّا ٱلْمِحْرَابَ وَجَدَ عِندَهَا رِزْقًا ۖ قَالَ يَـٰمَرْيَمُ أَنَّىٰ لَكِ هَـٰذَا ۖ قَالَتْ
هُوَ مِنْ عِندِ ٱللَّهِ ۖ إِنَّ ٱللَّهَ يَرْزُقُ مَن يَشَآءُ بِغَيْرِ حِسَابٍ

"Whenever Zakarīya entered the sanctuary to (see) her, he found food with her. He said: O Maryam! whence comes this to you? She said: It is from Allah. Surely Allah gives to whom He pleases without measure." (Sūrat Āli 'Imrān, 3:36)

Allah then stresses the importance of this place:

There did Zakariya pray to his Lord..." (Sūrat Āli 'Imrān, 3:37) as one in which prayers are answered, having become holy as Maryam's place of worship. Here we see that a place, whether a mosque or a sanctuary, once it becomes holy, can provide blessings and rewards to those who worship in it or send oil to, in the case of Masjid al-Aqṣā. This is for a place, consisting of nothing more than four inanimate walls, what then of asking a pious person for dua? That is the case of the intercession of the Prophet ﷺ.

> The Prophet was asked by Abū Dharr al-Ghifārī which was the first masjid placed on earth. The Prophet replied, "Al-Masjid al-Ḥarām." [The mosque Sayyidinā Ibrāhīm ؑ built in Mecca]. Then he asked which was next. "Masjid al-Aqṣā." [in Jerusalem]. Abū Dharr asked how much time was in between the two and he ﷺ replied, "Forty years. Sayyidinā Ibrāhīm ؑ established the Mosque in Mecca, Sayyidinā Yaʿqūb ؑ founded Masjid al-Aqṣā and his son Sayyidinā Sulaymān ؑ finished it." (Abū Dāwūd)

Spiritual Vehicles of the Prophet ﷺ

One of the great scholars of Qur'ānic exegesis, al-ʿAlāʾī said:

> On the Night of Ascension the Prophet had five different vehicles. The first was the Buraq, a winged creature which carried him from Mecca to Masjid al-Aqṣā. The second was the Ascension by which the Prophet ﷺ reached the sky of this world, *as-samāʾ ad-dunyā*.' There are two explanations for Miʿrāj: either the Buraq carried the Prophet ﷺ up or a ladder that descended and took the Prophet up very rapidly. 'The third vehicle was the wings of angels taking the Prophet up to the seventh heaven. The fourth vehicle was the wings of Jibrīl ؑ from the seventh heaven to *Sidrat al-Muntahā*. The fifth vehicle was *ar-raf raf* to *qaʿba qawsayn*.'

> The Prophet ﷺ stopped in ten different stations: the seven heavens with the eighth being at the Furthermost Lote Tree, *Sidrat al-Muntahā*. The ninth is where he heard the sound of the angels' pens writing people's actions. The tenth level was at the Throne. And Allah knows best.' (*Tafsīr Rūḥ al-Maʿānī* of al-Ālūsī)

Allah supports His prophets with miracles (*muʿjizāt*) to be able to go beyond the laws of physics and beyond the constraints of our human realities. If Allah grants a miracle we should not view it as something improbable otherwise we will be like scientists who cannot understand anything beyond the physical laws of the universe.

These miraculous events happened on the Night of the Night Journey and Ascension, Laylat al-Isrāʾ wa-l-Miʿrāj. The many hadith of Isrāʾ were authenticated by numerous *Ḥuffāẓ* (hadith masters) such as Al-Ḥāfiẓ ʿAbdul-Ghanī ibn Surūr al-Maqdisī said that it took place in Rajab. In *ar-Rawḍa*, Nawawī says it happened

10 years and 3 months after the beginning of the prophecy, while in his *Fatāwā* he states it was five or six years after prophecy began. Whatever the case, all scholars say that the Isrā' and Mi'rāj took place both in body and spirit.

Ibrāhīm's Vision; Sayyidina Muhammad's Reality

Allah said in the Holy Qur'ān

> 75. So also did We show Ibrāhīm the kingdom and glories behind the magnificent powers and laws of the physical universe that he might have certitude.
>
> 76. When the night covered over him he saw a star. He said 'This is my lord.' But when it set he said, 'I do not love those that set.'
>
> 77. When he saw the moon rising in splendor he said, 'This is my lord.' But when the moon set he said, 'Unless my Lord guides me I shall surely be among those who go astray.'
>
> 78. When he saw the sun rising in splendor he said, 'This is my lord.' But when the sun set he said, 'O my people, I am innocent and free from the sin of you giving partners to Allah.
>
> 79. 'For me I have set my face firmly and truly towards the One Who created the heavens and the earth, and I am not one who gives partners to Allah.' (Sūrat al-An'am 6:75-79).

Allah opened the kingdom of heavens and earth to Sayyidinā Ibrāhīm without an Isrā' or Mi'rāj. He opened Prophet Ibrāhīm's *basīra* (spiritual vision) to see the wonders of the universe from where he was on earth. Allah showed him what is beyond the laws of the physical universe through the eyes of his heart. Yet immediately after this verse where Allah has shown Ibrāhīm the glories behind the physical universe, in verse 76 Ibrāhīm sees a star and says, 'This is my lord!' In verses 77 and 78 he similarly "mistakes" the moon and sun for his lord.

Allah showed Ibrāhīm the truth, and he is conveying the heavenly message. If he tried to directly present unseen spirituality to those who worship only physical objects, they would not understand it. How could he explain the heavens and glorifying the Lord to those who only understand literal meanings and physicality and have no comprehension of interpretative meanings or spirituality? Ibrāhīm was trying to gently tell the people 'don't worship the stars, or moon, or sun. Go beyond what you can see physically.' Ibrāhīm knew the reality of the universe as Allah had shown it to him. The verses of the stars, moon, and sun are for the non-believers, to slowly build up their beliefs. They rejected anything beyond the comprehension of their minds. He wanted everyone to be under Allah's Mercy so he was trying to let them understand by a process of elimination that there is a spiritual dimension. He eliminated the star (something small), then the moon, then the sun (the biggest heavenly body). This means "Don't run after things of this worldly life but run after the spiritual dimension which surpasses the laws of the physical universe."

In our time, materialistic scientists and certain narrow-minded Islamic sects try to negate spirituality, that fourth dimension, which Allah showed to Ibrāhīm ﷺ. Those rejecting the spiritual dimension of Islam are falling into the same trap as the people of Ibrāhīm.

أَخْوَفُ مَا أَخَافُ عَلَى أُمَّتِي الشِّرْكُ الْخَفِيّ

> *Akhwafu mā akhāfu ʿalā ummatī ash-shirk al-khafī*
>
> The Prophet ﷺ said, "What I fear most for my community is the hidden *shirk* (associating partners with Allah)." (Musnad Aḥmad, Shuʿab al-ʾĪmān)

Hidden *shirk* is for a person to be prideful of himself. Sayyidinā Ibrāhīm ﷺ was shown the realities of this universe and tried to guide his people to Allah. Finally, in verse 79 he reaffirms his true belief in Allah and his turning away from worldly distractions. From his place on earth, Ibrāhīm was shown by Allah ﷻ the *malakūt* of heavens and earth.

Sayyidinā Mūsā ﷺ did not see this *malakūt*, but he was able to hear and talk to Allah from Mount Sinai. Although Ibrāhīm ﷺ was granted to see in spiritual dimensions, and Mūsā ﷺ was granted to hear Allah directly, both of their bodies were still on earth and subject to its physical laws. Sayyidinā Ibrāhīm's ﷺ vision and Sayyidinā Mūsā's ﷺ hearing went beyond the physical through the power of the soul, but their bodies did not move beyond the physical world.

However, Allah made Prophet Muhammad ﷺ to move in spiritual dimensions with his physical body in complete freedom from the physical laws. Allah called the Prophet, *Li-nūrīyahu min āyātinā "to show him from Our signs…"* (Sūrat al-Isrā' 17:1) Allah showed Ibrāhīm *malakūt* of this universe, but He showed Muhammad His signs. Allah moved the Prophet in body and spirit beyond the physical laws of this universe and showed him His signs *ayātinā* 'Our Signs.' This possessive form relating the signs as being Allah's directly indicates a greater honor and knowledge bestowed to the Prophet as opposed to knowledge about Allah's creation in general. The *malakūt* of *samawāt* (heavens or skies) and *arḍ* (earth) shown to Ibrāhīm were the workings of this physical universe and did not reach to Paradise. Allah's signs are directly related to Allah and are not associated with this world.

Imām Nawawī and the late Imām Muṭawallī Shaʿrāwī side with the majority of scholars in interpreting this to mean that the Prophet saw his Lord another time—not that he saw Jibrīl ﷺ another time as others assert. Nawawī relates in his commentary on *Ṣaḥīḥ Muslim*, "Most of the scholars say that the Prophet saw his Lord with the eyes of his head, *ra'a rabbahu bi 'aynay ra'sihi.*"

10 *Allah revealed to His servant what he revealed*
11 *The Prophet's heart in no way falsified what it saw.*
12 *Will you then dispute with him about what he saw?*
13 *And he saw Him again another time*
14 *at the Lote-tree of the utmost boundary*
15 *at the Garden of Abode*
16 *Behold the lote-tree was shrouded with what shrouds*
17 *His sight did not swerve or go wrong.* (Sūrat al-Isrā' 17:10-17)

Imām Shaʿrāwī asks, "What would make the Prophet's sight swerve? Some say it was Jibrīl ☞, but the Prophet had seen Jibrīl ☞ many times and Jibrīl ☞ was with him for the duration of the Night Journey and Ascension. It is irrelevant to say at this juncture that the Prophet's sight did not swerve or go wrong, because if this was in reference to Jibrīl ☞ the Prophet had many opportunities to see him already. Allah doesn't say anything irrelevant which is why I side with the majority of ʿulama (including Imām Nawawī) in saying that with his physical eyes the Prophet saw Allah ﷻ."

The Prophet came all the way to the Divine Throne (*ʿarsh*), reached *qāba qawsayni* (the distance of two bow lengths), and reached the Paradise of Jannat al-Maʾwa near the Lote-Tree (*sidrat al-muntahā*). After all this what could possibly make his sight swerve or go wrong? As mentioned above, the Isrāʾ and Miʿrāj took place several years after Jibrīl ☞ brought the first revelation to the Prophet ﷺ. Thus, it is illogical that after being seen by the Prophet ﷺ so many times that now Jibrīl ☞ would have the potential to make his sight swerve.

17 *His sight did not swerve or go wrong.*
18 *Indeed he saw the Greatest Signs of his Lord*
19 *Have you seen Lat and ʿUzza (two pagan idols)*
20 *And the third one Manat (another idol)* (Sūrat an-Najm, 53:17-20)

Why does Allah mention these three false deities here immediately after mentioning the "*Greatest Signs of his Lord*" in 53:18? Scholars say that verses 53:19-20 name the idols that people were worshipping in order to contrast them to Allah ﷻ mentioned in 53:18. If 53:18 referred to Jibrīl ☞ then it would not follow to mention the false idols after it.

That is the greatness of Sayyidinā Muhammad ﷺ. No one saw his Lord except for Muhammad ﷺ, so he is the only real *muwaḥḥid*. No one except Muhammad ﷺ has real *tawḥīd*, only imitation *tawḥīd*.

Prophet Abraham ﷺ was the father of the prophets and was granted spiritual vision to see the workings of the universe and Prophet Moses ﷺ was granted to speak with his Lord. But Allah moved Prophet Muhammad ﷺ with his physical body in defiance of the physical laws of the universe to the Unseen, a place where there is nothing and no possibility of anything to be there – *lā khalā wa lā malā*. Allah took Muhammad ﷺ there and revealed Himself to him, in the manner He wished. How this was we don't know. It is *ghayb* (unseen, unknown). But we know that this is not in reference to Jibrīl ﷺ who was seen by the Prophet ﷺ many times. We again recall the opinion of Imām Nawawī who said, "Most of the scholars say that the Prophet ﷺ saw his Lord with the eyes of his head *ra'ā rabbahu bi-ʿaynay rā'sihi."*

Looking at these verses in Sūrat Isrā' and Sūrat an-Najm we see that the Isrā' and Miʿrāj was not like Allah showing Ibrāhīm *malakūt* of the universe. Allah gave this universe to all of humanity whether in *dunyā* or *akhirā*. However Allah showed Muhammad ﷺ something related to Himself *ayātinā* "Our Signs."

The Reality of Prophet ﷺ in the Presence of Allah

كَلِمَتَانِ خَفِيفَتَانِ عَلَى اللِّسَانِ، ثَقِيلَتَانِ فِي الْمِيزَانِ، حَبِيبَتَانِ إِلَى الرَّحْمَنِ: سُبْحَانَ اللَّهِ وَبِحَمْدِهِ، سُبْحَانَ اللَّهِ الْعَظِيمِ

There are two words that are very easy to say, yet very heavy on the Scale, most beloved to The Merciful, "*Subḥānallāh wa bi-ḥamdihi, subḥānallāhi-l-ʿaẓīm.*" (Bukhārī and Muslim)

نَرْجُو اللَّهَ عَزَّ وَجَلَّ أَنْ يَغْفِرَ لَنَا ذُنُوبَنَا بِجَاهِ حَبِيبِهِ الْمُصْطَفَى وَأَهْلِ بَيْتِهِ الْكِرَامِ

Narjullāh ʿazza wa jalla an yaghfira lanā dhunūbanā bi jāhi ḥabībihi 'l-muṣṭafā wa ahli baytihi 'l-kirām.

It is easy to speak, but it is difficult to understand, because when you understand something it is necessary to rise up with that thing, but when you give a speech you don't necessarily rise up. Speech comes in this ear and we allow it to go out from the other ear, but if we close one ear then that understanding will stay inside. Allah gave us...if you look in the ear, how fine it is that Allah ﷻ gave us something in the ear like a drum. How? Did we ask ourselves how Allah ﷻ created Creation and how He created us? An ear, this (outer ear) is the dish and this inside is the LNB, it pulls the information that comes on the dish and transmits it in a language, it sends it inside as a magnetic wavelength moving a small bones inside that allow you to perceive someone speaking.

Not all people speak the same language. How many languages are there? In China there are thousands of languages; in India there are thousands of languages and in our Arab countries there are many different kinds of dialects. Yet one ear understands them all. Who is behind that? *Allahu Akbar!* He said:

لَخَلْقُ السَّمَاوَاتِ وَالْأَرْضِ أَكْبَرُ مِنْ خَلْقِ النَّاس

Truly the creation of the Heavens and the Earth is greater than the creation of Man. (Sūrat Ghāfir, 40:57)

He said, "The creation of Heavens and Earth is greater than the creation of human beings." Each one of us is a *maʿwjiza*, miracle, coming from a small dot in the womb of his mother, becoming a human being, *Allahu Akbar!* So we stand *ʿajiz* in front of all that, helpless, dumbfounded, for whatever we say:

وَفَوْقَ كُلِّ ذِي عِلْمٍ عَلِيمٌ

Above every knower is a (higher) knower. (Sūrat Yūsuf, 12:76)

Yet Allah ﷻ created us... "He did not create you for your beautiful eyes, He created you because He loves you." Allah loves His Prophet ﷺ, His Messenger and He loves His *Ahl ul-Bayt*, his Family. We have to love what He loves. If we don't love them we will be far away from Allah on the Day of Judgment.

وَكُلٌّ مِّن رَّسُولِ ٱللَّهِ مُلْتَمِسٌ

غَرْفًا مِّنَ ٱلْبَحْرِ أَوْ رَشْفًا مِّنَ ٱلدِّيَمِ

Wa kullun min rasūlillāhi multamisun,
gharfan min al-baḥri aw rashfan min ad-diyami.
All of them partake from the Prophet of God
a handful of his oceans or a sip from his continuous rains.
(Shaykh Muḥammad al-Busayrī, *Burdatu 'sh-Sharīf*)

What are you taking from the Prophet ﷺ? You are coming seeking him and what do you want? *Multamisun*, asking for what? Asking without stopping! "by pitchers from the ocean of the Prophet ﷺ" whose Reality is in *Baḥr al-Qudrah*, the Ocean of Divine Power. Grandshaykh ʿAbd Allāh al-Fā'iz al-Dāghestānī ق said in in one of his seclusions that what Allah created first is the Reality, the *Nūr,* Light of the Prophet ﷺ in *Baḥr al-Qudrah*, which He put in a Lamp, a heavenly *Zujāj,* transparent glass, "*which has been very well put together.*"

قَوَارِيرَ مِن فِضَّةٍ قَدَّرُوهَا تَقْدِيرًا

qawārīra min fiḍḍatin qaddarūhā taqdīrā,

Crystal-clear cups [made] of silver, which they have precisely measured. (Sūrat al-Insān, 76:16)

And he ق said Allah ﷻ kept that *Ḥaqīqat an-Nabī* ﷺ, Reality of the Prophet ﷺ under His Gaze for 70,000 heavenly light years of which every day is like 1,000 earthly years. After 70,000 years had passed, Allah ﷻ looked at him with another Divine Gaze for 500,000 years, and this was repeated five times, raising him from one level to another through another five levels: the first level was 70,000 and every level above that was 500,000 years.

At that time, the Reality of the Prophet ﷺ began to sweat, like drops of water condensing inside the glass, not outside, it is inside, as in winter when you have condensation on windows, or in hot countries when air conditioning is running it produces condensation. So with continuous condensation these drops began to appear on the inside of the heavenly Glass and from that Light of the condensation, He ﷻ created all the 124,000 prophets. Ibn ʿAbbās ؓ mentioned this number in *Tafsīr Sūrat al-Aʿrāf,* that when Sayyidinā Mūsā ؑ asked to see Allah ﷻ:

قَالَ رَبِّ أَرِنِي أَنظُرْ إِلَيْكَ قَالَ لَن تَرَانِي وَلَكِنِ انظُرْ إِلَى الْجَبَلِ فَإِنِ اسْتَقَرَّ مَكَانَهُ فَسَوْفَ تَرَانِي فَلَمَّا تَجَلَّى رَبُّهُ لِلْجَبَلِ جَعَلَهُ دَكًّا وَخَرَّ موسَى صَعِقًا

He said, "O my Lord! Show Yourself to me that I may look upon You." Allah said, "By no means can you see Me (directly), but look upon the mountain: if it abides in its place, then you shall see Me." When his Lord manifested His glory on the mount, He made it as dust and Moses fainted. (Sūrat al-Aʿrāf, 7:143)

Allah sent one Manifestation of one ray of the Light of Reality of Sayyidinā Muhammad ﷺ on that mountain, because Mūsā ؑ cannot carry the Reality of Allah—no one knows Allah's *Dhāt al-Buht*, the Divine Essence. Allah is only known by His *Asmā wa'ṣ-Ṣiffāt,* His Beautiful Names and Attributes. When that Reality shone down on the mountain, the mountain dissolved and Sayyidinā Mūsā ؑ fainted and when he awoke he saw 124,000 prophets following Prophet Muhammad ﷺ in prayers.

From these drops of *al-Nūr al-Muhammadī,* more *Nūr* is coming out making the condensation on the Glass and from that Allah ﷻ created the 124,000 prophets and from the core of that Light, Allah created his Family, *Ahlu 'l-Bayt.* That's why '*Bismillāhir-raḥmānir-raḥīm'* is the Key for Paradise as Prophet ﷺ said:

كُلُّ أَمْرٍ ذِي بَالٍ لَا يُبْدَأُ فِيهِ بِبِسْمِ اللَّهِ الرَّحْمٰنِ الرَّحِيمِ فَهُوَ أَقْطَعُ، أَوْ فَهُوَ الْأَبْتَرُ.

Any action which does not begin with '*Bismillāhir-raḥmānir-raḥīm*' is cut off; it has no continuity. (Musnad Aḥmad)

Every *ʿamal* must begin with *Bismillāhir-raḥmānir-raḥīm.* Your appearance in *dunyā* is with *Bismillāhir-raḥmānir-raḥīm* and everyone has a different *tajallī*, manifestation of *Bismillāhir-raḥmānir-raḥīm* through which he or she appears in *dunyā*. You did not choose your image. Everyone is under the *tajallī*, manifestation of *Bismillāhir-raḥmānir-raḥīm* in a different meaning that Allah knows best, and with that he or she appears. So every drop inside that heavenly glass began with *Bismillāhir-raḥmānir-raḥīm. And Bismillahi 'r-Rahmani 'r-Raheem* is comprised of nineteen Arabic letters, just as the names of *Ahlu 'l-Bayt* are comprised of nineteen letters: Sayyidinā ʿAlī, Sayyida Fāṭimah, Sayyidinā al-Ḥasan, Sayyidinā al-Ḥusayn and Sayyidinā Muḥammad ﷺ. So *Bismillāhir-raḥmānir-raḥīm* is manifested directly under those *Ahlu 'l-Bayt* whom Prophet ﷺ covered with his *jubbah*, cloak.

عَلِيٌّ، فاطِمَةُ، حَسَنٌ، حُسَيْنٌ، مُحَمَّدٌ

No one can understand the Reality of *Ahlu 'l-Bayt*: whatever they describe is outside of it, so that's why *Ahlu 'l-Ḥaqīqah*, *Awliyā'ullāh*, stand *ʿajizīn*, helpless.

They know they cannot know more than what has been given to them. So after the creation of the *Anbiyā 'ullah* from that *Nūr*, Allah created the remainder of creation, as mentioned in the hadith of *Khalqu 'n-Nabī,* the Creation of the [light of the] Prophet ﷺ:

رَوَاهُ عَبْدُ الرَّزَّاقِ بِسَنَدِهِ عَنْ جَابِرِ بْنِ عَبْدِ اللَّهِ بِلَفْظِ: قَالَ: قُلْتُ: يَا رَسُولَ اللَّهِ، بِأَبِي أَنْتَ وَأُمِّي، أَخْبِرْنِي عَنْ أَوَّلِ شَيْءٍ خَلَقَهُ اللَّهُ قَبْلَ الْأَشْيَاءِ. قَالَ: يَا جَابِرُ، إِنَّ اللَّهَ تَعَالَى خَلَقَ قَبْلَ الْأَشْيَاءِ نُورَ نَبِيِّكَ مِنْ نُورِهِ، فَجَعَلَ ذَلِكَ النُّورَ يَدُورُ بِالْقُدْرَةِ حَيْثُ شَاءَ اللَّهُ تَعَالَى.

When Jābir ؓ asked, "Let my father and mother be sacrificed for you, oh Prophet of Allah! What is the first thing that Allah ﷻ created?" the Prophet ﷺ said, "The first thing that Allah ﷻ created is the Light of your Prophet from His Light, O Jābir. Then He made that Light rotate as He ﷻ willed with His Power." (*Muṣannaf ʿAbdu 'r-Razzāq*)

The Light of the Prophet ﷺ was rotating in that heavenly Glass, creating more and more condensations of Light on the Glass, and from all that Allah created the *ʿArsh*, the *Kursiyy*, the Heavens, the Earth, the angels, jinn, human beings and all creation. Thus we are connected to him ﷺ:

قُلْ إِن كُنتُمْ تُحِبُّونَ اللهَ فَاتَّبِعُونِي يُحْبِبْكُمُ اللهُ وَيَغْفِرْ لَكُمْ ذُنُوبَكُمْ وَاللهُ غَفُورٌ رَّحِيمٌ

Say (O Muhammad), "If you (really) love Allah, then follow me! Allah will love you and forgive your sins, and Allah is Oft-Forgiving, Most Merciful." (Sūrat Āli ʿImrān, 3:31)

Allah says: *"tell them 'follow me.'"* Allah knows we cannot follow in *ʿamal*, because our deeds are a sour soup, a mix of good and bad deeds. It means, "Hold my cloak and come with me!" And who is under his cloak? *Ahlu 'l-Bayt*, so, "Hold fast to my *Ahlu 'l-Bayt* and come to me, *fattabiʿūnī*!" Because Prophet ﷺ is moving in Ascension and *Ahlu 'l-Bayt* are moving with him! That's why when the Prophet ﷺ was preparing to leave this *dunyā*, and Sayyidatinā Fāṭimah ؓ was crying, he whispered in her ear and she became happy. What did he tell her? Sayyidatinā ʿĀishah ؓ wanted to know what the Prophet ﷺ told her but she had promised not to tell. Then, after Prophet ﷺ left *dunyā* she told Sayyida ʿĀishah ؓ that he said, "You are going to follow me after six months," *fattabiʿūnī*. So the first *ʿittibā* was for Sayyidatinā Fāṭimah ؓ following her father.

The whole *Ummah* must follow *Ahlu 'l-Bayt* in order to reach and ascend with the Prophet ﷺ, because on *Laylat al-Isrā' wal-Miʿrāj*, when the Prophet ﷺ was invited for Ascension, he said, "*Yā Rabbī,* I need my *Ummah!*" The Prophet ﷺ would not leave his *Ummah* behind. Thus they were ascending with him according to their levels: first *Ahlu 'l-Bayt*, then his *Ṣaḥābah* ﷺ, then the rest of the *Ummah*. When you ascend, do you come back? When the Prophet ﷺ reached the Divine Presence, *Qāba Qawsayni aw Adnā* is it acceptable to say that the Prophet ﷺ left that position and then returned? *Awliyā'ullāh* say that one of his *Ḥaqīqas*, Realities, came back because the other Realities [are too much for this world to carry].

For Sayyidinā Mūsā ؏, when Allah ﷻ manifested that Light on the mountain it shattered to pieces, so what will happen if the Reality of Sayyidinā Muhammad ﷺ that reached *al-Isrā wa 'l-Miʿrāj* and *Qāba Qawsayni aw Adnā* returns? No one will be able to carry it!

Look at the story of Sayyidinā Aḥmad al-Badawī ق when that *Walī* appeared to him and poured into his heart the Reality of spiritual knowledge, *'Ilm*.

فَوَجَدَا عَبْدًا مِّنْ عِبَادِنَا آتَيْنَاهُ رَحْمَةً مِنْ عِندِنَا وَعَلَّمْنَاهُ مِن لَّدُنَّا عِلْمًا

Fa wajadā ʿabdan min ʿibādinā ātaynāhu raḥmatan min ʿindinā wa ʿallamnāhu min ladunnā ʿilma

So they found one of Our Servants on whom We had bestowed Mercy from Ourselves and whom We had taught knowledge from Our Own Presence. (Sūrat al-Kahf, 18:65)

Because of the Heavenly Knowledge that a *Walī* had poured into Aḥmad al-Badawī's heart, no one could look into his eyes or they would faint. For that reason he used to cover his eyes with a *burqā*. Therefore, what do you think would happen to the *Ummah* if the Prophet ﷺ came back with all these Realities? They would shatter completely! That is why Abū Hurayrah ؓ said in one Hadith:

حَفِظْتُ مِنْ رَسُولِ اللَّهِ صَلَّى اللَّهُ عَلَيْهِ وَسَلَّمَ وِعَاءَيْنِ : فَأَمَّا أَحَدُهُمَا فَبَثَثْتُهُ ، وَأَمَّا الآخَرُ فَلَوْ بَثَثْتُهُ قُطِعَ هَذَا الْبُلْعُومُ

I have been given two different types of knowledge from Prophet ﷺ: one I shared with everyone, but if I share the other, they will cut this neck of mine. (Bukhārī)

No one can understand the Reality of Sayyidinā Muhammad ﷺ: he is where he was and he will be where he will be, with no beginning to his Reality as a Servant to Allah ﷻ, *Maqām al-ʿAbdiyyah*, in the level of Servanthood to Allah which has no beginning and no end; he is *ʿAbd* from whenever Allah wanted him to be *ʿAbd* and he will be *ʿAbd* to whenever Allah wants him to be *ʿAbd*! Past, present, and future are the same for him.

May Allah open the hearts of Muslims and the *ʿulamā* of the *Ummah*, not to reject these *Awliyā'*. These are *shaṭaḥāt*, ecstatic statements. Yes, *ʿulamā* did not understand *Awliyā'ullāh* like Sayyidinā Muḥiyyidīn ibn ʿArabī ق, Sayyidinā Bāyazīd al-Bistāmī ق and Junayd al-Baghdādī ق, and all the other *Awliyā'ullāh*, in spite of being scholars. Like this very small story here, related by one of the *Awliyā'ullāh*, Shaykh Abā 'l-Khayr al-ʿAqṭaʿ ق.

قَالَ أَبُو الْخَيْرِ الْأَقْطَعُ: دَخَلْتُ مَدِينَةَ النَّبِيِّ صَلَّى اللَّهُ تَعَالَى عَلَيْهِ وَسَلَّمَ وَأَنَا بِفَاقَةٍ، فَأَقَمْتُ خَمْسَةَ أَيَّامٍ مَا ذُقْتُ ذَوَاقًا، فَتَقَدَّمْتُ إِلَى الْقَبْرِ، وَسَلَّمْتُ عَلَى النَّبِيِّ صَلَّى اللَّهُ تَعَالَى عَلَيْهِ وَسَلَّمَ وَعَلَى أَبِي بَكْرٍ وَعُمَرَ، وَقُلْتُ: أَنَا ضَيْفُكَ يَا رَسُولَ اللَّهِ، وَتَنَحَّيْتُ وَنِمْتُ خَلْفَ الْقَبْرِ، فَرَأَيْتُ فِي الْمَنَامِ النَّبِيَّ صَلَّى اللَّهُ تَعَالَى عَلَيْهِ وَسَلَّمَ، وَأَبُو بَكْرٍ عَنْ يَمِينِهِ، وَعُمَرُ عَنْ شِمَالِهِ، وَعَلِيُّ بْنُ أَبِي طَالِبٍ بَيْنَ يَدَيْهِ، فَحَرَّكَنِي عَلِيٌّ وَقَالَ: قُمْ، قَدْ جَاءَ رَسُولُ اللَّهِ صَلَّى اللَّهُ تَعَالَى عَلَيْهِ وَسَلَّمَ، فَقُمْتُ إِلَيْهِ وَقَبَّلْتُ بَيْنَ عَيْنَيْهِ، فَدَفَعَ إِلَيَّ رَغِيفًا، فَأَكَلْتُ نِصْفَهُ، وَانْتَبَهْتُ فَإِذَا فِي يَدِي نِصْفُ رَغِيفٍ

"I came to the city of the Prophet ﷺ and stayed five days by the Holy Grave of the Prophet ﷺ, not eating and not drinking. After that I approached with only *Dhikrullāh* and meditation."

Allah described such people:

إِنَّ فِي خَلْقِ السَّمَاوَاتِ وَالأَرْضِ وَاخْتِلاَفِ اللَّيْلِ وَالنَّهَارِ لآيَاتٍ لِّأُوْلِي الأَلْبَابِ الَّذِينَ يَذْكُرُونَ اللّهَ قِيَامًا وَقُعُودًا وَعَلَىَ جُنُوبِهِمْ وَيَتَفَكَّرُونَ فِي خَلْقِ السَّمَاوَاتِ وَالأَرْضِ رَبَّنَا مَا خَلَقْتَ هَذا اطِلاً سُبْحَانَكَ فَقِنَا عَذَابَ النَّارِ

Behold! In the creation of Heaven and Earth, and in the alternation of night and day, there are indeed signs for men of understanding, those who remember Allah (always, and in prayers) standing, sitting and lying down on their sides, and contemplate the creation of the Heavens and the Earth, (saying), "Our Lord! You have not created (all) this without purpose! Glory to You! Grant us salvation from the torment of the Fire." (Sūrat Āli ʿImrān, 3:190-191)

Shaykh Abā 'l-Khayr was contemplating the creation of Heavens and Earth. "After that I gave *salāms* to the Prophet ﷺ and to his Ṣaḥābah ؓ and then I said, 'I came to you, *yā Rasūlallāh,* as your guest.'"

Everyone who comes to Madinah is a guest, so what shall the host do? He hosts them! If you speak to any common Arab or Muslim, if a guest comes to him, what will he do? He will host him for three days, not asking him anything (of his plans), and he can sleep, eat and drink in comfort. So what do you think about the Prophet ﷺ? The people who come from around the world to visit him are his guests so he ﷺ will accommodate every one of them and give them whatever they need, and what each one needs is different from one person to another.

Also, Prophet ﷺ can see all of them at the same time, in the same moment, as they are coming to enter *Madīnatu 'l-Munawwarah* and *Bāb as-Salām*. He welcomes them just as he used to welcome heads of tribes, even though they were non-Muslim; they came to ask questions and some became Muslim. The Prophet ﷺ hosts them and welcomes them.

Shaykh Abā 'l-Khayr al-ʿAqṭaʿ ق said, "When someone comes to *Madīnatu 'l-Munawwarah*, they are your guests. I am your guest, so host me."

So with what will Sayyidinā Muhammad ﷺ host him? *Awliyā'ullāh* are granted miracles. He said, "I am your guest, *yā Sayyidī*, *yā Rasūlallāh*," and he sat on the side and slept behind the *minbar*; the same *minbar* which the Prophet ﷺ had touched; the same the *minbar* which, upon feeling the sweetness of his touch made *ṣalawāt* on the Prophet ﷺ, and when he left *dunyā* people heard the rail where he put his hand *ḥanīn*, as if the *minbar* was crying.

So Shaykh Abā 'l-Khayr al-ʿAqṭaʿ ق said, "I went behind the *minbar* and slept and I saw the Prophet ﷺ in my dream with Sayyidinā Abū Bakr as-Ṣiddīq ؓ and on his right Sayyidinā ʿUmar ؓ and on his other side Sayyidinā ʿAli (*karama 'llāhu wajhahu*) who told me, *Qūmū li-sayyidikum*,, 'The Prophet ﷺ came, so stand up!' I stood up and kissed him between his eyes. *Fa dafaʿa ʿalayya raghīfan, fa akaltu niṣfahu*, he pulled a loaf of bread from his pocket, and I ate half of it. When I woke up, I had the other half in my hand."

When I was in *Madīnatu 'l-Munawwarah,* I met one of the *Ḥabā'ib*, Ḥabīb ʿAsim an elderly person over 60 years old. He told me, "I was seven years old and my father used to be the one responsible to clean the inside of the Holy Grave, *Ḥujrah al-Sharīfah*. He swept and cleaned the *Maqām*. My mother came to see my father at his work and I was standing in front of the *Ḥujrat al-Sharīfah*, where there is a *fajwa*, circle in the door, and I put my hand in the opening while I was making *ṣalawāt*. I felt something in my hand and I pulled my hand out and found a bottle of *ʿattar*, perfume in it, which I showed to my mother. I said, 'Look what I got from inside!' My mother immediately said, 'Give it back.' I put my hand back inside and it disappeared. We went home and my mother told my father what had happened, and he said, 'Why did you tell him to give that back? That was a gift from the Prophet ﷺ to him.'"

Awliyā'ullāh have high levels that we must to know are impossible to comprehend!

وَفَوْقَ كُلِّ ذِي عِلْمٍ عَلِيمٌ

Above every knower is a (higher) knower. (Sūrah Yūsuf, 12:76)

This means *Awliyā'ullāh* are in a hierarchy in a golden chain and when one goes from the first one in the hierarchy to the top, all of them are connected to the Prophet ﷺ as links in a chain. Therefore I am not warning myself only but I am warning others, that we have to be very careful, because even the lowest *Walī* is a Saint and we have to respect him in his level, just as we respect the one at top of the chain.

لَا نُفَرِّقُ بَيْنَ أَحَدٍ مِّن رُّسُلِهِ

We do not distinguish between any of His messengers. (Sūrat al-Baqara, 2:285)

We don't differentiate between any Prophets, nor between any *Awliyā'*, nor between any *Mashayikh*. We say they are all our leaders whom we love and respect. However, if you have stronger love to your shaykh that does not mean you have to demean other *shuyukh*; that is not advisable. It's a big mistake that people might do when they begin to promote their *mashayikh*, which they don't realize makes the *mashayikh* feel shy in front of Prophet ﷺ. The *murīds* don't understand the sensitivity of saying something that might affect the heart of Prophet ﷺ because he loves all of them. Consider that if you take away any link in the chain the whole chain will collapse. If you hit the bottom of the chain it will ring to the top, and if you hit the top of the chain it will ring all the way down. Therefore do not say, "This one is better than the other," because all of them are beloved to Allah ﷻ and to the Prophet ﷺ.

Abū 'l-Khayr al-Daylamī ق relates the following story in Hilyat al-Awliyā':

> I was sitting in the store of Khayr an-Nassāj ق, one of Allah's *Awliyā'*, and a lady came to him and asked him to make her a towel and asked how much it will cost.
>
> He said, "I will make that towel, *mandīl*, for two *dirhams*."
>
> She said, "I don't have the money now, I will bring it to you tomorrow."
>
> He said, "If you come and don't find me, throw the *dirhams* in the River Dijla (Tigris), [the famous river along with al-Furāt (Euphrates)]. When I return I will take them, don't worry, *In shā'Allāh.*"
>
> She said, 'With love and respect, I will come and throw them in the River Dijla."
>
> That lady came the next morning and he was not in the store, so she waited one hour and he did not come, so she took the two *dirhams* and put them in a *khirqa*, small piece of cloth, and threw them in the Djila. At that moment a *salt'an*, crab came and pulled the cloth and dove into the water. After two hours, Khayr an-Nassāj ق was sitting by the beach making *wuḍū*,

then that crab came out of the water holding the cloth and approached the shaykh and handed him the *khirqa*, which the shaykh took and the crab went back to the water!

These are *Awliyā'ullāh*! This is a lesson for us that when your love exceeds certain limits towards Allah ﷻ and His Prophet ﷺ, then the whole *dunyā* will be under your command:

وَسَخَّرَ لَكُم مَّا فِي السَّمَاوَاتِ وَمَا فِي الْأَرْضِ جَمِيعًا مِّنْهُ

He made everything in the Heavens and everything in the Earth subservient to you. (Sūrat al-Jāthiyah, 45:13)

Then in every action you make must be a miracle. May Allah ﷻ make our lives miracles in the love of Prophet ﷺ, in the love of *Awliyā'ullāh*, and of course in the love of Allah ﷻ.

May Allah forgive us and if I said something wrong forgive me. What I heard from Grandshaykh ق I mentioned. *Awliyā'ullāh's* knowledge is not limited. What *Awliyā'ullāh* know is vast from East to West with no limitations, from *dunyā* to *Ākhirah*! You might ask, "Why don't we see such people today?" They are there, but they are not allowed to show themselves. When Grandshaykh ʿAbd Allāh al-Fā'iz al-Dāghistānī ق entered seclusion by the order of his shaykh, Shaykh Sharafuddīn ق, for five years he ate one piece of bread the size of half your palm and seven olives daily, with as much water as he liked. He said, "I entered very big, and I was very slim when I came out. To test me more when I came out of that seclusion, Shaykh Sharafuddīn did not let me go back to my family; he sent me a message, 'Don't come to see me!'

Grandshaykh ق went in at age 18 and came out 23 years old. After seclusion, you are yearning to come to see your shaykh and your family. Shaykh Sharafuddīn told him "Go spend 40 days with Ibrāhīm Effendī (who was *majdhūb*) and listen to his *ṣuḥbah,* then you can come to see me."

Grandshaykh told me, "I went and stayed with Ibrāhīm Effendī and respected him as I respect my shaykh, and listened to whatever he said of nonsense to me and he was teaching me through his *jadhbah* and after 15 days many miracles began to appear to me. Anything I did became a miracle. I went to see my shaykh, Shaykh Sharafuddīn, who was also my uncle, and he said, 'I want you to divorce *karāmāt*, miracles, six *ṭalāqāt!*'"

In the Naqshbandi Order you must not show any miracles directly, you must only show you are weak and helpless before Allah, although you may show them indirectly by making a *duʿā'* that is answered. However, now people say, "Where are the *Awliyā'ullāh* miracles?" They are there, but you have to find them.

The time is approaching when all that power is hidden in the hand of one whom the whole *Ummah* is awaiting! May Allah give us life to see that heavenly peace come on Earth and to see him, the great-great-grandson of the Prophet ﷺ, about whom he mentioned:

لَا تَقُومُ السَّاعَةُ حَتَّى تَمْتَلِئَ الْأَرْضُ ظُلْمًا وَعُدْوَانًا، ثُمَّ يَخْرُجُ رَجُلٌ مِنْ عِتْرَتِي، أَوْ مِنْ أَهْلِ بَيْتِي، يَمْلَؤُهَا قِسْطًا وَعَدْلًا، كَمَا مُلِئَتْ ظُلْمًا وَعُدْوَانًا

> The hour will not arise until the Earth is filled with oppression and enmity, then a man will come from my descendants and will fill it with fairness and justice as it was previously filled with oppression and enmity. (Aḥmad, Ibn Ḥibbān)

In shā' Allāh, as Allah ﷻ said:

وَقُلْ جَاءَ الْحَقُّ وَزَهَقَ الْبَاطِلُ إِنَّ الْبَاطِلَ كَانَ زَهُوقًا

Say (O Muhammad), "Ḥaqq (Truth) has come and bāṭil (falsehood) has perished." (Sūrat al-Isrā', 17:81)

The Immense Greatness of Prophet Muhammad ﷺ

Sayyidinā ʿĪsā ؑ came to a civilization in Bayt al-Maqdis. Sayyidinā Mūsā ؑ came to a civilization in the land he lived, in Egypt. But Sayyidinā Muhammad, Allah said, I am going to make his name on every tongue. That is why Allah ﷻ said:

إِنَّا أَعْطَيْنَاكَ الْكَوْثَرَ

'Innā aʿṭaynāka al-Kawthar,

[O Muhammad] We have given you a lot. (Sūrat al-Kawthar, 108:1)

Al-Kawthar derives from *al-kathīr*, which means 'too much' or 'a lot'. And Kawthar is a river in Paradise with no beginning and no end. The cups around its shores are made from pearls while its shores are made from gold and its bed is made from rare precious gems. Its water is perfectly clear like a diamond and just as pure. Anyone who drinks a cup from it or even one sip will be dressed with the manifestations of Allah's Beautiful Names and Attributes. And Kawthar was given for eternal life to anyone drinks from it.

And that Kawthar is a message, the message that is continuous forever in *dunyā* and *ākhirah*. It is the way of gnosticism, *maʿrifah*.

Allah brought Sayyidinā Muhammad ﷺ from an arid place, a desert everywhere you look, with that immense message:

إِنَّ الدِّينَ عِندَ اللَّهِ الْإِسْلَامُ

Inna 'd-dīna ʿinda Allāhi 'l-Islām

Indeed, the religion in the sight of Allah is Islam. (Sūrat Āli ʿImrān, 3:19)

Sayyidinā Muhammad ﷺ, Allah sent him:

إِنَّا أَرْسَلْنَاكَ شَاهِدًا وَمُبَشِّرًا وَنَذِيرًا

Innā arsalnāka shāhidan wa mubashshiran wa nadhīran

Indeed We have sent you [O Muhammad] as a witness, a bearer of good news, and a warner. (Sūrat al-Fatḥ, 48:8)

We have sent you O Muhammad ﷺ, as a witness, to witness on everything. Someone who is witnessing will give you guidance. "We have sent you as a witness!" A teacher is a witness on his students on what they are doing. If he sees something wrong, he will correct them.

Allah sent Sayyidinā Muhammad ﷺ as a witness. He is seeing and witnessing everything that we are doing. Allah gave him that power, *shāhidan.*

A witness is a guide; if he sees anything wrong he will correct it. That is why Allah said:

وَاعْلَمُوا أَنَّ فِيكُمْ رَسُولَ اللَّهِ

Wa ʿlamū anna fīkum Rasūlullāh.

Know that the [light of the] Prophet is in you. (Sūrat al-Ḥujurāt, 49:7)

That light will guide you to what is right and what is wrong. His presence is with us. It is with us since Allah ﷻ sent him

وَمَا أَرْسَلْنَاكَ إِلَّا رَحْمَةً لِّلْعَالَمِينَ

Wa mā arsalnāka illā raḥmatan lil- ʿālamīn.

And We have not sent you [O Muhammad] except as a mercy to the worlds. (Sūrat al-Anbiyā', 21:107)

When was he ﷺ sent? There is no limit or restriction on sending. It means: "We have sent you to earth. We have sent that light that was in forehead of Ādam ؑ, that went to the forehead of Sayyidinā Nūḥ ؑ that went to the forehead of Sayyidinā Ibrāhīm ؑ, that went to Sayyidinā Mūsā's ؑ forehead that went to Sayyidinā ʿĪsā's ؑ forehead. The light of the Prophet ﷺ was there with all these prophets. Because Allah said to the other prophets, "If Muhammad ﷺ comes in your time you must follow him."[2] They were taking from his knowledge. That is why he ﷺ said,

أَنَا سَيِّدُ وَلَدِ آدَمَ يَوْمَ الْقِيَامَةِ، وَلَا فَخْرَ، وَبِيَدِي لِوَاءُ الْحَمْدِ، وَلَا فَخْرَ، وَمَا مِنْ نَبِيٍّ يَوْمَئِذٍ إِلَّا آدَمُ، فَمَنْ سِوَاهُ إِلَّا تَحْتَ لِوَائِي، وَأَنَا أَوَّلُ مَنْ تَنْشَقُّ عَنْهُ الْأَرْضُ، وَلَا فَخْرَ.

Ādam wa-man dūnahu taḥta liwāʾī yawma al-qiyāmah.

Ādam ؑ and whoever is other than him are under my flag on the Day of Judgment. (Sunan al-Tirmidhī, Musnad Aḥmad, Sunan Ibn Mājah)

That light was passing through all the Prophets until it reached his father ʿAbdullāh ؑ and finally passed to the womb of Sayyida Amīnah ؑ. There was a lady who was a relative of ʿAmīnah who was hoping to be a wife to ʿAbdullāh. One day she stopped asking him to be her husband. They asked her why? She said, "I saw that that light had transferred from ʿAbdullāh ؑ to the womb of Sayyida Amīnah ؑ" [i.e. she had gotten married, and that light shone forth].

2

وَإِذْ أَخَذَ اللَّهُ مِيثَاقَ النَّبِيِّينَ لَمَا آتَيْتُكُم مِّن كِتَابٍ وَحِكْمَةٍ ثُمَّ جَاءَكُمْ رَسُولٌ مُّصَدِّقٌ لِّمَا مَعَكُمْ لَتُؤْمِنُنَّ بِهِ

And [remember] when Allah took the covenant of the prophets, [saying], "Whatever I give you of the Scripture and wisdom—then there comes to you a Messenger confirming what is with you—you must believe in him and support him." Sūrat Āli ʿImrān (3:81)

People are happy when they have a child. They celebrate from the day of its birth. Why we are not happy with Sayyidinā Muhammad's ﷺ birth? With his birth Islam came. With his birth light came. With his birth mercy came. With his birth knowledge came.

O Muslims! Be happy with the birth of Sayyidinā Muhammad ﷺ. Rejoice in what Allah has given us. Be happy in his mercy because Sayyidinā Muhammad ﷺ is the mercy. He is the mercy for everyone. Allah has granted him and gifted him gifts that he has not given to anyone.

He has gifted him different levels and al-Ālā'ī in his *tafsīr* of Sūrat an-Najm mentioned that when Allah called Sayyidinā Muhammad ﷺ to His Divine Presence on the Night of Ascension, Sayyidinā Muhammad ﷺ was conveyed in Isrā' and Miʿrāj on five different vehicles. The first vehicle that Allah ﷻ has sent to Sayyidinā Muhammad ﷺ a was the Burāq, a heavenly creature that carried Sayyidinā Muhammad ﷺ from Mecca to Bayt al-Maqdis, Jerusalem.

The second vehicle was from the *samā ad-dunyā*, the first level of the atmosphere, up through the skies. That was a different one from the first one. That is why it is called a Miʿrāj. The golden stairway was a certain heavenly creature that carried the Prophet in his Miʿrāj, going to heavens.

The third vehicle, which carried Sayyidina Muhammad ﷺ as far as the seventh paradise were the wings of the angels.

The fourth vehicle was the wing of Sayyidinā Jibrīl. Sayyidinā Jibrīl ؑ has 600 wings and he has opened them all and carried Sayyidinā Muhammad ﷺ. With Sayyidinā Jibrīl ؑ he landed at Sidrat al-Muntahā. Finally the fifth vehicle was the Rafraf, a luminous green carpet, which was continuously making a sound and which carried him up to *Qāba Qawsayni aw Adnā*, 'two bow's-length or nearer.'

O Muslims! Allah has granted to Sayyidinā Muhammad ﷺ in *Qāba Qawsayni* to hear the writing of the pens, that write all that human beings are doing, by angels. Then he reached the highest level, which is ʿArsh al-Rahmān and that is where he made *sajda*. That was the station of *Qāba Qawsayn*. That is where Allah gave Sayyidinā Muhammad ﷺ something from the 'great amount' which is the Fount of Kawthar.

To whom other than Muhammad did Allah send a physical vehicle? To no one else. But He ﷻ sent Sayyidinā Muhammad ﷺ five different vehicles to carry him from one level to another. Allah has granted him something that he gave no one else. So, be happy that he is our prophet, that we believed in him and that we followed in his footsteps.

Anyone who follows in the footsteps of the Prophet ﷺ, Allah will love him, as Allah said:

إِن كُنتُمْ تُحِبُّونَ اللَّهَ فَاتَّبِعُونِي يُحْبِبْكُمُ اللَّهُ

In kuntum tuḥibbūna Allāha fa-ttabiʿūnī yuḥbibkumullāh

If you truly love Allah, then follow me, and Allah will love you. (Sūrat Āli ʿImrān, 3:31)

We are still in the month of the Prophet, the month of happiness, the month in which the Prophet was born, Rabīʿ al-Awwal. May Allah make every month Rabīʿ al-Awwal, and make every night the birth night of Sayyidinā Muhammad ﷺ. May Allah forgive us for the sake of Sayyidinā Muhammad ﷺ.

Wa min Allāhi 't-tawfīq, bi ḥurmati 'l-ḥabīb, bi ḥurmati 'l-Fātiḥah.

And with Allāh is success, for the honor of the Beloved, and by the sanctity of al-Fātiḥah, the opening chapter of the Qur'ān.

ولئن صبرتم لهو خير للصابرين

We Can Never Give the Prophet ﷺ His Rights

It is the month of the Prophet ﷺ, the month of Creation. You might ask why is it the month of Creation? It is because Allah ﷻ created the Prophet ﷺ first. He was asked by Jābir ؓ, "When did Allah ﷻ create you?" and the Prophet ﷺ said, "What Allah created first is my Light."

رَوَاهُ عَبْدُ الرَّزَّاقِ بِسَنَدِهِ عَنْ جَابِرِ بْنِ عَبْدِ اللّهِ بِلَفْظِ: قَالَ: قُلْتُ: يَا رَسُولَ اللّهِ، بِأَبِي أَنْتَ وَأُمِّي، أَخْبِرْنِي عَنْ أَوَّلِ شَيْءٍ خَلَقَهُ اللّٰهُ قَبْلَ الْأَشْيَاءِ. قَالَ: يَا جَابِرُ، إِنَّ اللّٰهَ تَعَالَى خَلَقَ قَبْلَ الْأَشْيَاءِ نُورَ نَبِيِّكَ مِنْ نُورِهِ، فَجَعَلَ ذَلِكَ النُّورَ يَدُورُ بِالْقُدْرَةِ حَيْثُ شَاءَ اللّٰهُ تَعَالَى.

> Jābir ؓ relates that he asked the Prophet ﷺ, "Let my father and mother be sacrificed for you, O Prophet of Allah! What is the first thing that Allah ﷻ created before all other things?" The Prophet ﷺ said, "The first thing that Allah ﷻ created is the Light of your Prophet from His Light, O Jābir." (<u>*Mūsannaf ʿAbdu 'r-Razzāq*</u>)

It is the Light of Sayyidinā Muhammad ﷺ that Allah ﷻ created first and put under His Gaze, as *Awliyā'* say, for 500,000 light years and a second time for another 500,000 light years, and a third time for 500,000 light years, and then a fourth and fifth time each of 500,000 years. No one was there except him, *taḥta tarbiyyat al-Ḥaqq*. Allah ﷻ was raising him in *Baḥr al-Qudrah*, the Ocean of Power. After the five sets of 500,000 years, Prophet ﷺ, that Light began to sweat drops of *Nūr* and from that sweat Allah created Creation. For this reason, the most difficult subject to speak about is the Prophet ﷺ, because he is above everyone's understanding. Whatever description one makes of him is within limits, but Allah ﷻ describes His Prophet ﷺ without limits as Allah's Light has no limits. Therefore the Prophet's *Rūḥ*, his holy soul, has no limits!

Allah ﷻ gave him what He did not give anyone. He wants to show his *Ummah* the greatness of their prophet, so He invited him for the Heavenly Night of *Isrā'* and *Miʿrāj*, the Night Journey and Ascension. Imagine! Think about what happens to someone who goes to the top of the Himalayas: he could faint in that environment, his blood pressure would change and some people die immediately. What if you were in a spaceship? If you were to go outside, your body would disintegrate. But the Prophet ﷺ passed all that and went through the universe with his physical body and nothing happened to him. He went with his body to the First Heaven all the way up to *Qāba Qawsayni aw Adnā*, and this is a fact.

As Muslims, we believe at the invitation of Allah ﷻ. Sayyidinā Muhammad ﷺ went through *Mi'rāj* himself and his companion was Jibrīl ﷺ. Allah wants to show him His Greatness that He has not shown anyone else. He took the Prophet ﷺ through the route of all the Paradises, although He could have taken him directly to the station of *Qāba Qawsayni aw Adnā*, but He did not. He took him to the First Heaven to dress him ﷺ from its Light and the Realities of the Beautiful Names and Attributes manifesting in that Heaven, preparing him for that immense meeting. All angels knew about his coming and were preparing for it with their heavenly *ṣalawāt*.

I heard that a group made their target completing 1 billion *ṣalawāt* on Prophet ﷺ, which *In shā'Allāh* might be equivalent to 100 billion *ṣalawāt*. Do you know how many millions of angels do *ṣalawāt* on Prophet? Our *ṣalawāt* compared to theirs has limits but their *ṣalawāt* has no limits. How many angels made *ṣalawāt* on Prophet? All of them, of course, because they are under the order of Allah ﷻ!

إِنَّ اللَّهَ وَمَلَائِكَتَهُ يُصَلُّونَ عَلَى النَّبِيِّ يَا أَيُّهَا الَّذِينَ آمَنُوا صَلُّوا عَلَيْهِ وَسَلِّمُوا تَسْلِيمًا

Verily, Allah and His angels send praise on the Prophet. O Believers! Pray upon him and greet him with a worthy salutation. (Sūrat al-Aḥzāb, 33:56)

Allah and His angels are making *ṣalawāt* continuously, non-stop, and Allah is bringing the greatness of Prophet ﷺ higher and higher. Allah ordered the angels to decorate the Heavens to receive Prophet ﷺ in his *Mi'rāj*. He went in one speed, passing the universe in moments.

If you look at Google Sky you can view the constellations. As you zoom in you see so many stars, lights and galaxies that you cannot count. The Prophet ﷺ passed through all that in one moment and understood the reality of everything he saw! That is why Allah ﷻ gave him the knowledge of *'Ulūm al-Awwalīn wa 'Ulūm al-Ākhirīn*, the great knowledge, not what we read, write and speak of, but heavenly knowledge that we don't know.

وَمَا أُوتِيتُم مِّنَ الْعِلْمِ إِلَّا قَلِيلًا

You have been given from knowledge not but a little. (Sūrat al-Isrā', 17:85)

What has been given to us is mere drops of Sayyidinā Muhammad's ﷺ knowledge! O Muslims!

$$\text{وَلَمَّا خَلَقَ اللَّهُ الْقَلَمَ، قَالَ لَهُ: اكْتُبْ مُحَمَّدٌ رَسُولُ اللَّهِ، قَالَ الْقَلَمُ: وَمَا مُحَمَّدٌ الَّذِي قَرَنْتَ اسْمَهُ بِاسْمِكَ؟ فَقَالَ اللَّهُ: تَأَدَّبْ يَا قَلَمُ، وَعِزَّتِي وَجَلَالِي، لَوْلَا مُحَمَّدٌ مَا خَلَقْتُ أَحَدًا مِنْ خَلْقِي.}$$

When the Pen was first ordered to write, it wrote *'Lā ilāha illa-llāh'* for 2,000 years as some scholars say, while others say for 70,000 years. Allah then ordered it to write *'Muhammad Rasūlallāh'*. The Pen said, *Yā Rabbī*, who is 'Muhammad' whose name you put with Yours?" Allah said, *Yā Qalam law lā Muhammad mā khalaqtu ahadan min khalqī*, "O Pen! If not for Muhammad, I would not have created anything from My Creation."

So what can we say? We are helpless and weak, only by *salawāt* are we strong. How did the Ṣaḥābah ؓ become strong? By looking at the face of Prophet ﷺ! They saw that Light attracting them and it became strong and they gave themselves completely to Allah ﷻ and His Prophet ﷺ! How can we become strong? We become strong by making *salawāt*, because we are not able to see Prophet ﷺ, although he is not far from us, he is present in this *masjid;* who knows, it might be that he is observing us now.

$$\text{قَالَ رَسُولُ اللَّهِ ﷺ: حَيَاتِي خَيْرٌ لَكُمْ، تُحَدِّثُونَ وَيُحْدَثُ لَكُمْ، وَمَمَاتِي خَيْرٌ لَكُمْ، تُعْرَضُ عَلَيَّ أَعْمَالُكُمْ، فَإِنْ وَجَدْتُ خَيْرًا حَمِدْتُ اللَّهَ، وَإِنْ وَجَدْتُ غَيْرَ ذَلِكَ اسْتَغْفَرْتُ لَكُمْ.}$$

The Prophet ﷺ said:

> My life is a great good for you: you relate from it and narrations are related to you. And my death contains good for you as well, for I observe the *'amal* of my Ummah. If I find good I thank Allah and if I see other than that, bad, I ask forgiveness for you. (*Musnad al-Bazzār*)

It means he is looking at our *'amal*, at what we are doing every moment, in every inspiration or gossip, detecting everything that comes to our hearts. He can see it. This is our *'Aqīdah*, belief, that Prophet ﷺ is *ḥāḍir* and *nāẓir*, present and witnessing, and without him there is no way to reach the Divine Presence!

The Prophet ﷺ reaching the Divine Presence means the entire Ummah reached it with him, because all his life he was saying, "*Ummatī, Ummatī*, my Ummah, my Ummah!" On the day he passed away he was saying "*Ummatī, Ummatī*," concerned about his Ummah. In his Holy Grave he is saying, "*Ummatī, Ummatī*. On *Yawm al-Maḥshar*, the Day of Resurrection, he will say, "*Yā* Jibrīl, what happened to my *Ummah*?" and Jibrīl ؑ will say, "*Yā Rasūlallāh*, don't worry, you are the first to be called." Who is being called to present us to Allah ﷻ? It is enough for us: when *Rasūlallāh* ﷺ is called to present to Allah ﷻ, be sure that all his *Ummah* is going to be forgiven or why will Allah call him? To forgive the *Ummah*! Prophet ﷺ said as soon as he entered the Divine Presence he went into *sajda,* asking Allah ﷻ to forgive his *Ummah.*

As we mentioned many times, *Rasūlallāh* ﷺ said in that *sajda* Allah opens for him *ʿUlūm al-Awwalīn wa 'l-Ākhirīn,* the Knowledge of the Firsts and the Lasts and he opened to him special *duʿās* that He never before opened to Prophet's heart. He said he never knew that before, although he has immense knowledge. For example all the mystical letters in the Qur'ān that Allah revealed: *'Alif, Lām, Mīm*, etc. When Jibrīl ﷺ revealed the first letter of Sūrat Maryam, *Kāf*, to Prophet ﷺ he said, "*ʿalimtu*, I knew," and the same for *Ḥā', ʿAyn, Yā, Ṣād*; for each letter he said, "I knew." Jibrīl ﷺ wondered what he knew. The Prophet ﷺ knew the secret meaning of these letters that Allah hid from Jibrīl ﷺ and everyone else. The Prophet ﷺ said when he goes into that *sajda* on the Day of Resurrection, Allah opens to his heart *duʿās* that He never opened before. What 'before' and what did He never open? In Arabic, we know it as 'from beginning to end', but Arabic language has limit. There are millions of words, but what *duʿā's* will Allah ﷻ open to Prophet ﷺ that he never knew before, and what kind of words? We don't know. With what will Allah recompense him because he did his best for the *Ummah*, for humanity?

عَنْ أَبِي هُرَيْرَةَ رَضِيَ اللهُ عَنْهُ، قَالَ: قَالَ رَسُولُ اللهِ ﷺ: إِنَّمَا بُعِثْتُ لِأُتَمِّمَ مَكَارِمَ الْأَخْلَاقِ.

> The Prophet ﷺ said, "I have been sent to perfect the best of conduct (your behavior and character)." (Imām Bukhārī's al-Adab al-Mufrad, Imam Malik's al-Muwaṭṭaʾ, al-Ḥākim's Mustadrak, Imām Aḥmad's Musnad)

So in that *sajda*, what does Prophet ﷺ say to Allah ﷻ that He answers, "*Yā* Muhammad, it is enough! Raise your head, I will give you whatever you want! What do you want from Me?" The Creator and His Servant are speaking to each other.

They say Mūsā ﷺ is '*Kalīmullāh*', to whom Allah spoke directly. Muhammad is *Ḥabībullāh,* Allah's Beloved, *Khalīlullāh,* Allah's Friend, and *Kalīmullāh*, to whom Allah spoke! All these descriptions are for Prophet ﷺ and he is speaking with Allah ﷻ on the most important day, the Day of Resurrection, when you either go to Paradise or Hellfire. It is more important than when Mūsā ﷺ spoke with Allah ﷻ in the Valley Ṭūwā. Prophet ﷺ is speaking for all humanity and Sayyidinā Mūsā ﷺ spoke for himself. In his *sajda,* Sayyidinā Muhammad ﷺ is asking for the *Ummah*, "*Yā Rabbī*, I want my *Ummah*!" Allah ﷻ says, "Don't worry, *yā* Muhammad, I am giving you your *Ummah*. Take one-third of them to Paradise with no account." Are we going to be in that one-third? *In shā'Allāh.*

Then Prophet ﷺ goes into *sajda* another time and he said Allah opened for him *du'ās* He didn't open for him in the first one. He asks, "*Yā Rabbī, Ummatī, Ummatī!*" Allah ﷻ says, "*Yā* Muhammad, raise your head and I will give you what you want. What do you want?' He says, 'I need my *Ummah*. Already one-third are there, but I need the rest." Allah gives him half of the rest.

Then he goes into *sajda* a third time and asks the same and Allah gives him the whole *Ummah* to take to Paradise except one person. That's why we are clean already. As long as we do our obligations, by our *nawāfil*, voluntary worship, with the *barakah* of the Prophet ﷺ, Allah ﷻ will erase all our sins! Allah ﷻ gave him the whole *Ummah* to be forgiven except one. Then Allah calls that one and says, "What will I do with you?" *Al-Ḥamdu lillāh* Allah speaks to that one, he is honored, "Do you want My Punishment or My *Raḥmah*?" Of course he says he wants His *Raḥmah*, and Allah ﷻ says, 'I am *Arḥam ar-Rāḥimīn*. You are from the *Ummah* of the Prophet ﷺ, go!" The whole *Ummah* enters Paradise. That is narrated in <u>*Ṣaḥīḥ Bukhārī*</u>.

O Muslims! We, the *Ummah*, is lost in too much ignorance nowadays. From the Signs of the Last Days that Prophet ﷺ mentioned, knowledge will be lifted up. The Ṣaḥābah ؓ asked if the Qur'ān will be lifted up, and he said, "No, the sincere *'ulamā* will die with no substitute (they will not be replaced)." We are lacking *'ulamā* today; before you could speak about thousands of them and today there remain only hundreds. Most of them passe away and now most *Awliyā'ullāh* are hidden. We are left without them, *yā Sayyīdī, yā Rasūlullāh, yā Raḥmatan li 'l-'Ālamīn!*

Al-Ḥamdu lillāh they have restored the Mawlid in every mosque today, and *Al-Ḥamdu lillāh* we are seeing the Mawlid in Madinah (where it was previously banned). We have to say may Allah bless the people of the Indian Subcontinent, because they initiated this movement. Before people used to say Mawlid is *bid'a*, yet now the majority of mosques identify with being Sufi. They knew the reality cannot be changed, Prophet ﷺ came with *Tazkiyyat an-Nafs,* Purification of the Self, which is *Tasawwuf*!

May Allah ﷻ keep us under the wings and arms of Prophet ﷺ in *dunyā* and *Ākhirah*. We are asking Allah ﷻ to grant us to inherit from the good manners of Prophet ﷺ.

One man came to Prophet ﷺ and said, "Advise me." Prophet ﷺ said, "Don't get angry," because anger kills the person; when someone gets angry he doesn't know what he's doing. Islam is to avoid anger. When you avoid anger, hate, and jealousy, Allah ﷻ will open from the good manners He dressed His Prophet ﷺ with:

وَمَا أَرْسَلْنَاكَ إِلَّا رَحْمَةً لِّلْعَالَمِينَ

(O Muhammad!) We have sent you not except as a Mercy for all the Worlds. (Sūrat al-Anbiyā, 21:107)

O Muslims! The time is running. I would like to say look very closely to any of the six *ṣaḥīḥ* books of Hadith on the Signs of the Last Days and you will see what Prophet ﷺ mentioned and predicted is now happening, which you will understand. Prophet ﷺ said in a famous Hadith:

قالَ: فَأَخْبِرْنِي عَنِ السَّاعَةِ، قالَ: ما المسْؤُولُ عَنْهَا بِأَعْلَمَ مِنَ السَّائِلِ، قالَ: فَأَخْبِرْنِي عَنْ أَمارَاتِهَا، قالَ: أَنْ تَلِدَ الأَمَةُ رَبَّتَهَا، وَأَنْ تَرَى الحُفَاةَ العُرَاةَ العَالَةَ رُعاءَ الشَّاءِ يَتَطَاوَلُونَ فِي البُنْيَانِ.

> He (Jibrīl) said [to the Prophet ﷺ], "Inform me about the Hour." The Prophet ﷺ said, "About that the one questioned knows no more than the questioner." So he said, "Inform me about the Signs of its coming." The Prophet ﷺ said, "They are the slave-girl will give birth to her mistress and you will see the barefooted, naked, destitute shepherds arrogantly building high buildings." (Muslim, Bukhārī and others)

Allah ﷻ gave them the wealth of Arabian Peninsula oil and they turned that into high-rise buildings, like Prophet ﷺ said 1400 years ago. Today if you go to these countries, what do you see? High buildings. Open your minds, open your hearts! If you are in a difficult situation, Prophet ﷺ said:

عَنْ أَبِي مُوسَى الْأَشْعَرِيِّ ، قَالَ : قَالَ رَسُولُ اللَّهِ صَلَّى اللَّهُ عَلَيْهِ وَسَلَّمَ : " إِنَّ بَيْنَ يَدَيِ السَّاعَةِ فِتَنًا كَقِطَعِ اللَّيْلِ الْمُظْلِمِ يُصْبِحُ الرَّجُلُ فِيهَا مُؤْمِنًا وَيُمْسِي كَافِرًا ، وَيُمْسِي مُؤْمِنًا وَيُصْبِحُ كَافِرًا ، الْقَاعِدُ فِيهَا خَيْرٌ مِنَ الْقَائِمِ ، وَالْمَاشِي فِيهَا خَيْرٌ مِنَ السَّاعِي ، فَكَسِّرُوا قِسِيَّكُمْ وَقَطِّعُوا أَوْتَارَكُمْ وَاضْرِبُوا سُيُوفَكُمْ بِالْحِجَارَةِ ، فَإِنْ دُخِلَ يَعْنِي عَلَى أَحَدٍ مِنْكُمْ فَلْيَكُنْ كَخَيْرِ ابْنَيْ آدَمَ " .

> Before the Hour comes, there will be a tribulation like patches of dark night. A man will get up a Believer and go to sleep an unbeliever, or will go to sleep a Believer and wake up an unbeliever. The one who sits at that time will be better than one who stands and the one standing will be better than the one walking and the one walking will be better than one running. Break your bows, cut their strings and strike your swords against stones. If someone comes to kill any of you, then be like the better of the two sons of Ādam. (Abū Dāwūd, Ibn Mājah, narrated by Abū Mūsā al-Ashʿarī)

Don't interfere and don't be part of that *fitna*. *In shā 'Allāh* may Allah take that *fitna* away and bring the name of Islam up, because our honor is the honor of Islam, the honor of Prophet ﷺ!

كُنتُمْ خَيْرَ أُمَّةٍ أُخْرِجَتْ لِلنَّاسِ تَأْمُرُونَ بِالْمَعْرُوفِ وَتَنْهَوْنَ عَنِ الْمُنكَرِ وَتُؤْمِنُونَ بِاللَّهِ

You were the best of Nations evolved for Mankind, enjoining what is right, forbidding what is wrong and believing in Allah. (Sūrat Āli 'Imrān, 3:110)

It is our duty to call for good! May Allah ﷻ forgive us and bless us, and make this event tonight alive in His Divine Presence! *Awliyā'* who pass away are alive in the presence of their Lord: they hear, they see, they can talk, because Allah ﷻ gave them a life in the grave that is from Heaven. May Allah give us that life until the Day of Resurrection when we will be forgiven from any mistakes.

May Allah ﷻ forgive all of us and turn our *ṣalawāt* into the *ṣalawāt* of angels!

As-salāmu 'alaykum wa Raḥmatullāhi wa barakātuh.

Wa min Allāhi 't-tawfīq, bi ḥurmati 'l-ḥabīb, bi ḥurmati 'l-Fātiḥah.

And with Allāh is success. For the sake of the Beloved, for his sake we recite the opening chapter of Holy Qur'ān.

وإنك لعلى خلق عظيم

'Alif is for "Allah" and Mīm is for "Muhammad ﷺ"

O Muslims and Believers, the followers of Sayyidinā Muhammad ﷺ, may Allah ﷻ bless us from His Light from His *Nūr* and may Allah ﷻ dress us from the Light of Sayyidinā Muhammad ﷺ.

'Aẓamat al-Nabī ṣallallāhu 'alayhi wa-sallam lā yumkinu sharḥuhā. No one can explain the Greatness of Sayyidinā Muḥammad ﷺ. *'Aẓamatuhu khāṣṣatan bihi.* His greatness, He is the only one to know about it.

'Aẓamat al-Nabī ﷺ min 'Aẓamatillāh. Fataḥa Allāhu 'alayhi min hādhihi l-'aẓama 'Ulūm al-Awwalīn wa-l-Ākhirīn kamā qāla Allāhu subḥānahu wa-ta'ālā, the *'aẓamah* of the Prophet ﷺ is from *'Aẓamatullāh*.

Allāh ﷻ opened for him from His *'Aẓamah*, from the *Anwār*, the Lights of this *'Aẓamatullāh*, dressed it to the Prophet ﷺ where he was appearing always with that Greatness in the Divine Presence.

When you go to see someone important you dress the best dress. What do you think about the Prophet ﷺ who is always in the Divine Presence, always in Allāh's Presence? What kind of dress must he dress? Allāh dresses him with His *'Aẓamah* in order that he can be facing Him and getting from what Allāh wants to open to him.

'Aẓamat al-Nabī ﷺ lā yumkin waṣfuhā illā bi-waṣf al-muḥīṭ, al-muḥīṭ alladhī lā qā'ra lah. We cannot describe the *'Aẓamah* of the Prophet ﷺ except we can say he is an ocean that has no bottom; as much as you dive down, the ocean is still farther down. As much as you dive and dive, that ocean is greater and greater, you cannot limit it. So *'Aẓamat al-Nabī ﷺ* cannot be limited, because it was given by Allāh ﷻ.

'Aẓamat al-Nabī ﷺ hiya ka 'l-ātī: maraja 'l-baḥrayni yaltaqiyān.

When Jibrīl ؏ came to the Prophet ﷺ asking about Islam, he mentioned the Five Pillars of Islam. From within these Five Pillars, he mentioned *Maqām al-'īmān*; from within the Five Pillars of Islam and the Six Pillars of *'īmān*, he mentioned the core and the essence of Islam and faith, the essence of all this is *Maqām al-Iḥsān*. So all these three different elements: *Islam, 'īmān, Iḥsān,* begin with the letter *'Alif*. Islam belongs to Allah, *'īmān* belongs to Allah, *Iḥsān* belongs to Allah, because it is *'Alif*. Allah ﷻ dressed the Prophet ﷺ from them. That's why Prophet ﷺ becomes *muḥsin, mu'min,* which begins with *Mīm*, referring to the Prophet ﷺ, as he is the *Muslim, mu'min,* and *muḥsin*. So these three, and the other three that Allah ﷻ owns, Islam, *'īmān, Iḥsān,* and Prophet ﷺ owns Muslim, *mu'min* and *muḥsin*, from them something special comes out.

A question: is it possible for sweet water to come from out from salt water? The answer is yes! If Allah wants sweet water to come from salt water He can make it happen. Sayyidinā Muḥammad ﷺ from all the bad manners and the sins of the *Ummah,* is turning them from salty to sweet. [*Allāhu Akbar*!]

Can Allah ﷻ bring sweet from salt? Yes. Can the Prophet ﷺ change our *sayyi'āt* to *ḥasanāt* sins into good deeds by asking forgiveness, *istighfār* on our behalf. Can he? Yes!

Today they found deep in the bottom of the oceans, that Allah ﷻ created *yanaabi'*, sources, springs of sweet water coming from within salty water. The ocean contains salt water, yet there is sweet water coming out from the middle of these holes in the bottom of the ocean that you can drink and it has no salt in it! They take bottles or pitchers to the ocean, dive down fill bottles and drink that water. It is sweeter than the water coming from waterfalls, *shalālāt* like Niagara Falls.

That water is enough to bring it out with pipes. It needs no transformation, only to place a pipe down in the hole, because the sweet water is coming up. Get a pipe, take it to the desert, and you can turn a desert into an oasis.

Be happy, because the Prophet ﷺ is turning our salty sins from within the sin itself, into a sweetness of good manners and good behaviors! Any sin you do the Prophet ﷺ will turn that sin into a *ḥasanah*, good deed. Allah gave him the *shafā'ah* intercession, to turn it into a sweet element and the bad manners to disappear, one after the other, taking them away from every one of us!

Here is a simple example of *'Aẓamat al-Nabī* ﷺ, only to help give us an understanding. Ask the *Angel Healing* group to stand up. Okay, I am asking one person who will be the volunteer to do something. Can he give me all their names quickly right now? He is one of them, but no one can give the names of 20-30 people at the same time together.

عَنْ أَبِي هُرَيْرَةَ رَضِيَ اللهُ عَنْهُ، قَالَ: قَالَ رَسُولُ اللهِ ﷺ:تُعْرَضُ عَلَيَّ أَعْمَالُكُمْ، فَمَا رَأَيْتُ مِنْ خَيْرٍ حَمِدْتُ اللَّهَ، وَمَا رَأَيْتُ مِنْ شَرٍّ اسْتَغْفَرْتُ لَكُمْ

> The Prophet ﷺ said: "Your deeds are presented to me; whatever I see of good, I praise Allāh for it, and whatever I see of evil, I ask Allāh's forgiveness for you." (al-Bazzār in his Musnad)

"I observe the *'amal* of my *Ummah*. I know my *Ummah* one-by-one by their names. At the same time, I know all of them: in one moment I can count all of them, all the Creation!" Here, we were not able to count a single one. Two of them said 'no.' But the Prophet ﷺ knows everyone by name, what he is doing and whether he is good or bad, and he will carry on in cleaning that human being.

If you ask me about Shaykh Mustafa, what he has of good tidings of *ḥasanāt*, can I know? Can I count his *ḥasanāt*, can I count your *ḥasanāt*? It is impossible. I don't know them. Can I count your *sayyi'āt* no, it is impossible! I don't know them. But the Prophet ﷺ knows everything; he knows what we are doing of good and bad. If he knows of what I do good and bad, and if he sees we are doing something good he praises Allah *ḥamdan lillāhi*, and if he sees us doing something bad, he makes *istighfār* for them. Who can do that, angels? They cannot. No one can do that. That is why he said: "…I observe the *ʿamal* of my ummah."

They cannot deny that hadith, it shows the greatness of the Prophet ﷺ. He said, "I observe the *ʿamal* of my *Ummah*." He checks everyone and what they are doing. "If I see good, I say 'thank you *yā Rabbī*,' if I see bad I ask *istighfār* on their behalf." All of them. How? Two people were not able to know their names? Look at the greatness Allah gave to the Prophet ﷺ to know everyone's names, he knows them sitting here now, one by one with their names. Don't say, "That is *shirk*," that is not *shirk*. Allah gave him that and the hadith is stating that.

He knows everyone, one by one, and checks on their notebooks: how many *sayyi'āt* and *ḥasanāt* they did. He knows everything about us. In a blink of an eye he can see the whole Creation on Earth. Allah gave him *quwwat malakūtiyya,* Heavenly Power, with Heavenly Power you can do everything. And that is why Allah said about *Awliyā'ullāh*:

بَلْ أَحْيَاءٌ عِندَ رَبِّهِمْ يُرْزَقُونَ

They are alive provided for by their Lord (Sūrat Āli ʿImrān, 3:169)

Allah ﷻ said regarding *Shuhadā'*, the martyrs, Ṣaḥābah ؓ, the Companions, *Awliyā'* and *al-A'immah*, the Imāms, "*They are alive provided for by their Lord.*" They are not provided with candies and food, but provided from *Anwār Allāh ʿazza wa-jall*, they are provided from what Allah dressed them with the Lights of His Beautiful Names and Attributes. They are provided from the oceans of knowledge Allah opened for them. One *Walī* can turn this *dunyā* upside down when the permission comes.

None of us can guarantee that he can enter Paradise without the *shafāʿah* of the Prophet ﷺ. No one must think that they will enter Paradise by praying and fasting, no! The Prophet ﷺ asked the Ṣaḥābah ؓ:

قَالَ النَّبِيُّ ﷺ لِأَصْحَابِهِ : «أَتَدْرُونَ مَنِ الْمُفْلِسُ؟»

قَالُوا: «يَا رَسُولَ اللهِ، الْمُفْلِسُ فِينَا مَنْ لَا دِرْهَمَ لَهُ وَلَا مَتَاعَ.»

قَالَ: «لَيْسَ ذَلِكَ الْمُفْلِسَ، وَلَكِنَّ الْمُفْلِسَ مَنْ يَأْتِي يَوْمَ الْقِيَامَةِ بِحَسَنَاتٍ أَمْثَالِ الْجِبَالِ، وَيَأْتِي وَقَدْ ظَلَمَ هَذَا، وَلَطَمَ هَذَا، وَأَخَذَ مِنْ عِرْضِ هَذَا، فَيَأْخُذُ هَذَا مِنْ

حَسَنَاتِهِ، وَهَذَا مِنْ حَسَنَاتِهِ، فَإِنْ بَقِيَ عَلَيْهِ شَيْءٌ، أُخِذَ مِنْ سَيِّئَاتِهِمْ، فَرُدَّ عَلَيْهِ، ثُمَّ صُكَّ لَهُ صَكٌّ إِلَى النَّارِ.»

> The Prophet ﷺ said: Do you know who the *muflis* (bankrupt one) is? The *muflis* from my Ummah is one who comes on the Day of Judgment having performed prayer, fasting and giving zakat. However, along with all of this, he abused this person and slandered that person, ate the wealth of this person and unlawfully spilled the blood of that person. These people will take from his good deeds. If, however, his good deeds become exhausted, then their sins will be put upon him and he will be thrown into the Fire. (Tirmidhī)

Man al-muflis? "Who is the bankrupt one?" Ṣaḥābah ؓ were not expecting that the Prophet ﷺ would ask them something like that. They were stunned, and astonished when he asked this question. They said:

Al-muflisu man lā māla lah, "the *muflis* is the one who has no money."

Are all of us bankrupt, *muflis,* or not? Are we *muflis*? No? Okay we'll show you that we are *muflis.* We are *muflis* by what we do, but rich by the Prophet's ﷺ intercession. So are we *muflis* or are we wealthy?

When they said the *Al-muflisu man lā māla lah,* the *muflis* is the one that has no wealth, the Prophet ﷺ said, "No, the *muflis* is the one that has no *ʿamal.*" That is because he is going to be in Allah's Presence for judgement and Allah will say to him, "You have no *ʿamal*, go to Hellfire." Ṣaḥābah ؓ said, "*Yā Rasūlallāh*, is he *muflis*, bankrupt with no *ʿamal*, even though he fasts and prays?" The Prophet ﷺ said, "Even if he fasts and prays he has no *ʿamal.*"

So our *ʿamal* is gone. We pray, we fast, but we have no *ʿamal*. The Prophet ﷺ said to them, "Anyone who backbites his brother, his father, his mother, his friend, anyone who backbites people, there is no *ʿamal* for him, his *ʿamal* disappears." Allah said in the Holy Qur'ān:

يَا أَيُّهَا الَّذِينَ آمَنُوا إِن جَاءَكُمْ فَاسِقٌ بِنَبَإٍ فَتَبَيَّنُوا أَن تُصِيبُوا قَوْمًا بِجَهَالَةٍ فَتُصْبِحُوا عَلَى مَا فَعَلْتُمْ نَادِمِينَ

Yā ayyuhā alladhīna āmanū in jā'akum fāsiqun binaba'in fatabayyanū an tuṣībū qawman bijahālatin fatuṣbiḥū ʿalā mā faʿaltum nādimīn.

O you who believe! If a corrupt person comes to you with something wrong, ascertain the truth unless you harm people unwittingly and afterwards become full of repentance for what you have done. (Sūrat al-Ḥujurāt, 49:6)

"O *mu'mins,* if a corrupted person, a *munāfiq*, comes to you with news, check it before taking a decision, because he might be lying." The *ayah* continues, "You might fall into the trap of attacking someone when you are ignorant of what he has done. Then you will regret it." Allah ﷻ said, *Bismillāhir-raḥmānir-raḥīm:*

يَا أَيُّهَا الَّذِينَ آمَنُوا اجْتَنِبُوا كَثِيرًا مِّنَ الظَّنِّ إِنَّ بَعْضَ الظَّنِّ إِثْمٌ ۖ وَلَا تَجَسَّسُوا وَلَا يَغْتَب بَّعْضُكُم بَعْضًا ۚ أَيُحِبُّ أَحَدُكُمْ أَن يَأْكُلَ لَحْمَ أَخِيهِ مَيْتًا فَكَرِهْتُمُوهُ ۚ وَاتَّقُوا اللَّهَ ۚ

Yā ayyuhā alladhīna āmanū ijtanibū kathīran mina al-ẓanni inna baʿḍa al-ẓanni ithmun wa-lā tajassasū wa-lā yaghtab baʿḍukum baʿḍan a-yuḥibbu aḥadukum an ya'kula laḥma akhīhi maytan fakarihtumūhu

O you who believe! avoid suspicion as much (as possible): for suspicion in some cases is a sin: and spy not on each other, nor speak ill of each other behind their backs. Would any of you like to eat the flesh of his dead brother? No, you would abhor it. (Sūrat al-Ḥujurāt, 49:12)

O *mu'mins*, and all of you here are *mu'mins*, the evidence is that you are coming to the *masjid*. If you are not *mu'min,* then why do you have to come here?

"*O believers avoid too much doubting people,*" You are doubting people a lot, avoid that suspicion, because you might believe something that is wrong., "*and don't spy on each other, don't back bite each other.*" Allah says in Holy Qur'ān:

أَيُحِبُّ أَحَدُكُمْ أَن يَأْكُلَ لَحْمَ أَخِيهِ مَيْتًا فَكَرِهْتُمُوهُ ۚ

a-yuḥibbu aḥadukum an ya'kula laḥma akhīhi maytan, fa-karihtumūhu.

Would one of you like to eat the flesh of his brother when dead? You would detest it. (Sūrat al-Ḥujurāt (49:12)

"Do you like to eat the flesh of your brother raw and his dead body?"

Allah is saying that the one who backbites and the one who spread rumors is as if he is eating the raw flesh of his dead brother, he is snatching it and biting his brother.

So who is the rich one now? The rich one is the one who always doesn't backbite, speak about others or spread rumors, *dhāka huwa al-rajulu al-mu'min*, that person is a *mu'min.*

Are there any angels here? How many? There are too many. Can you count them? I can. Infinite number of angels. [laughter]

عَنْ أَبِي هُرَيْرَةَ رَضِيَ اللهُ عَنْهُ، قَالَ: قَالَ رَسُولُ اللهِ صَلَّى اللهُ عَلَيْهِ وَسَلَّمَ: «إِنَّ لِلّٰهِ مَلَائِكَةً يَطُوفُونَ فِي الطُّرُقِ يَلْتَمِسُونَ أَهْلَ الذِّكْرِ، فَإِذَا وَجَدُوا قَوْمًا يَذْكُرُونَ اللهَ تَنَادَوْا: «هَلُمُّوا إِلَى حَاجَتِكُمْ». قَالَ: «فَيَحُفُّونَهُمْ بِأَجْنِحَتِهِمْ إِلَى السَّمَاءِ الدُّنْيَا».

قَالَ: «فَيَسْأَلُهُمْ رَبُّهُمْ وَهُوَ أَعْلَمُ مِنْهُمْ: مَا يَقُولُ عِبَادِي؟» قَالُوا: «يَقُولُونَ: يُسَبِّحُونَكَ، وَيُكَبِّرُونَكَ، وَيَحْمَدُونَكَ، وَيُمَجِّدُونَكَ». قَالَ: «فَيَقُولُ: هَلْ رَأَوْنِي؟» قَالُوا: «لَا وَاللهِ، مَا رَأَوْكَ». قَالَ: «فَكَيْفَ لَوْ رَأَوْنِي؟» قَالُوا: «لَوْ رَأَوْكَ كَانُوا أَشَدَّ لَكَ عِبَادَةً، وَأَشَدَّ لَكَ تَمْجِيدًا وَتَحْمِيدًا، وَأَكْثَرَ لَكَ تَسْبِيحًا». قَالَ: «فَمَا يَسْأَلُونِي؟» قَالُوا: «يَسْأَلُونَكَ الْجَنَّةَ». قَالَ: «وَهَلْ رَأَوْهَا؟» قَالُوا: «لَا وَاللهِ يَا رَبِّ، مَا رَأَوْهَا». قَالَ: «فَكَيْفَ لَوْ أَنَّهُمْ رَأَوْهَا؟» قَالُوا: «لَوْ أَنَّهُمْ رَأَوْهَا، كَانُوا أَشَدَّ عَلَيْهَا حِرْصًا، وَأَشَدَّ لَهَا طَلَبًا، وَأَعْظَمَ فِيهَا رَغْبَةً». قَالَ: «فَمِمَّ يَتَعَوَّذُونَ؟» قَالُوا: «مِنَ النَّارِ». قَالَ: «وَهَلْ رَأَوْهَا؟» قَالُوا: «لَا وَاللهِ يَا رَبِّ، مَا رَأَوْهَا». قَالَ: «فَكَيْفَ لَوْ رَأَوْهَا؟» قَالُوا: «لَوْ رَأَوْهَا، كَانُوا أَشَدَّ مِنْهَا فِرَارًا، وَأَشَدَّ لَهَا مَخَافَةً». قَالَ: «فَأُشْهِدُكُمْ أَنِّي قَدْ غَفَرْتُ لَهُمْ». قَالَ: «يَقُولُ مَلَكٌ مِنَ الْمَلَائِكَةِ: فِيهِمْ فُلَانٌ لَيْسَ مِنْهُمْ، إِنَّمَا جَاءَ لِحَاجَةٍ». قَالَ: «هُمُ الْجُلَسَاءُ، لَا يَشْقَى بِهِمْ جَلِيسُهُمْ».

Abū Hurayra ؓ reported that the Prophet of Allah ﷺ said, "Allah Almighty has angels who travel the highways and by-ways seeking out gatherings of remembrance (*dhikr*) in the earth. When they find a gathering of remembrance, they enfold them with their wings stretching up to the heaven. Allah asks them, 'From where have you come?' They reply, 'We have come from Your slaves who are glorifying You, praising You, proclaiming Your oneness, asking of You and seeking refuge with You.' He says, and He knows better than them, 'What are they asking Me for?' They reply, 'They are asking You for the Garden.' He says, 'Have they seen it?' They reply, 'No, our Lord.' He says, 'How would it be if they were to see it?' Then He asks, and He knows better than them, 'What are they seeking refuge from?' 'From the Fire,' they reply. He asks, 'Have they seen it?' 'No,' they reply. Then He says, 'How would it be if they were to see it?' Then He says, 'I testify to you that I have forgiven them, I have given them what they ask Me for, and I give them the refuge which they ask of Me.'

> They say, 'Our Lord, among them is a wrongdoer who is sitting with them, but is not one of them.' He says, 'I have forgiven him as well. The one sitting with these people will not be wretched.'" (Bukhārī, Muslim, al-Tirmidhī, al-Ḥākim)

Allah has angels that roam in the street looking for such an association, associations of *Dhikrullāh*, this meeting is *Dhikrullāh.* Allah ordered angels where there are circles like this one, to sit with them and they make *istighfār* on their behalf. So, that's why by sitting in such associations and such meetings, you will never have any sin, they will erase it, they will sit with you asking Allah for forgiveness on our behalf. Be happy! Be happy that you are Muslim, be happy that you are *mu'min*, be happy that you are *muḥsin*, be happy that Allah revealed the Holy Qur'ān on the Prophet ﷺ and you are reading it. May Allah forgive us and bless us,

Wa min Allāhi 't-tawfīq, bi ḥurmati 'l-ḥabīb, bi ḥurmati 'l-Fātiḥah.

And with Allāh is success, for the honor of the Beloved, and by the sanctity of al-Fātiḥah, the opening chapter of the Qur'ān.

بسم الله الرحمن الرحيم

The Light of Muhammad ﷺ is the Fabric of All Creation

Allāh said:

وَمَا أَرْسَلْنَاكَ إِلا رَحْمَةً لِّلْعَالَمِينَ

Wa-mā arsalnāka illā raḥmatan li'l-ʿālamīn "We sent you not, but as a Mercy for all creatures." (Sūrat al-Anbiyā' 21:107)

There are two meanings for the Arabic word *ʿālamīn*. It can refer to humankind and jinn, or it can mean everyone and everything. Everything that Allāh ﷻ has created is included in *ʿālamīn*. As Allāh said in the opening of the *Qur'ān* (Sūrat al-Fātiḥa):

الْحَمْدُ للهِ رَبِّ الْعَالَمِينَ

Al-ḥamdu li'Llāhi Rabbi'l-ʿālamīn "All praise is for Allāh, Lord of the Worlds." (Sūrat al-Fātiḥa 1:1)

ʿĀlamīn means Allāh is the Lord of everything. The Prophet ﷺ, as a mercy to the worlds (*ʿālamīn*), is correspondingly sent as a mercy to all of Allāh's creation. Anything and everything that is other than Allāh is a recipient of His mercy and blessings through the Prophet ﷺ.

عَنْ جَابِرِ بْنِ عَبْدِ اللهِ بِاللَّفْظِ، قَالَ: قُلْتُ: «يَا رَسُولَ اللهِ، بِأَبِي أَنْتَ وَأُمِّي، أَخْبِرْنِي عَنْ أَوَّلِ شَيْءٍ خَلَقَهُ اللهُ قَبْلَ الْأَشْيَاءِ».قَالَ: «يَا جَابِرُ، إِنَّ اللهَ تَعَالَى خَلَقَ قَبْلَ الْأَشْيَاءِ نُورَ نَبِيِّكَ مِنْ نُورِهِ، فَجَعَلَ ذٰلِكَ النُّورَ يَدُورُ بِالْقُدْرَةِ حَيْثُ شَاءَ اللهُ، وَلَمْ يَكُنْ فِي ذٰلِكَ الْوَقْتِ لَوْحٌ، وَلَا قَلَمٌ، وَلَا جَنَّةٌ، وَلَا نَارٌ، وَلَا مَلَكٌ، وَلَا سَمَاءٌ، وَلَا أَرْضٌ، وَلَا شَمْسٌ، وَلَا قَمَرٌ، وَلَا جِنِّيٌّ، وَلَا إِنْسِيٌّ .فَلَمَّا أَرَادَ اللهُ أَنْ يَخْلُقَ الْخَلْقَ، قَسَمَ ذٰلِكَ النُّورَ أَرْبَعَةَ أَجْزَاءٍ: فَخَلَقَ مِنَ الْجُزْءِ الْأَوَّلِ الْقَلَمَ، وَمِنَ الثَّانِي اللَّوْحَ، وَمِنَ الثَّالِثِ الْعَرْشَ . ثُمَّ قَسَمَ الْجُزْءَ الرَّابِعَ أَرْبَعَةَ أَجْزَاءٍ: فَخَلَقَ مِنَ الْجُزْءِ الْأَوَّلِ حَمَلَةَ الْعَرْشِ، وَمِنَ الثَّانِي الْكُرْسِيَّ، وَمِنَ الثَّالِثِ بَاقِيَ الْمَلَائِكَةِ. ثُمَّ قَسَمَ الْجُزْءَ الرَّابِعَ أَرْبَعَةَ أَجْزَاءٍ: فَخَلَقَ مِنَ الْأَوَّلِ السَّمَاوَاتِ، وَمِنَ الثَّانِي الْأَرْضِينَ، وَمِنَ الثَّالِثِ الْجَنَّةَ وَالنَّارَ. ثُمَّ قَسَمَ الرَّابِعَ أَرْبَعَةَ أَجْزَاءٍ: فَخَلَقَ مِنَ الْأَوَّلِ نُورَ أَبْصَارِ الْمُؤْمِنِينَ، وَمِنَ الثَّانِي نُورَ قُلُوبِهِمْ وَهِيَ الْمَعْرِفَةُ بِاللهِ، وَمِنَ الثَّالِثِ نُورَ إِنْسِهِمْ وَهُوَ التَّوْحِيدُ: لَا إِلٰهَ إِلَّا اللهُ، مُحَمَّدٌ رَسُولُ اللهِ».

an Jābir ibn 'Abd Allāh bi-lafẓ: Qāla qultu: yā Rasūl Allāh, bi-abī anta wa-ummī, akhbirnī 'an awwal shay'in khalaqahu Allāh qabla al-ashyā'. Qāla: yā Jābir, inna Allāha ta'ālā khalaqa qabla al-ashyā' nūra nabiyyika min nūrihi, fa-ja'ala dhālika al-nūr yadūru bi'l-qudra ḥaythu shā'a Allāh, wa-lam yakun fī dhālika al-waqt lawḥun wa-lā qalamun wa-lā janna wa-lā nārun wa-lā malakun wa-lā samā'un wa-lā arḍun wa-lā shamsun wa-lā qamarun wa-lā jinnī wa-lā insī...

It is related that Jābir ibn 'Abd Allāh ※ said to the Prophet ﷺ, "O Messenger of Allāh, may my father and mother be sacrificed for you, tell me of the first thing Allāh created before all things." He said:

O Jābir, the first thing Allāh created was the light of your Prophet from His light, and that light remained[3] in the midst of His Power for as long as He wished. At that time, there was no Tablet (*lawḥ*), no Pen (*qalam*), no Paradise (*Jannah*), no Fire (*nār*), no angel (*malak*), no heaven (*samā'*), no earth (*arḍ*)...

When Allāh wished to create creation, He divided that Light into four parts:

From the first, He created the *qalam*, the Pen,

From the second, the *lawḥ*, the Preserved Tablet,

From the third, the *'arsh*, the Throne,

Then He divided the fourth into four parts and created:

ḥamalat al-'arsh, the bearers of the Throne,

kursī, the Footstool,

The rest of the *malā'ika*, angels,

Then the heavens, *samāwāt*, the earths, *arḍīn*, Paradise and Hell, *Jannata wa 'n-nār*)

Then the light of the believers' sight, the light of the believers' hearts (*ma'rifa bi 'Llāh*), and the light of the believers' human essence (*ins*) which is *tawḥīd*: Lā ilāha illa'Llāh Muḥammad Rasūl Allāh. ('Abd al-Razzāq in his *Mūsānnaf*. Bayhaqī in *Dalā'il al-nubūwwa*.)

The Prophet ﷺ told Jābir ※: "O Jābir! The first thing that Allāh created is the light of your Prophet." If we heed what modern physics teaches, then that light must be the source of the great *Big Bang*. Physicists say that before that event, there was nothing. Then Allāh said: *Kun!* (Be!) and *fayakūn* (it was).

When the Prophet ﷺ says, "The first thing that Allāh created is my light," and from it everything else was created, it follows from Allāh's saying: *"We have sent you (O Prophet) not but as a mercy to humanity (or the worlds)."*

---

[3] Literally: "turned."

> The Prophet ﷺ said: "That light turned in the midst of His Power for as long as He wished."

Allāh caused that light to turn (*yadūru*) around the Essence of the Divine Attribute of Power—*baḥr al-qudra*—just as people circumambulate the *Kaʿba*, and just as electrons turn around the nucleus of the atom.

As the light of the Prophet ﷺ turned in the Divine Presence, it accumulated immense energy. Eventually, Allāh ﷻ ordered it to explode in what is known as the *Big Bang*.

The expansion of that light and energy continues even now. Thus, the Prophet Muḥammad ﷺ is the center of light. Allāh ﷻ created the light of the Prophet ﷺ and endowed him with vast energy from His *Ocean of Power*.

If the essence of all creation comes from Divine Light, then all existence is the result of the Mercy of Allāh ﷻ. Mercy is the ocean in which all creation swims.

The *Ocean of Power* is from the *Essence*—no one knows its reality, not even the Prophet ﷺ. This is the meaning of:

Allāh*u waḥdahu lā sharīka lah* — Allāh is One with no partner.

لَيْسَ كَمِثْلِهِ شَيْءٌ وَهُوَ السَّمِيعُ البَصِيرُ

Laysa ka-mithlihi shay'un wa-huwa al-Samīʿ al-Baṣīr

"There is nothing whatever like unto Him, and He is the One that hears and sees (all things)." (Sūrat ash-Shūrā 42:11)

سُبْحَانَ اللَّهِ عَمَّا يَصِفُونَ

Subḥāna'Llāhi ʿammā yaṣifūn

Glory to Allāh. (He is free) from the (sort of) things they attribute to Him!" (Sūrat al-Mu'minūn 23:91)

Here Allāh ﷻ names the Divine Essence. He revealed what He wished of His Attributes, Names, and Acts to the Prophet ﷺ, but knowledge of His Absolute Essence He did not show to anyone.

To delve into the spiritual understanding of the Big Bang is to penetrate something of the *Ḥaqīqa Muḥammadiyya* (Muhammadan Reality) ﷺ. In issuing the command *"Kun!"*, Allāh was giving form to a sound, the vibrations of which constituted the Prophet ﷺ.

Existence was formed from the very Reality that instantiates physical being. The creation of the *Ḥaqīqa Muḥammadiyya* took place even before the creation of the angels. According to the ḥadīth transmitted from Ibn ʿAbbās, the Muhammadan Reality passed from prophet to prophet (*min nabiyyin ilā nabiyyin*) until Allāh ﷻ caused it to emerge (*akhraja*) as the historical Prophet Muḥammad ﷺ.

Shaykh ʿAbd al-Qādir al-Jīlānī (d. 561 AH), in his book Sirr al-Asrār fī mā yaḥtāju ilayhi al-Abrār, said:

> Know that since Allāh first created the soul of Muḥammad ﷺ from the light of His Beauty, as He said: "I created Muḥammad from the light of My Face," and as the Prophet said: "The first thing Allāh created is my soul," and "The first thing Allāh created is the Pen," and "The first thing Allāh created is the Intellect"—what is meant by all this is one and the same: the *Ḥaqīqa Muḥammadiyya.*
>
> It was named *nūr* (light) because it is purified from darkness, as Allāh said: *"There has come to you from Allāh a Light and a manifest Book."*
>
> It was named *ʿaql* (intellect) because it is the cause for the transmission of knowledge, and the *qalam* (pen) is its medium in the world of letters.
>
> The *Rūḥ Muḥammadiyya* (Muhammadan soul) is the quintessence of all created things and their origin. As the Prophet ﷺ said: "I am from Allāh and the believers are from me."
>
> Allāh created all souls from him in the spiritual world in the best form. After its creation by four thousand years, Allāh created the *ʿarsh* (Throne) from the light of Muḥammad ﷺ, and from it the rest of creation.

However, what Allāh ﷻ created and gave to the Prophet ﷺ at that time no one knows. He said:

اللَّهُ نُورُ السَّمَاوَاتِ وَالْأَرْضِ مَثَلُ نُورِهِ كَمِشْكَاةٍ فِيهَا مِصْبَاحٌ الْمِصْبَاحُ فِي زُجَاجَةٍ الزُّجَاجَةُ كَأَنَّهَا كَوْكَبٌ دُرِّيٌّ يُوقَدُ مِن شَجَرَةٍ مُّبَارَكَةٍ زَيْتُونِةٍ لا شَرْقِيَّةٍ وَلا غَرْبِيَّةٍ يَكَادُ زَيْتُهَا يُضِيءُ وَلَوْ لَمْ تَمْسَسْهُ نَارٌ نُّورٌ عَلَى نُورٍ يَهْدِي اللَّهُ لِنُورِهِ مَن يَشَاءُ وَيَضْرِبُ اللَّهُ الأَمْثَالَ لِلنَّاسِ وَاللَّهُ بِكُلِّ شَيْءٍ عَلِيمٌ

Allāhu nūru al-samāwāti wa'l-arḍ. Mathalu nūrihi ka-mishkātin fīhā miṣbāḥ. Al-miṣbāḥ fī zujāja. Al-zujāja ka-annahā kawkabun durrīy yuqādu min shajaratin mubārakatin zaytūna lā sharqīyya wa-lā gharbīyya yakādu zaytuhā yuḍīʾu wa-law lam tamsas-hu nār. Nūrun ʿalā nūr. Yahdī Allāhu li-nūrihi man yashāʾ. Wa-yaḍrib Allāhu al-amthāl li'l-nās. Wa-Allāhu bi-kulli shayʾin ʿalīm.

Allāh is the Light of the heavens and the earth. The similitude of His light is as a niche wherein is a lamp. The lamp is in a glass. The glass is as it were a shining star. (This lamp is) kindled from a blessed tree, an olive neither of the East nor of the West, whose oil would almost glow forth (of itself) though no fire touched it. Light upon light. Allāh guides unto His light whom He will. And Allāh speakes to mankind in allegories, for Allāh is Knower of all things." (Sūrat al-Nūr 24:35)

"*Allāh is the light of the heavens and the earth*" means He is the Creator of everything other than Himself. Whatever is other than Allāh is called *mā siwā Allāh.* Allāh created everything: the *qalam*, heavens, earth, *janna*, angels, universes, galaxies, stars, planets, and the smallest objects.

"*And the similitude to His light*" is given by Allāh as an example for us to understand as "a niche wherein is a lamp." *Mishkāt* is usually translated as niche, but in fact it is a bundle like those in which garlic comes, tied together. *Mathalu nūrihi ka-mishkātin* can be translated: "the example of His light is like a bundle." Within the bundle there is a *miṣbāḥ. Miṣbāḥ* comes from *ṣabāḥ*, meaning an instrument that produces light, as in His saying to the Prophet Lūṭ ﷺ:

أَلَيْسَ الصُّبْحُ بِقَرِيبٍ

Alaysa al-ṣubḥu bi-qarīb

"Is not the light of dawn near?" (Sūrat Hūd 11:81)

Kāʿb al-Aḥbār ؓ makes the entire verse refer to Muḥammad ﷺ—it is a metaphor of the light of Muḥammad. The Messenger of Allāh ﷺ is the niche, the lamp is *nubuwwa*, the glass is his heart, the blessed tree is the *waḥy* and the angels who brought it, the oil are the proofs and evidences which contain the revelation.

True scholars and *awliyā'* say that this verse refers to the Prophet ﷺ. ʿAlī al-Qārī, commenting upon the Prophet's title says:

سِرَاجاً مُّنِيراً

Sirājan munīran

A lamp spreading light." (Sūrat al-Aḥzāb 33:46)

> Muḥammad... is a tremendous light and the source of all lights. He is also a book that gathers up and makes clear all the secrets. *Sirājan munīran* means a luminous sun, because of His saying:
>
> تَبَارَكَ الَّذِي جَعَلَ فِي السَّمَاءِ بُرُوجاً وَجَعَلَ فِيهَا سِرَاجاً وَقَمَراً مُّنِيراً
>
> *Tabāraka alladhī jaʿala fī al-samā' burūjan wa-jaʿala fīhā sirājan wa-qamaran munīran*
>
> *"He has placed therein a great lamp and a moon giving light."* (Sūrat al-Furqān 25:61)
>
> This verse indicates that the sun is the highest of the material lights and that other lights are outpourings from it. Similarly, the Prophet is the highest of the spiritual lights and other lights are derived from him by virtue of his mediating connection and pivotal rank in the overall sphere of creation.

> This is also inferred from the tradition: "The first thing Allāh created is my light." (Sharh al-shifā').

Allāh is giving an example of His Light—not of His *Dhāt* (Essence). Allāh here is not describing Himself; for nothing can describe His Essence. Rather, He is describing one of His Attributes—al-Nūr—a Name that reveals His Light.

Here the light of the Prophet ﷺ, which was the source of the Big Bang, the source of the light of the heavens and earth, is compared to a lighted bundle holding an instrument that gives light—and that light is the Prophet ﷺ.

He said, "*the lamp is in a glass,*" the lamp is shining in the glass, and "*the glass is as it were a shining star.*" It means that the light within has not yet emerged. Still, that reality of the Prophet—the *Ḥaqīqat al-Muḥammadiyya*—illumined, pearl-like, a veritable constellation glowing "as if it were a shining star," remains within.

That light of the Prophet ﷺ is the light of *Muḥammadun Rasūl Allāh*. That is *al-Ḥaqīqat al-Muḥammadiyya*, the Muhammadan Reality, whose internal character signifies that it reflects the Heart of the Essence, since the Prophet's heart moves without restriction in the orbit of the ninety-nine Names and Attributes. He has been blessed by being adorned by the ninety-nine Names, inside of which is a glowing pearl not yet come forth.

So the Muhammadan Reality has never appeared—it is still hidden and it is not emerging. But what is manifested in this life is *Muḥammadun Rasūl* Allāh.

Thus *Lā ilāha illa Allāh* in the testimony of faith represents the Creator, and *Muḥammadun Rasūl Allāh* symbolizes the entirety of creation.

The *kāf* in *kun* of Allāh's Order represents *Lā ilāha illa Allāh*, and the *nūn* represents *Muḥammadun Rasūl Allāh* in Allāh's Order which lies between the *kāf* and the *nūn*. Allāh's Order for creation proceeded from the Divine Essence and resulted in the creation of the Muhammadan Reality. Allāh is the One who caused it to expand in the way that He liked.

Thus the Prophet's light exists in everything, for which Allāh ﷻ said:

وَاعْلَمُوا أَنَّ فِيكُمْ رَسُولَ اللَّهِ

Wa'lamū anna fīkum Rasūl Allāh
And know that within you is Allāh's Messenger." (Sūrat al-Ḥujurāt 49:7)

Al-Khāṭib Abū al-Rab'ī Muḥammad ibn al-Layth, in his book Shifā' al-Ṣudūr, says:

> The first thing Allāh created is the light of Muḥammad ﷺ, and that light came and prostrated before Allāh. Allāh divided it into four parts and created from the first part the Throne (*'arsh*), from the second the Pen

> (*qalam*), from the third the Tablet (*lawḥ*), and then similarly He subdivided the fourth part into parts and created the rest of creation.

Therefore the light of the Throne is from the light of the Prophet ﷺ, the light of the Pen is from the light of the Prophet ﷺ, the light of the Tablet is from the light of the Prophet ﷺ, the light of day, the light of knowledge, the light of the sun and the moon, and the light of vision and sight are all from the light of the Prophet ﷺ.

Al-Khāṭīb also says:

> The first thing Allāh created is the light of Muḥammad ﷺ and that light came and prostrated before Allāh. Allāh divided it into four parts and created from the first part the Throne, from the second the Pen, from the third the Tablet, and then similarly He subdivided the fourth part into parts and created the rest of creation. Therefore the light of the Throne is from the light of the Prophet ﷺ, the light of the Pen is from the light of the Prophet ﷺ, the light of the Tablet is from the light of the Prophet ﷺ, the light of day, the light of knowledge, the light of the sun and the moon, and the light of vision and sight are all from the light of the Prophet ﷺ.(Ibn al-Hajj al-Abdarī's al-Madkhal.)

عَنْ ابْنِ عَبَّاسٍ: إِنَّ قُرَيْشًا (فِي بَعْضِ النُّسَخِ: رُوحُهُ يَعْنِي الرَّسُولَ صَلَّى اللهُ عَلَيْهِ وَسَلَّمَ) كَانَتْ نُورًا بَيْنَ يَدَيِ اللهِ تَعَالَى قَبْلَ أَنْ يَخْلُقَ آدَمَ بِأَلْفَيْ عَامٍ. يُسَبِّحُ ذَلِكَ النُّورُ، وَتُسَبِّحُ الْمَلَائِكَةُ بِتَسْبِيحِهِ، فَلَمَّا خَلَقَ اللهُ آدَمَ أَلْقَى ذَلِكَ النُّورَ فِي صُلْبِهِ.

> Ibn ʿAbbās ﷺ said: Verily the spirit of the Prophet ﷺ was a light in front of Allāh two thousand years before He created Ādam. That light glorified Him and the angels joined in its glorification. When Allāh created Ādam, He cast that light into his loins. (Ibn Abi ʿUmar al-ʿAdanī relates it in his Musnad.)
>
> ʿAlī ibn al-Ḥusayn ﷺ related from his father, who related from his grandfather, who said that the Prophet ﷺ said: "I was a light in front of my Lord for fourteen thousand years before He created Ādam." (Imām Āhmad's Fadā'il al-ṣaḥāba, al-Dhahabī's Mīzān al-i'tidāl, al-Tabarī's al-Riyāḍ al-nādirā)

It is this light, which was sent to this earth, which became manifest when the Prophet was born.

Al-Qurṭubī says: "*Kindled from a blessed tree, an olive*," can be taken to refer to the Prophets, in which case Ādam would be the blessed tree, or Ibrāhīm because Allāh called him "blessed."

It is that blessed familial tree from which its most blessed fruit, our master Prophet Muḥammad ﷺ was born.

> Ibn Jubayr ؓ and Kaʿb al-Āḥbār ؓ said, "What is meant by the second light [in 'light upon light'] is the Prophet ﷺ because he is the Messenger and the Expositor and the Conveyor from Allāh of what is enlightening and manifest." (Imām al-Suyūṭī said in al-Riyāḍ al-anīqa)
>
> Kaʿb, referring to "*whose oil would almost glow forth (of itself) though no fire touched it,*" said, "Its oil well nigh would shine because the Prophet well nigh would be known to the people even if he did not say that he was a prophet, just as that oil would send forth light without a fire."
>
> In that regard the Prophet ﷺ said, "The night I was delivered my mother saw a light that lit the castles of Damascus so that she could see them." (Al-Ḥākim in his Mustadrak, *Āhmad* in his Musnad, and Bayhaqī in Dalā'il al-nubūwwa.)

The light of the Prophet ﷺ is the source of the light of all believers, for while all things were created from his light, the believers were created in a special way.

Al-Qurṭubī relates in Jamʿ li-aḥkām al-Qur'ān from *Anas* ؓ who said that the Prophet ﷺ said:

> Allāh created me from light and He created Abū Bakr from my light, and He created ʿUmar and ʿĀ'isha from the light of Abū Bakr, and He created the male believers of my community from the light of ʿUmar and He created the female believers of my community from the light of ʿĀ'isha. Whoever does not love me or love Abū Bakr, ʿUmar and ʿĀ'isha has no light.

This ḥadīth explains the tremendous love the Prophet ﷺ bore towards Abū Bakr al-Ṣiddīq ؓ, who was his sole companion when he migrated from Meccah to Madīnah and who was his companion in the cave, for which Allāh revealed:

إِلَّا تَنصُرُوهُ فَقَدْ نَصَرَهُ اللَّهُ إِذْ أَخْرَجَهُ الَّذِينَ كَفَرُوا ثَانِيَ اثْنَيْنِ إِذْ هُمَا فِي الْغَارِ إِذْ يَقُولُ لِصَاحِبِهِ لَا تَحْزَنْ إِنَّ اللَّهَ مَعَنَا

If ye help not (your leader), (it is no matter): for Allāh did indeed help him, when the Unbelievers drove him out: he had no more than one companion; they two were in the cave, and he said to his companion, "Have no fear, for Allāh is with us." (Sūrat al-Tawbah 9:40)

This magnificent reality applies to those who have no blood relation with the Prophet ﷺ but indicates how close the believers are to him by virtue of their love for him. Through these *aḥadīth*, the Prophet ﷺ demonstrated his love for those with whom he had no blood connection, but whom he loved for their link to him through spirituality, their piety and their sincerity towards Allāh.

On the other side, in the station of self-sacrifice, was the Prophet's son-in-law to be, and future father of his grandchildren, Sayyidinā ʿAlī ☘. For during the migration from Meccah, when the unbelievers were conspiring to kill the Prophet, Sayyidinā ʿAlī ☘ took the Prophet's place in his bed. Sayyidinā ʿAlī ☘ willingly accepted to lie down in the Prophet's place—expecting to be killed by the ferocious Quraysh. This spirit of sacrifice was expressed repeatedly by the Family of the Prophet ☘ throughout the life of the Ummah, up to the present day; for their love of the Prophet ☘ they bore unfathomable burdens by means of which the Community was relieved, protected and preserved.

And Allāh said in regard to the family of the Prophet ☘:

قُل لَّا أَسْأَلُكُمْ عَلَيْهِ أَجْرًا إِلَّا الْمَوَدَّةَ فِي الْقُرْبَىٰ

Say: I do not ask of you any reward for it but love for my near relatives.
(Sūrat al-Shūrā 42:23)

This shows the two sides of love of the Prophet ☘—on the one hand love for his family, and on the other hand love for the Ummah, in particular the sincere, guided and perfected ones who hold fast to the Sunnah.

In respect of the first love, the Prophet ☘ said, "I have left among you two matters by holding fast to which, you shall never be misguided: Allāh's Book and the Sunnah of His Prophet." (al-Bayhaqī in *al-Sunan al-kubrā*, al-Ḥākim and Mālik in *al-Muwaṭṭā*') Another version adds: "And these two shall never part ways until they show up at the Pond." (al-Ḥākim and al-Bayhaqī in *al-Madkhal*.)

حَدَّثَنَا ابْنُ نُمَيْرٍ، حَدَّثَنَا عَبْدُ الْمَلِكِ بْنُ أَبِي سُلَيْمَانَ، عَنْ عَطِيَّةَ الْعَوْفِيِّ، عَنْ أَبِي سَعِيدٍ الْخُدْرِيِّ، قَالَ: قَالَ رَسُولُ اللَّهِ ﷺ: «إِنِّي قَدْ تَرَكْتُ فِيكُمْ مَا إِنْ أَخَذْتُمْ بِهِ لَنْ تَضِلُّوا بَعْدِي، الثَّقَلَيْنِ، أَحَدُهُمَا أَكْبَرُ مِنَ الْآخَرِ: كِتَابُ اللَّهِ، حَبْلٌ مَمْدُودٌ مِنَ السَّمَاءِ إِلَى الْأَرْضِ، وَعِتْرَتِي أَهْلُ بَيْتِي، أَلَا وَإِنَّهُمَا لَنْ يَفْتَرِقَا حَتَّى يَرِدَا عَلَيَّ الْحَوْضَ»

Other versions state: I am leaving among you that which if you hold to it, you shall never go astray, one of them greater than the other: Allāh's Book—a rope extended down from the heaven to the earth—and my mantle (*'itra*), the People of my House. These two shall never part ways until they come to me at the Pond. Look well to how you act with them after me. (al-Tirmidhī and al-Ḥākim, al-Nasā'ī in *al-Sunan al-kubrā*.)

The five mentioned here are known as *Ahl al-ʿabāʾa*, for Jibrīl covered them with the cloak (*ʿabāʾa*) of the Prophet, and they were given importance as Ahl al-Bayt in two incidents mentioned in the Qurʾān:

عَنْ عَامِرِ بْنِ سَعْدٍ، عَنْ أَبِيهِ، قَالَ: سَمِعْتُ رَسُولَ اللهِ ﷺ يَقُولُ لَهُ وَخَلَفَهُ فِي بَعْضِ مَغَازِيهِ، فَقَالَ: «يَا عَلِيُّ، أَتَخَلَّفُنِي مَعَ النِّسَاءِ وَالصِّبْيَانِ؟» قَالَ: «يَا عَلِيُّ، أَمَا تَرْضَى أَنْ تَكُونَ مِنِّي بِمَنْزِلَةِ هَارُونَ مِنْ مُوسَى، إِلَّا أَنَّهُ لَا نُبُوَّةَ بَعْدِي؟» وَسَمِعْتُهُ يَقُولُ يَوْمَ خَيْبَرَ: «لَأُعْطِيَنَّ الرَّايَةَ رَجُلًا يُحِبُّ اللهَ وَرَسُولَهُ، وَيُحِبُّهُ اللهُ وَرَسُولُهُ.» فَتَطَاوَلْنَا لَهَا، فَقَالَ: «ادْعُوا لِي عَلِيًّا.» فَأُتِيَ بِهِ أَرْمَدَ، فَبَصَقَ فِي عَيْنِهِ، وَدَفَعَ الرَّايَةَ إِلَيْهِ، فَفَتَحَ اللهُ عَلَيْهِ. وَلَمَّا نَزَلَتْ هَذِهِ الْآيَةُ: «نَدْعُ أَبْنَاءَنَا وَأَبْنَاءَكُمْ»، دَعَا رَسُولُ اللهِ ﷺ عَلِيًّا، وَفَاطِمَةَ، وَالْحَسَنَ، وَالْحُسَيْنَ، فَقَالَ: «اللَّهُمَّ هَؤُلَاءِ أَهْلِي.»

> ʿĀmir ibn Saʿd ibn Abī Waqqāṣ reported on the authority of his father that Muʿāwiyah ibn Abī Sufyān appointed Saʿd as the governor and said: "What prevents you from abusing Abū Turāb (ʿAlī)?" At this he said: "It is because of three things which I remember Allāh's Messenger ﷺ having said about him that I would not abuse him and even if I find one of those three things for me, it would be more dear to me than the red camels. …(The third occasion is) when the (following) verse was revealed: *Let us summon our children and your children.* Allāh's Messenger ﷺ called ʿAlī, Fāṭimah, Ḥasan and Ḥusayn and said: O Allāh, they are my family. (Sahīh Muslim and another narration in Āhmad's Musnad.)

It is established that when the verse of mutual invocation of curses (*mubāhala*) was revealed:

فَمَنْ حَآجَّكَ فِيهِ مِن بَعْدِ مَا جَاءَكَ مِنَ الْعِلْمِ فَقُلْ تَعَالَوْا نَدْعُ أَبْنَاءَنَا وَأَبْنَاءَكُمْ
وَنِسَاءَنَا وَنِسَاءَكُمْ وَأَنفُسَنَا وَأَنفُسَكُمْ ثُمَّ نَبْتَهِلْ فَنَجْعَل لَّعْنَتَ اللَّهِ عَلَى الْكَاذِبِينَ

And whoso disputes with you concerning him, after the knowledge which has come unto you, say (unto him): Come! We will summon our sons and your sons, and our women and your women, and ourselves and yourselves, then we will pray humbly (to our Lord) and (solemnly) invoke the curse of Allāh upon those who lie. (Sūrat Āli ʿImrān, 3:61)

عَنْ عَامِرِ بْنِ سَعْدٍ، عَنْ أَبِيهِ، قَالَ: لَمَّا نَزَلَتْ هَذِهِ الْآيَةُ: ﴿فَقُلْ تَعَالَوْا نَدْعُ أَبْنَاءَنَا وَأَبْنَاءَكُمْ﴾ دَعَا رَسُولُ اللَّهِ ﷺ عَلِيًّا وَفَاطِمَةَ وَحَسَنًا وَحُسَيْنًا فَقَالَ: «اللَّهُمَّ هَؤُلَاءِ أَهْلِي».

The Prophet ﷺ summoned ʿAlī, Fāṭimah, al-Ḥasan, and al-Ḥusayn, and said: "O Allāh! These are my Family" (*Allāhumma hā'ulā'i Ahlī*). (Muslim, al-Tirmidhī, al-Hākim and others.)

He repeated this act when the verse of the cleansing of the People of the House was revealed:

إِنَّمَا يُرِيدُ اللَّهُ لِيُذْهِبَ عَنكُمُ الرِّجْسَ أَهْلَ الْبَيْتِ وَيُطَهِّرَكُمْ تَطْهِيرًا

Allāh only desires to keep away the uncleanness from you, O People of the House! and to purify you a (thorough) purifying. (Sūrat al-Aḥzāb 33:33)

As mentioned in the following ḥadīth:

عَنْ أَبِي سَعِيد ﷺ قَالَ قَالَ رَسُول اللَّه ﷺ « نَزَلَتْ هَذِهِ الآيَة فِي خَمْسَة : فِيَّ وَفِي عَلِيّ وَحَسَن وَحُسَيْن وَفَاطِمَة ﴿ إِنَّمَا يُرِيد اللَّه لِيُذْهِب عَنْكُمْ الرِّجْس أَهْل الْبَيْت وَيُطَهِّرَكُمْ تَطْهِيرًا﴾ »

Abū Saʿīd ﷺ related that the Prophet ﷺ said: This verse was revealed regarding five: regarding myself; regarding ʿAlī and Ḥasan and Ḥusayn and Fāṭimah, *"Allāh only desires to keep away the uncleanness from you, O People of the House! and to purify you a (thorough) purifying."* (Ibn Abī Ḥātim).

Lexically, the term *ʿitra* was defined as "A man's relatives such as his children, grandchildren, and paternal cousins," while in the context of the present hadiths it was explained to mean "Those of the Prophet's Family who follow his Religion and cling to his commands." (al-Tahāwī, Sharḥ mushkil al-āthār) What emerges from these meanings together with the two wordings of the ḥadīth "I have left among you two matters" is firm evidence that there is an inseparable connection, until the Last Day, between the Qur'ān, the Sunnah, and the Family of the Prophet.

Know that the light of the Prophet ﷺ is in you, for Allāh said:

وَاعْلَمُوا أَنَّ فِيكُمْ رَسُولَ اللَّهِ

And know that Allāh's Messenger is within you. (Sūrat al-Ḥujurāt 49:7)

Through this verse, and the preceding narrations, we must know that Prophet Muḥammad ﷺ was informing us that his light is within every believer; with a particular emphasis on the qualities of perfect character exemplified by Sayyidinā Abū Bakr ﷺ and Sayyidinā ʿUmar ﷺ, while those related to the Prophet ﷺ through blood have the specialty of being from his family, whom Allāh favored in a tremendous way—particularly the descendants of *Ahl al-ʿabā'a*, the children of Sayyidinā ʿAlī ﷺ

The Unique Station of Ḥabībullāh ﷺ

Dastūr, madad yā Sulṭān al-Awliyā', Mawlānā Shaykh Muḥammad Nāẓim al-Ḥaqqānī. Dastūr, madad yā Sulṭān al-Awliyā', Mawlānā Shaykh 'Abd Allāh al-Fā'iz ad-Dāghistānī.

As-salāmu 'alaykum wa Raḥmatullāhi wa barakātuh. Allah ﷻ gave us life to thank Him. He didn't give us life to forget about Him. And He gave us this *amānah,* trust, to keep intact, pure. Not to disturb it, and not to make it dirty. But unfortunately we are people who are not up to the level of clean, to be clean and to be responsible. We are irresponsible. If someone is sick in *dunyā,* you see lot of doctors looking after him or after her. You try your best to keep in contact with your doctors to make sure you live a healthy life. You see from the behavior of people that everyone is trying to eat healthy. And they tell you today not to eat oil, not to eat butter, not to eat ghee, don't eat this or that. What do you want to eat? Everything must be boiled! Is it not? (They say:) "Then you live longer."

Allahu akbar. How can they live longer when Allah ﷻ said:

"فَإِذَا جَاءَ أَجَلُهُمْ لاَ يَسْتَأْخِرُونَ سَاعَةً وَلاَ يَسْتَقْدِمُونَ"

fa-idhā jā'a ajaluhum lā yasta'khirūna sā'atan wa-lā yastaqdimūn

When their appointed term has come there is no way to increase your life by one hour or to decrease it by one hour. (Sūrat al-A'rāf, 7:34)

People run to the doctor, since they think they can increase their life. But Allah ﷻ made doctors as instruments to make sure the person whom they are treating will reach the right moment of death. That means the doctor is part of the system of the age that Allah ﷻ gave to you. The doctor is playing a role in it, that the right time of age Allah ﷻ gave to you will be completed. That doctor Allah ﷻ made him to look after your illness in order to come to the right time frame to die. Then when the time of death comes, no doctor can say, "Stay." You are leaving. You are not listening to anyone at that time, except to that voice that is calling you. Come! You will go. You cannot say, "No."

So as we look at our bodies to be healthy with the help of doctors and nutritionists, and this and that. We must also look for spiritual doctors. And by spiritual doctors I mean the real ones, not the fake ones. There are too many fake ones. Too many, you cannot count them. The real ones are the ones that are really connected through their hearts with the Prophet ﷺ without a doubt. Those spiritual doctors keep this sunnah of the Prophet ﷺ in every action they do. Not like these pseudo doctors, murshid this murshid that, shaykh this, shaykh that. No. Those, if they ask they will be answered. Those, when they say, "*Yā Rabbī*!" They hear the voice "*Yā 'Abdī*!" They hear,

$$\text{ادْعُونِي أَسْتَجِبْ لَكُمْ}$$

ud'ūnī astajib lakum

Ask Me! I will respond to you; (Sūrah Ghāfir, 40:60)

From whom can it be accepted? Who is the one that has the title that whatever he asks, he will be given? The one, that if you love someone, if he asks you, you give.

You love your son, if he asks you, you give. Even if you don't have what he wants, you try to get it to give it to him. You give to your daughter. If a man's wife asks, he will not give, but if his daughter asks he will give. Some people give freely to their wives as well. But both wife and husband, if their child requests something, they try their best to find a way to give what was requested.

So it means anything the *ḥabīb*, the beloved requests will be given. What is the difference between *ḥabīb* and *khalīl*? *Khalīl* is different and *ḥabīb* is different. *Khalīl* is the one you feel close and intimate with, a true friendship. The one that is your friend, is in need of you. He is the one that if he is in need asks of you something, you will give it to him. But *ḥabīb* is the one that without asking you give. A lover—someone you love—you go and buy jewelry, even if they don't ask. But for your friend you don't buy jewelry unless he asks. The *khalīl*, you give if he asks. The *ḥabīb*, without asking you give.

So Khalīlullāh is different and Ḥabībullāh is different. Khalīlullāh is Sayyidinā Ibrāhīm ⬥ and Ḥabībullāh is Sayyidinā Muhammad ﷺ, and between Khalīlullāh and Ḥabībullāh there are many different levels that others may have, but the only one who is Ḥabībullāh is Sayyidinā Muḥammad ﷺ. He is the one entitled to *maḥabbah*. Allāh ﷻ loved him ﷺ, because He created him to be loved. He created him with that reality and He dressed him with that reality. Allāh ﷻ wants His servant to be loved by Him. That is why he is called Ḥabīb ar-Raḥmān; no one else is called Ḥabīb al-Raḥmān, except Sayyidinā Muḥammad ﷺ.

Sayyidinā Ibrāhīm ⬥ is called Khalīlullāh, "Friend of Allāh" ﷻ and saints are friends of Allāh ﷻ. That is not like friends between people—rather they are *Rijāl-Allāh*. If they ask something, Allāh ﷻ gives them. If in their heart inspirations come, then Allāh ﷻ makes those realities for them. If they ask, Allāh ﷻ will give.

$$\text{رِجَالٌ صَدَقُوا مَا عَاهَدُوا اللَّهَ عَلَيْهِ فَمِنْهُم مَّن قَضَىٰ نَحْبَهُ وَمِنْهُم مَّن يَنتَظِرُ وَمَا بَدَّلُوا تَبْدِيلًا}$$

rijālun ṣadaqū mā 'āhadū Allāha 'alayhi fa-minhum man qaḍā naḥbahu wa-minhum man yantaẓiru wa-mā baddalū tabdīlā

Men that kept their covenant with Allah ﷻ and some have passed and some are waiting and they did not change in the least. (Sūrat al-Aḥzāb, 33:23)

They never changed, they are always on Ṣirāṭ al-Mustaqīm, the Straight Path. They are always on the right path. This is their path, they have to go through that way. Allah ﷻ created that Ṣirāṭ al-Mustaqīm and no one can pass it, except there is one at the end who doesn't need to pass. He passed it already. Allah ﷻ said about him,

إِنَّا فَتَحْنَا لَكَ فَتْحًا مُّبِينًا لِيَغْفِرَ لَكَ اللَّهُ مَا تَقَدَّمَ مِن ذَنبِكَ وَمَا تَأَخَّرَ وَيُتِمَّ نِعْمَتَهُ عَلَيْكَ وَيَهْدِيَكَ صِرَاطًا مُّسْتَقِيمًا

innā fataḥnā laka fatḥan mubīnan li-yaghfira laka Allāhu mā taqaddama min dhanbika wa-mā ta-akhkhar wa-yutimma niʿmatahu ʿalayka wa-yahdiyaka ṣirāṭan mustaqīman

We have granted you a manifest victory in order that Allah may forgive you your faults of the past and those to follow; fulfil His favour to you; and guide you on the Straight Way. (Sūrat al-Fatḥ 48:1,2)

Allah ﷻ granted to him without him asking. *"That Allah may forgive you"* is a big opening for him; it means, "You don't need to ask, *yā* Muhammad ﷺ. We have made a huge opening for your victory against Shayṭān and for anything in *dunyā* and by giving you forgiveness."

"That Allah may forgive what you what you did before and after." What did the Prophet ﷺ do? He didn't make a sin. But Allah ﷻ wants to give him responsibility over human beings, jinn and angels. *Mā taqadama* means "what happened before". That means, "*Yā* Muhammad ﷺ! You are My beloved one and you are My lover. And I am giving you that Creation under your responsibility and in the Day of Promises I asked them, 'Who am I?' and they said, 'You are our Lord.' But they didn't keep that responsibility. So the sins they made are your responsibility and so I made for you an opening to forgive for you all the sins you have done."

We know that Prophet ﷺ didn't do any sin. So whose sins are they? They are the sins of the Ummah. Just as Sayyidinā Ādam ؑ ate from the fruit and he was *maʿṣūm* (innocent). In reality, it was not him who ate, but the *dhurriyyah* (offspring) of Bani Ādam ؑ behind his back who made his arm to move to eat.

So the Prophet ﷺ took that responsibility. "Since I love you, you are My *Ḥabīb*, I am forgiving all sins from before. I am forgiving your ummah. That is why I gave you *shafāʿah*, intercession." So what happened before the sins refers to what happened in the world of souls, before *dunyā*. Not as they translate, "what sins you have done before in your life." No, the Prophet ﷺ as we all know, did not sin in his life. Therefore, this is referring to the time when Sayyidinā Ādam ؑ was married to Sayyida Hawā and their children. Allah ﷻ has forgiven all their children of their sins without the Prophet ﷺ asking. This is the greatness of Prophet Muhammad ﷺ, the sincere servant of Allah ﷻ. So there is huge difference between Ḥabībullāh and Khalīlullāh. *Ḥabīb* is the one who without asking will be given. But *khalīl* is the one given when he asks. You must be happy that Allah ﷻ created us from Ummat an-Nabī ﷺ! We are not following prior prophets, but we are following Sayyidinā Muhammad ﷺ. Why can we say, "*Muhammadu Ḥabībullāh*" and you can say, "*Allah Ḥabību Muhammad* (Allah is beloved of Muhammad)"? Can you say that or not? Yes, and you can also say, "*Allahu Ḥabību Muhammad.*"

One person stands up every time the Prophet's ﷺ name is mentioned. So in Indonesia we often had 5000 people in attendance and she would stand up and I stood up as well, because I was shy, so all were standing and sitting, standing and sitting! (laughter)

So we can say "*Muhammad Ḥabībullāh*" and "*Allah Ḥabību Muhammad,*" but we cannot say "*Allah Khalīl Ibrahīm*", no. We can say "*Ibrahīm Khalīlullāh*" but not the reverse. You cannot say that Allah ﷻ is friend of Sayyidinā Ibrahīm ﷺ. But you can say "Muhammad ﷺ is the beloved of Allah ﷻ." That is why we say: *Huwa al-ḥabībulladhī turjā shafā'atuhu*, "He is the beloved one to Allah ﷻ that humanity are always in need of and seeking his intercession." Intercession is not for him, intercession is for the Ummah.

Can you say "*Muhammad Ḥabīb al-Ummah*?" Yes. Can you say "*al-Ummah Ḥabību Muhammad*?" Yes; it is the reality of Sayyidinā Muhammad ﷺ. Allah ﷻ gave him the total love. So you can say whatever you like about the love of Prophet ﷺ for Allah ﷻ, and the love of Allah ﷻ for Prophet ﷺ. But you cannot say "*Allah Khalīl 'Ibrahīm.*" So for Sayyidinā Muhammad ﷺ you can reverse the equation. You cannot say "*Allah Khalīl Ibrahīm.*" That is why we say: *Huwa al-Ḥabīb alladhī turjā shafā'atuhu*, "he is the beloved one that everyone seek his intercession." Who is everyone? Is it us? No, it is everyone. It means jinn and *ins*. Not one is excluded because everyone is need of *shafā'ata an-Nabiyy* ﷺ. *Yarḥamuka'llāh*. He is the one that everyone needs his *shafā'ah*, human beings and jinn.

So you can reach your lover without a doorkeeper, *bi-lā wāsiṭah*, is it not so? With no means you reach your lover. But you cannot reach your friend, your *khalīl*, without a means. That is why Sayyidinā Muhammad ﷺ went to the station of *Qāba Qawsayni aw Adnā,* Two Bow's Length or Nearer, without a means. Sayyidinā Jibrīl ﷺ said, "You go on without me." Without a means and with no doorkeeper, the Prophet ﷺ continued his way. But *khalīl*, a friend, needs a means. (Sayyidinā 'Ibrahīm made *du'ā*':)

وَالَّذِي أَطْمَعُ أَن يَغْفِرَ لِي خَطِيئَتِي يَوْمَ الدِّينِ

wa-alladhī aṭma'u an yaghfira lī khaṭī'atī

"And the One in Whom I hope will forgive my sin on the Day of Judgment." (Sūrah ash-Shu'arā', 26:82)

"I wish that Allah will forgive my sins." To forgive a sin what do you need? You need intercession, someone to intercede. Sayyidinā Ibrahīm ﷺ, the father of the three (monotheist) religions, is saying, "I am in the need for Allah to forgive me." But for Prophet ﷺ:

آدَمُ وَمَنْ دُونَهُ تَحْتَ لِوَائِي يَوْمَ الْقِيَامَةِ

Ādam wa man dūnahu taḥta liwā'ī yawma 'l-qiyāmah

He ﷺ said, "Ādam and those beneath him will be under my banner on the Day of Judgment." (Sunan al-Tirmidhī)

Do you understand? The *ḥabīb* reaches without means. The *khalīl* needs a means. So on Judgment Day they need intercession of Sayyidinā Muhammad ﷺ.

There is a story about Imām al-Ghazali ؓ. He said, *kuntu fī dārin khārij al-balda*, "One night I came to a village and at night when I was performing my *tahajjud* prayer, I am awake and praying. Through *mukāshafah*, vision that Allah ﷻ opened to my heart, I saw all the people in this village sleeping. Not one was up praying. All of them were sleeping. *wa-lam yakun aḥadun minhum fī 'ibādati Rabbihi aw ṭā'ati Khāliqihi*, "Not one was praying or working in obedience to Allah ﷻ."

So look and don't say it is too much; even *Awliyā'ullah* can fall into mistakes. There is no *Walī* that is *ma'ṣūm*, free of sin. They make mistakes; if they didn't make mistakes they would be prophets. But you have to have *ḥusn aẓ-ẓann*, good thoughts about him because by good intention, not by bad intention, he did it. His intention is pure, but a mistake happened. So like Imām al-Ghazali ؓ here, he saw everyone sleeping, and not praying. His ego began to speak with him, telling him, "O, you are better than them. (I am adding that.) You are better, you are praying and they are not praying."

(Imām Ghazali's narration continues,) "And I said to myself *law kuntu qādiran 'alā ḥarq hādhihi al-balda laḥaraqtu kullahā*, If I was able to burn this village as they are not worshipping their Creator, I will burn them all!" Look how much the self can play with everyone! Major. Who are you to say this? I am not saying that for him, he is a big *Walī*, but for the self. The self is talking and struggling with the ego.

(Imām Ghazali's narration continues), "And I thought, 'Who are you to say, "I will burn them'? Who gave you that authority?" I was thinking and struggling between my soul and my ego, and inspirations came to me that *iḥrāq al-'ibād mukhtaṣan bi-llāhi binafsihi,* "No one can burn anyone; the Only One who has right to burn is Allah ﷻ!"

That is why the Prophet ﷺ prohibited burning anyone dead or alive. That is suicide bombings, killing with fire and explosions is forbidden; it is not accepted in Islam. The Prophet ﷺ prohibited burning someone with fire. You cannot burn even a worm with fire, or even a fly, or any small animal, even an insect—you are not allowed to burn by fire. People in villages often collect rubbish and burn it. There might be ants there which die from such a fire. So we do many things that are not accepted and we don't even think about it. How many ants are you killing by burning up trash on a farm? How many souls are you killing?

So Imām Ghazali ؓ said to himself, "Burning can only be done by Allah ﷻ! So how did I give such a wrong decision to myself? Immediately I backed out of that inspiration that came to my heart. (Then he said,) *law kunta shāfiʿan la-shafaʿta li-kulli wāḥidin minhum*, "If I was an intercessor, I would have interceded for everyone of them without looking at their deeds! (Then I said to myself,) "That is another mistake for me! *Shafaʿh* is only for Sayyidinā Muhammad ﷺ, not for anyone else!"

Then came to me *nidāʾun*, a voice (saying), *yā shaykh, law lā turjaʿ ʿalā hādhā al-qawl*, "O Shaykh! It is good that you backed up from that inspiration that came to your heart also, because if you didn't back out from that, I would have put you in the deepest possible point in Earth, and I would have stripped your name completely from *Awliyāʾullah*! You would no longer be a *Walī* to Me, because *shafaʿh* is to My Beloved. That is *ṣifat al-Ḥabīb*, the attribute of Sayyidinā Muhammad ﷺ!"

So we are in need for *Shafāʿat an-Nabī* ﷺ to be saved, and that *shafāʿah* is that the Prophet ﷺ wants to catch one good thing you have done in your life in order to intercede for you!

Wa min Allāhi 't-tawfīq, bi ḥurmati 'l-ḥabīb, bi ḥurmati 'l-Fātiḥah.

And with Allāh is success, for the honor of the Beloved, and by the sanctity of al-Fātiḥah, the opening chapter of the Qur'ān.

محبة الله

Allah's Possessiveness

Tonight coincides with the first of Rabīʿ al-Awwal. As time is passing we are approaching our destiny. No one can take the destiny of another. His destiny is that way and yours is that way.

But all of them are going to be in the same place where they have to meet. They cannot go on forever. If they were parallel to each other they would go on forever but at some point they are going to make an intersection. *Taqāṭuʿ*. They are going to have an intersection. Everyone is going to have his own space to move but at the end it is going to intersect with everyone else.

Our Lord Allah knows, knows that we are weak and we are helpless and we are oppressors to ourselves. That is what he described us, as ignorant. If Allah says.

إِنَّا عَرَضْنَا الْأَمَانَةَ عَلَى السَّمَاوَاتِ وَالْأَرْضِ وَالْجِبَالِ فَأَبَيْنَ أَنْ يَحْمِلْنَهَا وَأَشْفَقْنَ مِنْهَا

وَحَمَلَهَا الْإِنسَانُ ۖ إِنَّهُ كَانَ ظَلُومًا جَهُولًا

innā ʿaraḍnā al-amānata ʿalā as-samāwāti wal-arḍi wal-jibāl fa-abayna an yaḥmilnahā wa-ashfaqna minhā wa-ḥamalahā al-insān, innahu kāna ẓalūman jahūlā

"Indeed, We offered the Trust to the heavens and the earth and the mountains, but they refused to bear it and feared it; yet man undertook it. Indeed, he was unjust and ignorant. (Sūrah Al-Aḥzāb, 33:72)

Allah described us as *"oppressors to ourselves and ignorant*" because we claim we can carry the Trust: "*Yā Rabbī*, O our Lord we are going to save it and protect it." But we didn't; instead we lost it." When you lose that, you become a loser and you are lost. You will be lost in such a way that you cannot find yourself anymore.

Allah described us as 'oppressor and ignorant' so what do you expect from the one Allah described this way? People look at themselves as so great, so proud and so arrogant. What you know and what human beings know from sciences and from religion is merely a drop in an ocean. And with that drop they became drunk and thought they reached the highest level of understanding. It is the ego that makes us think like that.

Allah knows that, therefore He described us as 'ignorant'. If we were not 'ignorant', we would have been on the road of saints. In this association we are struggling to achieve something that is valuable. But we are not. As the Prophet ﷺ said and as *Awliyā'ullāh* said, from the notes in front of me, scholars counted 300,000 *aḥadīth marfūʿīn li-r-rasūl*, hadiths that are connected and related from one transmitter to another back to the Prophet ﷺ, from what he said. And *Awliyā'ullāh* know that there are 300,000 or even as some scholars say 500,000 *aḥādīth*. And how many do we know? How many did they write in books and say, "We take these and leave the rest." The Prophet ﷺ is saying to *Awliyā'ullāh* as *Awliyā'ullāh* understood, that one hadith from whatever they took while leaving the rest, is higher by 7000 levels than the *aḥadīth* of other prophets to their nations.

So that is one hadith. One hadith of the Prophet ﷺ is 7000 times higher than a hadith by other prophets.

And to whom has that been given? Do you think when the Prophet ﷺ says one hadith and that is 7000 times higher than other prophets' *aḥadīth*, will not all these lights and manifestations will be dressed on you? That is why reading the hadith is important even if you don't understand them. You don't need to read the *takhrīj* "this Ṣaḥābah related to this one,"— that is for scholars. But for normal people like us when you read [the text of] one hadith you will be dressed with whatever is coming with that hadith from the manifestation of the Beautiful Names and Attributes that Allah ﷻ opened to Sayyidinā Muhammad ﷺ. If you read it you get that.

The Prophet ﷺ wanted that mercy. That is the meaning of mercy. The Prophet ﷺ wanted that great mercy that Allah ﷻ gave to him through the different manifestations that Allah ﷻ made to appear on him that are unknown to us; and he ﷺ wanted to dress these manifestations on the Ummah. So the Prophet ﷺ opened and spoke relating these revelations that were coming to him according to the incident that was happening to him at that time.

So how are you going to build yourself up, struggling against your desires, and improving your behavior? To do that you have to read what the Prophet ﷺ gave to us, and whatever the Prophet ﷺ gave to us is immense. As the Prophet ﷺ opened his mouth to address us, he gave to us what was 7000 times higher than the level of any prophet before him. So imagine, where are you reaching with 300,000 hadith?!

These are secrets given to the Ummah. These are secrets given to *Awliyā'ullāh* in order to guide their students and to encourage them. That is why he said:

قَالَ: لَا يَشْقَى جَلِيسُهُمْ

qāla: lā yashqā jalīsuhum

"Who sits with them will not suffer (hardship)." (*op cit.*)

Allah sends His *malā'ikatahu yaṭūfūna fī al-arḍ*, "angels roaming through the earth." They are encircumambulating, they roam with you going about and searching for these associations that are doing *Dhikrullāh.* When they find them Allah ordered them to sit with them and Allah asks the angels, "What are they doing?" The angels reply that they are seeking His mercy. Then at the end of that long hadith, Allah ﷻ says:

فَاشْهَدْ أَنِّي قَدْ غَفَرْتُ لَهُمْ

fa-sh-had annī qad ghafartu lahum

"so bear witness *that I have forgiven them."*

They are sitting remembering Him. They are not watching TV. Where we do our *dhikr* today? In front of the tv. Even that, do think your *dhikr* will not be rewarded. It will be rewarded.

وَرَحْمَتِي وَسِعَتْ كُلَّ شَيْءٍ ۚ فَسَأَكْتُبُهَا لِلَّذِينَ ءَامَنُوا وَكَانُوا يَتَّقُونَ

wa-raḥmatī wasi'at kulla shay', fa-sa'aktubuhā li-lladhīna āmanū wa-kānū yattaqūn

My mercy encompasses all things. So I shall decree it for those who believe and have (piety).'"

My mercy encompasses everything. There is *jīm* there, it isn't connected.

So some people argue that *Raḥmat* is for those who do these and this. But here is a *waqf, a stopping pause,* there. "My mercy has encompassed everything." So don't stop doing *dhikr*, even you are doing anywhere keep doing it.

So Allah says,"O my angels, witness that I have forgiven them."

When Allah says, "I have forgiven them" the angels say, "Stop, stop, O our Lord." Why are you trying to stop that *Raḥmat*. They complained about Sayyidinā Ādam. They criticized and said:

قَالُوا أَتَجْعَلُ فِيهَا مَن يُفْسِدُ فِيهَا وَيَسْفِكُ الدِّمَاءَ وَنَحْنُ نُسَبِّحُ بِحَمْدِكَ وَنُقَدِّسُ لَكَ

a-taj'alu fīhā man yasfiku al-dimā'

"How are you going to put someone in the earth who is going to shed blood?" (Sūrat al-Baqarah, 2:30)

O Angels! Why do you want to interfere? Interfere when Iblīs pushed Ādam to eat from the tree. They didn't do anything. Why they didn't stop him? They only know how to say, "*they are going to make bloodshed on earth.*"

So here is an authentic hadith of the Prophet, and to us, they are all authentic. But in this case, it is a Bukhārī hadith. They said, "O our Lord there is one there not from among them. He only came to take something from another and then leave." Allah said, "No problem. Even that one; never mind. For their sake I forgave him."

That visitor does not even believe in all they are doing. Why was he forgiven? Because that manifestation of Allah's Beautiful Names and Attributes and Lights is coming on him. It hit him and he was dressed with it.

So be certain that any kind of association around the world where people are remembering Allah the Creator, and reading and studying, will be rewarded greatly and more and more will be opened to their hearts and they will be forgiven. That is according to that one in hadith of the Prophet ﷺ. That visitor is forgiven and sent to Paradise. So what about when you sit in an association of *dhikr*. Do you think Allah won't forgive you and make you as clean as they day you were born? Guaranteed, no sins. Grandshaykh said, "This is a cleansing process, as the washing machine cleans your clothes *Dhikrullāh,* the remembrance of Allah, cleans the human being of everything that he or she has done." That is why it is good to make *Dhikrullāh* every day. Then your sins are gone.

Do you think that you are not doing sins every day? You are doing sins. You are lying. You are not lying to people but to your own self. And you are conspiring with yourself, with your shaytan, the devil that is inside you. When you sign a contract you cannot breach it. How many of us breached our contract between us and our Lord. Before we were sent to *dunyā* we had a contract. When Allah created us, He asked us, "Am I not your Lord?" We all said, "Yes, You are our Lord." And that is why we said *Ashhadu an lā ilāha illa-llāh, wa ashhadu anna Muḥammadan Rasūlu-llāh.*

If you breach a contract here with a bank what happens? You pay a penalty. Is it a big penalty or a small one? It is a big penalty. So what you think with your Creator the One Who created everyone? There is a penalty; a big one. But it is a penalty that can be erased.

Now they are paying 900 billion dollars for what? To recover and erase all these national debts. To return money that was borrowed in order for the people not to pay.

So Allah ﷻ will erase all your sins. On Judgment Day you will say, "O Allah if I own this whole *dunyā* I would give it away for You to forgive us." Allah already forgave us. He knows we are oppressors. Are you not an oppressor or ignorant one? Khan, Abdul Kabir, myself: there is no one who can raise his nose and say, "I am not an oppressor." Therefore, those who are inheritors from the Prophet ﷺ are worried and afraid.

It says that one hadith that comes from the Prophet ﷺ is higher than the hadith of other prophets by 7,000 times. Now how much time does it take for one breath to go out and come in? A very short time. That one short breath goes out from the mouth of the Prophet ﷺ when he is giving his Ṣaḥābah a hadith and from the Ṣaḥābah it goes out to everyone. How many breaths does it take to say one hadith? One hadith might take 3 minutes to 5 minutes to speak. How many breaths come in and go out. One breath of the Prophet ﷺ is better than the entire life of any other messenger. If a messenger lived 70 years one of the Prophet's ﷺ breath is better than that 70 years. That is why on Judgment Day all prophets are going to be seeking the intercession of the Prophet ﷺ for themselves and for their Ummas.

Sayyidinā Nūḥ ﷺ had the longest lifetime of any *Nabī mursal*—he lived 950 years, as is mentioned in Holy Qur'ān. That means that one breath of the Holy Prophet ﷺ is more valuable than 950 years, because you must take the longest lifetime of a *Nabī mursal*. So one breath of the Prophet ﷺ is better than the lifetime of Sayyidinā Nūḥ.

Why is that so? Because he is giving that hadith according to the reality of *al-Ḥaqīqah al-Muḥammadiyyah,* not according to our level but according to the level he is saying it. And we mentioned before that the Prophet ﷺ when he gives a hadith it must come according to the level he is at for that hadith. That will be either at *al-Maqām al-Muhammadiyya* or the level of the Ummah or the level of the *Awliyā'ullāh.*

So one hadith is going to go higher and higher in levels.

Kāna an-nabī yataḥarak famahu bil-ḥadīthu ... kāna yadūbu. The Prophet ﷺ when he moves his mouth with that hadith he is under the manifestation of that hadith in the station of the lamp that is the house that Allah has put for the Prophet ﷺ in the Divine Presence. If any of the *tajallīs* would come on the prophets from the hadith at that level all of them would faint.

He is explaining that when Isrāfīl is ordered to blow in the trumpet at the end of this *dunyā*, what will happen. Everyone will vanish. Not because of the trumpet but because of the manifestation of *qahr,* destruction, that comes with it. They vanish.

So when the hadith emerges from the mouth of the Prophet ﷺ they cannot take it and they faint away. So just as Allah ﷻ is giving the knowledge of the Holy Qur'ān to the Prophet ﷺ when He taught Sayyidinā Muhammad ﷺ the Qur'ān, *'Allam al-Qur'ān,* from Sayyidinā Muhammad ﷺ Allah gave to other prophets, then He created creation.

Here I would like to mention something about which we have to be very careful. Ibn 'Aṭā' Allāh al-Sakandarī was one of the great saints to appear on this earth. He came from Morocco along with Abī al-'Abbās al-Mursī, his shaykh for whom he was calipha. He used to hold an association with 12,000 people present, and at that time there were no microphones and no speakers but everyone of the 12,000 attendees was hearing when he spoke. How were they hearing?

Today if you don't have that microphone everyone will call out, "we are not hearing!" Before, when *Awliyā'ullāh* would speak, everyone could hear them, near or far. Allah ﷻ gives power to saints so their voices can reach everyone without increasing the volume of their voices but speaking normally. Everyone can hear.

So one time his students were all listening to his speech and suddenly he stopped. He said, "I am not continuing because Iblīs is between you now." He felt that presence of the evil one.

What this means is that when the Shaykh is giving a speech everyone must be focused on listening, not even moving. Often people come in from the door and everyone turns to look at them. Are you interested in who is coming or are you interested in what is being said? Many times Grandshaykh and Mawlana Shaykh Nazim said to us, "Don't look at anyone who is coming or going. And if anyone enters they must not greet the shaykh; rather he must sit wherever he finds a place without speaking to the people."

He also said that if anyone makes a movement to scratch their nose that brings the level of the association down seven levels.

So he stopped the lecture. There were some people whose hearts were not with the association. Respect is important, discipline is important. That is why they never allowed someone to come to the association in their work clothes. They come and change to white clothes out of respect. So give respect to Allah ﷻ and give respect to the Prophet ﷺ.

We have to be clean, not coming dirty, without taking ablution. Don't you feel shy? Then Iblīs can come and then that association is zero. Next time you must have complete ablution. If you lose it, you must jump and go make a fresh ablution not to wait.

Wa min Allāhi 't-tawfīq, bi ḥurmati 'l-ḥabīb, bi ḥurmati 'l-Fātiḥah.

And with Allāh is success, for the honor of the Beloved, and by the sanctity of al-Fātiḥah, the opening chapter of the Qur'ān.

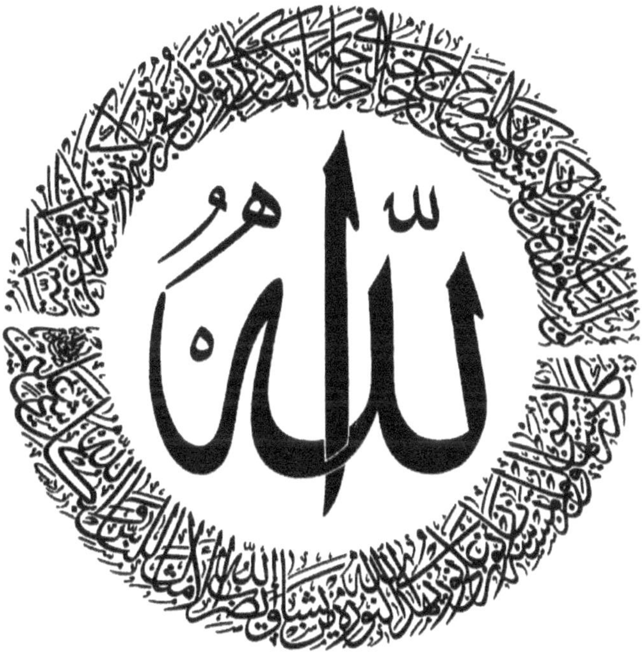
الله

Secrets of Isrā' and Mi'rāj

We mentioned before in the previous session that Allah ﷻ has invited his Prophet Sayyidinā Muhammad ﷺ for Laylat al-Isrā' wa'l-Mi'rāj. What was the purpose of inviting him? For sure we don't know. Allah ﷻ and His Prophet ﷺ know best. But what Grandshaykh said is that there is a huge treasure and that treasure has to be given to someone. Allah does not need that treasure for Himself. Allah is the creator who is creating treasures. So these treasures that are continuously being created have to be given out for the benefit of human beings. And who is the one who can keep these treasures in trust? Not everyone; only none. That one is none other than the Seal of Messengers Sayyidinā Muhammad ﷺ. That is why it is very important to know and realize that behind every step of Sayyidinā Muhammad ﷺ there are wisdoms, not only one wisdom but an infinite number of wisdoms.

Awliyā'ullāh say and it is from Grandshaykh and Mawlana Shaykh's saying, that if a *Walī* scratched his face, a minimum of at least wisdom of 12,000 wisdoms is in that. If a *Walī* moves his finger like that, there are at least 12,000 wisdoms behind that. They don't move anything. Because when someone moves from cold weather to hot weather he will be shaking. And if that weather gets colder he will freeze and then he cannot move forward or backward. Forget about cold weather, what is someone sees something beyond imagination? What will happen to them? They will freeze; no movement.

You are a doctor, if something happened beyond imagination what happens? They freeze; they are stunned, they cannot say anything. And when *Awliyā'ullāh* enter the presence of Sayyidinā Muhammad ﷺ they freeze. And when the Prophet ﷺ entered and comes with the *Awliyā'ullāh* to the Divine Presence, they are as if frozen. *Awliyā'ullāh* freeze. They are in complete submission, no movement. They are stunned it is something immense that is changing everything they knew before. Whatever they knew before when they entered the Divine Presence everything they learned before has to be dumped. There is no comparison between what they are now receiving and what they learned before from different kinds of teachings. That is why we say the knowledge spread between people today is like kindergarten. So they knew that is spread between *Awliyā'ullāh* and they want to raise them to their level; to enter their students there and make them frozen there.

What can you say when you reach there? You can say nothing. That living example and living reality and living level is a livelihood level that keeps you in continuous full ecstasy that you cannot see better than that in the Divine Presence. Those manifestations of heavens, paradises and whatever angelic manifestations that Allah will manifest on you and the appearances of Allah's Beautiful Names and Attributes will cause you to feel that *rāsha*, that shivering of ecstasy. Then you feel you don't want anything of *dunya*; you only want that heavenly pleasure that will be opened in the Divine Presence.

That is what *Awliyā'ullāh* are after. When the Prophet ﷺ was invited for Laylat al-Isrā' wa'l-Mi'rāj, Allah invited him to give to the Ummah. He is not hiding those treasures. What did He create it for? To give to Sayyidinā Muhammad ﷺ, for the Prophet ﷺ to follow it up. And Grandshaykh said, ق, when Sayyidinā Muhammad ﷺ was invited and he was approaching more and more until he reached a level with Jibrīl where Jibrīl said, "*Yā Rasūlullāh!* I cannot go further. I cannot move."

The hidden wisdom is that Allah ﷻ wants to give Sayyidinā Muhammad ﷺ the hidden treasure, whatever there are of divinely treasures that Allah created for *Jibrīl wa mā dūnahu*, Jibrīl and whatever is under him, whatever is known from the First Paradise up to level of Jibrīl, Allah wants to give to Sayyidinā Muhammad ﷺ. The realities of soul and spirit are uncountable. That is why at the level of Jibrīl, you can differentiate between them, but not below his level. There are three levels of knowledge: the level below Sayyidinā Jibrīl, the level Sayyidinā Jibrīl ؑ is in, and then a level above that. At the level of Sayyidinā Jibrīl ؑ one can differentiate soul from spirit—they are completely different. The meaning of soul is one thing and the meaning of spirit is something else.

إِنَّا لِلَّهِ وَإِنَّا إِلَيْهِ رَاجِعُونَ

Inna lillāhi wa inna ilayhi rāji'ūn
Surely we belong to God, and surely to Him we return.(Sūrat al-Baqarah, 2:156)

We mix between soul and spirit. But for Sayyidinā Jibrīl ؑ who is standing at that level in Paradise, the meaning of soul and the meaning of spirit is different. There is a level above that. Allah called the Prophet ﷺ to Sayyidinā Jibrīl's level first to give him what is up to that level. Then second is what is at the level of Sayyidinā Jibrīl ؑ and last is what is above the level of Sayyidinā Jibrīl. That is not opened.

So whatever is at the level of Sayyidinā Jibrīl ؑ and below the Prophet ﷺ shared with creation. All that knowledge was given to Sayyidinā Muhammad ﷺ and the Prophet ﷺ shared that knowledge and distributed it. But at the level of Sayyidinā Jibrīl ؑ and beyond, is not opened. We need the road to be paved first. That needs a special container that can contain and understand that knowledge.

What Sayyidinā Muhiyyidīn ibn 'Arabī ق wrote astonished scholars, not only common people. What Sayyidinā Jalāluddīn ar-Rūmī astonished not only common people but scholars as well, yet what he revealed is but a drop of an ocean that *Awliyā'ullāh* of the Naqshbandī Golden Chain are keeping in that turbine of Divine Knowledge. That turbine is rotating at a very high speed. That rotation is producing all these different levels of knowledge. There are turbines for water in order to create energy to make engines to run. As these engines run they are creating energy. The *Walī* is a turbine by himself. Don't look at the *Walī* as a normal person. Rather look at him as a turbine, turning non-stop, generating continuous knowledge from what is coming into his heart. When these knowledges go into the heart of that *Walī* that heart is moving like a turbine producing knowledge that everyone can take according to the size of the container of his or her heart.

Allah wanted to give to Sayyidinā Muhammad ﷺ so he gave him in three different levels. The first level he gave to the whole Ummah, *mā dūn maqām Jibrīl,* "all knowledge below that of Jibrīl." Allah gave that knowledge to the Prophet ﷺ in one shot. And he was able to differentiate all of its parts in one shot. In one moment he was able to receive and understand all that knowledge and understanding one portion of that knowledge does not affect understanding any other portion.

These days it is easy to understand. Do you not see digital receivers that are able to receive thousands of channels at the same time? Does not Sayyidinā Muhammad ﷺ have the capacity to receive all the knowledge into his heart in one shot? His heart is a receiver. All the receivers in *dunyā* and in *ākhirah* are not like one drop of the receivers of the Prophet ﷺ.

If I am going to explain these realities, some people will say, "Oh, that is not acceptable. It is beyond our understanding," as they did to Sayyidinā Abū Hurayrah ؓ:

عَنْ أَبِي هُرَيْرَةَ، قَالَ: حَفِظْتُ مِنْ رَسُولِ اللَّهِ ﷺ وِعَاءَيْنِ، فَأَمَّا أَحَدُهُمَا فَبَثَثْتُهُ، وَأَمَّا الْآخَرُ فَلَوْ بَثَثْتُهُ قُطِعَ هَذَا الْبُلْعُومُ.

> Sayyidinā Abū Hurayrah ؓ who said, "I receive two containers of knowledge from the Prophet ﷺ; one of them I revealed to people and the other if I were to reveal it they would cut my neck." (*Sahīh al-Bukhārī*)

That was in the station of Sayyidinā Jibrīl. There he was in that level. Therefore the Prophet ﷺ says in the hadith, *kuntu atadārisu 'l-Qur'ān ma' Jibrīl,* "I used to study the Holy Qur'ān with Jibrīl." It was as if the two of them were sitting and discussing and sitting and reciting and memorizing, from the Prophet ﷺ to Jibrīl and from Jibrīl to the Prophet ﷺ. At that level where Jibrīl heard the revelation, the Prophet ﷺ was hearing the same as Jibrīl heard, because that is the level at which Sayyidinā Jibrīl ؑ was receiving revelation. So he was hearing at that level, the same voice and the same understanding.

Now Jibrīl is the head of all the angels. If a general has an army he knows everyone of his army, and what kind of weapons each soldier is carrying. What do you think of Sayyidinā Jibrīl ؑ who is head of all the angels? He must know every angel and what every angel is doing. So that means when Sayyidinā Muhammad ﷺ reached that station he knew everything that Jibrīl has known. Today they bring two remote controls together and one can program the other—it passes all its knowledge to the other. *Subḥānallah* in everything nowadays you can give an example from spirituality.

So the Prophet ﷺ took that knowledge from Jibrīl and Jibrīl knew every knowledge of Paradise. That happened in one second; in one shot. No need for more than one second. So as soon as Jibrīl said, "I cannot ascend further with you *yā Muḥammad,*" the Prophet ﷺ began to rise up, and as soon as he was ascending the third level of knowledge appeared, which was, as Grandshaykh used to call it, the Station of Khāmis al-Qur'ān, the fifth Qur'ān. There is not a different Qur'ān but that level is called Khāmis al-Qur'ān. We have the remainder of the revealed books: Tawrāt, Injīl, Zabūr and Qur'ān. There are four heavenly books. Khāmis al-Qur'ān is the fifth 'book' without being another book or a different Qur'ān. Rather it is the secret of the Holy Qur'ān.

What Ṣaḥābah heard is what the Prophet ﷺ gave to them; they did not hear from Jibrīl. But above that level... the Prophet ﷺ heard something different. A different voice at a different station adn that is called Khāmis al-Qur'ān. There is no fifth book, but *Awliyā'ullāh* describe it as 'fifth' because it is the secret of Holy Qur'ān with which Sayyidinā al-Mahdī ؑ will appear.

The Prophet ﷺ said, *Afḍal al-Ummah akhyār al-Ummah ākhir al-Ummah*, "the best of my Ummah, the most honored of my Ummah are the last of the Ummah." That is because they are going to get the secret of revelation from Sayyidinā al-Mahdī ؑ. That did not come before except to heart of the Ṣaḥābah when the Prophet ﷺ wants to give them. The grandson of the Prophet ﷺ, that is Sayyidinā al-Mahdī ؑ, will be giving out that knowledge which, compared to whatever knowledge is currently known in this universe is but a drop of knowledge from that knowledge. He said from every letter of Holy Qur'ān 24,000 oceans of knowledge will open. There are 300,000 letters, and each letter will contain 24,000 oceans of knowledge of which there is no limit to the depth of each ocean. That is why *Awliyā'ullāh* always pray "O Allah let us to be in time of Mahdī ؑ."

Wa min Allāhi 't-tawfīq, bi ḥurmati 'l-ḥabīb, bi ḥurmati 'l-Fātiḥah.

And with Allāh is success, for the honor of the Beloved, and by the sanctity of al-Fātiḥah, the opening chapter of the Qur'ān.

ورحمتي وسعت كل شيء
١٤٠٢

Secrets of Isrā' and Miʿrāj, Part2

Allah gave *Awliyā'ullāh* a knowledge that astonished scholars, *tuḥayyir al-ʿulamā*. Scholars know what they read. Scholars know 'this one said this' and 'this one said that.' Beyond that their knowledge is restricted and their knowledge is limited.

But there is no limitation on the knowledge of *Awliyā'ullāh* because it is *ʿUlūm al-ḥaqā'iq*, knowledge of realities. A reality cannot be restricted. It has to give its essence. It has to come up from something that is real. *ʿUlamā'* when they write a fatwa or read something, they are not sure if what they are writing is going to be a correct fatwa. This understanding is based on the hadith:

الحلالُ بيِّنٌ والحرامُ بيِّنٌ

al-ḥalālu bayyinun wa al-ḥarāmu bayyinun.

The permitted is known and the forbidden is known… (*Ṣaḥīḥ al-Bukhārī* and *Ṣaḥīḥ Muslim*)

So in between *ḥalāl* and *ḥarām* is where the *fatwa* of scholars comes in. Sometimes they are not certain of what they are giving a *fatwa* on, but they build their *fatwa* on the principles of what is between *halal* and *haram*. They seek to avoid what is *haram* and to approach as much as possible what is *halal* but still there is a methodology which they use to build their *fatwa*. Therefore the Prophet ﷺ continued the hadith:

إِذَا اجْتَهَدَ الْحَاكِمُ فَأَصَابَ فَلَهُ أَجْرَانِ، وَإِذَا اجْتَهَدَ فَأَخْطَأَ فَلَهُ أَجْرٌ

idhā ajtahad al-ḥākim fa-aṣāba fa-lahu ajrāni, wa in lam yuṣib fa-lahu ajrun

"If the judge gives a ruling and he is correct he gets double the reward and if he is incorrect then he gets one reward."

This is what we call *ʿUlūm al-ʿulamā'*. The knowledge of *Awliyā'* is completely different. The knowledge of *Awliyā'* is astonishing, it leaves *ʿulamā* stunned. That is why they were stunned with what Sayyidinā Muḥiyyidīn ibn ʿArabī ق said. They were astonished by what Sayyidinā ʿAbd al-Qādir al-Jīlānī ق said. They could not understand what Sayyidinā Bāyazīd al-Bisṭāmī ق said. They could not understand what Rābiʿa al-ʿAdawiyya said. It is very difficult. So what we are discussing here is something from those traces Grandshaykh ق, and Mawlana Shaykh Nazim Adil ق, may Allah grant him long life, were expressing to us from these knowledges and these knowledges were coming from inspirations and these inspirations become like real facts because they are taking it from the heart of the Prophet ﷺ, through the chain of secrets from the heart of one shaykh to another.

This is a small introduction. We said in the previous session that Allah called His Prophet on Laylat al-Isrā' wal-Mi'rāj to deliver to him his trusts. He gave them all these realities of whatever is below the station of Sayyidinā Jibrīl ﷺ and lower in order that he will be able to save his ummah from wrongdoing. That is why he related the hadith:

قَالَ رَسُولُ اللهِ صَلَّى اللهُ عَلَيْهِ وَسَلَّمَ: حَيَاتِي خَيْرٌ لَكُمْ، تُحَدِّثُونَ وَيُحْدَثُ لَكُمْ، وَمَمَاتِي خَيْرٌ لَكُمْ، تُعْرَضُ عَلَيَّ أَعْمَالُكُمْ، فَإِنْ وَجَدْتُ خَيْرًا حَمِدْتُ اللهَ، وَإِنْ وَجَدْتُ غَيْرَ ذَلِكَ اسْتَغْفَرْتُ لَكُمْ.

> *Qāla Rasūlullāhi ṣallallāhu 'alayhi wa sallam: ḥayātī khayrun lakum tuḥaddithūn wa yuḥdathu lakum, wa mamātī khayrun lakum tu'raḍu 'alayya a'mālukum, fa-in wajadtu khayran ḥamidtullāh fa in wajadtu ghayra dhālika astaghfartu lakum.*
>
> My life is a great good for you: you relate from it and narrations are related to you. And my death contains good for you as well, for I observe the *'amal* of my Ummah. If I find good, I thank Allah, and if I see other than that, whatever is bad, I ask forgiveness for you. (al-Bazzār in his Musnad)

That is to save the Ummah from punishment.

Anything which is from the station of Jibrīl and *dūnahu,* down, is from *'Ulūm ash-shara'* because Jibrīl was revealing to the Prophet ﷺ. And from that station and above is from the *'Ulūm al-ḥaqā'iq* knowledge of realities that Allah ﷻ has given to the Prophet ﷺ when Sayyidinā Jibrīl ﷺ said to him: "I cannot go any further I reached the limit. You go on ahead."

And Grandshaykh said that in that journey as the Prophet ﷺ was moving from the station of Jibrīl to the Divine Presence Allah was sending and revealing to him the secret of the Holy Qur'ān. Because from Jibrīl and down is Holy Qur'ān what we read and understand from the explanation of the Prophet ﷺ and from what different Ṣaḥābah heard from the Prophet ﷺ. But from the level of Jibrīl and above, there is on every one of the 300,000 letters of the Holy Qur'ān an ocean that you cannot dive in and find its bottom. Allah was opening, revealing to the Prophet ﷺ from these knowledges and from the secrets He ﷻ was opening to him the manifestation of the 99 Names which *lā sharīka lahu,* has no partner."

That is why *'ulamā* say that the real worshipper the real *muwaḥḥid*, the one who testified to the Oneness of Allah truly is Sayyidinā Muhammad ﷺ because he saw the revelations of these manifestations of these Divine Names and from all the appearances that manifest to him he understood the Divine Oneness from the appearance of these 99 Holy Names.

That is why *Awliyā'ullāh* say that the real worshipper, the real *muwwaḥid*, the one that testified to the Oneness of Allah ﷻ truly is Sayyidinā Muhammad ﷺ. That is because he saw that the revelation of the manifestations of all these Names and he understood the reality of Oneness through the understanding of these 99 Names.

Whatever you add turns out to be 9. Take 99. It is a nine and another nine: 9 + 9 = 18. Take the digits of 18, they are a one and an eight. 1+8 = 9. And 9 in numerology is zero. Nothing exists except Allah's ﷻ Existence. So the real *muwwaḥid* to testify *ash-hadu an lā ilāha ill-Allāh* is Sayyidinā Muhammad ﷺ. He is the only one that can be described as the *muwwaḥid*. Not as we typically describe everyone. We are *muwwaḥid* according to the station we are in. What is our station? Our station is struggling between good and bad. Our station is *thumma āmanū thumma kafarū - One day in belief, one day in unbelief.* We have not yet reached the level of belief. Only Sayyidinā Muhammad ﷺ has.

Allah ﷻ did not speak to the Prophet ﷺ in the understanding of Rasūlullāh ﷺ. Rasūlullāh is the one who is carrying the message, that message that Prophet ﷺ is bringing to humanity, is from station of Jibrīl ﷺ and down. But above, what Allah has granted to the Prophet ﷺ is higher than that. He isn't Rasūlullāh ﷺ to humanity only. He is Rasūlullāh ﷺ to angels also. He is also Rasūlullāh ﷺ to all creation that has been creation. So they have a different knowledge and what that knowledge is we don't know, but it is from the Appearance of the 99 Names. Allah ﷻ spoke to him from Khāmis al-Qur'ān. He talked to him as the guardian of these secrets which are above the position of Sayyidinā Jibrīl ﷺ.

So Khāmis al-Qur'ān is something huge, which we cannot see and we cannot understand and he said "*wa lā yushāriku fīhi aḥadā.*" It is only for him ﷺ and he has no partner in it, not any other prophet ﷺ and not *Awliyā'ullāh* except according to their capacity. No one can be partner to Sayyidinā Muhammad ﷺ in that knowledge. He said for that reason He ﷻ called him to deliver those treasures. And everything that the Prophet ﷺ took is between him and Allah ﷻ; no one knows what has been given. So the meaning of what we are saying is that no one knows that secret that happened between Allah ﷻ and the Prophet ﷺ on Laylat al-Isrā' wa'l-Miʿrāj except Sayyidinā Muhammad ﷺ. That is a secret that happened between them. As mentioned in the *seerah*, the Prophet ﷺ in the Laylat al-Isrā' wa'l-Miʿrāj has seen his Creator with the eyes of his head - that means physically. That means that manifestation of the Essence that Allah wanted Sayyidinā Muhammad ﷺ to know about, that reality of the manifestation of the Divine Essence was seen by the Prophet ﷺ with his eyes, not with his spirit. It was his physical eyes. As contemporary scholars mentioned, especially Shaykh Shaʿrawi and earlier scholars, such as Imām an-Nawawī related that the Prophet ﷺ "saw his Lord with the eyes of his head." Physically.

When Sayyidinā al-Mahdī ؑ comes, traces from the secret of the Holy Qur'ān, *Khāmis al-Qur'ān,* the fifth 'book' of the heavenly books which include the Holy Qur'ān, will be given to the Ummah at that time.

That is why Sayyidinā 'Umar ؓ asked, when the Prophet ﷺ was describing that, he asked, "Are those people going to be prophets?" The Prophet ﷺ said, "No, they are not prophets. He said, what are they then, that they have such high levels we didn't hear about it. The Prophet ﷺ said, "They are normal people. When they go to pray, they don't know how many *rak'āts* they prayed." They pray 3, 4 or 5 or 7 *rak'āts*. They think 'did I pray 2 or 3, then add one or two and it becomes six.' Then they are distracted and they forgot how many *rak'āts* they prayed."

Don't think it didn't happen. It happened. With me even. It happens with everyone that is not something strange. Prophet describing: "They are going to be like that," Prophet ﷺ said. But Allah's Mercy will be so huge at that time, it cannot be described. Because of that huge mercy Allah ﷻ will give them things that others did not see. And as we said, before the rank of Ṣaḥābah no one can reach, they are Ṣaḥābah. He said that at that moment what happened between Allah ﷻ the Creator what He gave to his Prophet ﷺ what took place and what secret went there, no one knows and Allah ordered Sayyidinā Muhammad ﷺ and gave permission to the Prophet ﷺ to call and to speak to his Ummah.

According to the voice of Holy Qur'ān:

لَا يُكَلِّفُ اللَّهُ نَفْسًا إِلَّا وُسْعَهَا ۚ

lā yukallifu llāhu nafsan illā wus'ahā.
Allah does not burden a soul beyond its capacity. (Sūrat al-Baqarah, 2:286)

Allah said to Sayyidinā Muhammad ﷺ, "I gave you the secrets and gave you everything, but I revealed to you in the Holy that Allah does not burden anyone more than he can take. According to what they take, you deliver. What can we take? Nothing. We took only a little of what happened that night. And what we take is from level of Jibrīl ؑ and down. Since we were not able to take, whatever that *miqdār*, amount, was not more than the manifestation of the Beautiful Name ar-Raḥmān. From that manifestation of that name ar-Raḥmān, all this knowledge you see and that has been given and even all knowledge of prophets, and knowledge of Ṣaḥābah and *Awliyā'*, all that they are bringing and what they are stunned from what they say and *'ulamā* are stunned with what they say, they are still only from the drop of that ocean of the name ar-Raḥmān.

Allāhu lā ilāha illā Huwa, al-Raḥmānu al-Raḥīm.

All we see in books and universities, Arabic, English, Persian, Hindu, Japanese, all are appearances from the manifestations of the appearances of that Name. And still more to come and that part is only a drop.

The reality of Divine knowledge has not been opened, except to the Prophet ﷺ. It will not open until the power of Sayyidinā Mahdī ؏ comes because that [power] has to back up its appearance. Then in the Last Days these knowledges will appear quickly. You cannot study at that time. When that reality comes all that they are teaching in the university becomes like the alphabet: *alif bā*. as when you first go to school what *do* they teach you? They teach you "A is for apple, B is for boy and C is for candy and D is for donkey." That is it.

That is what we are learning. When Sayyidinā Mahdī ؏ comes all the huge knowledge of universities of science and physics and astronomy will stop and will no longer be of importance. It is obsolete. And he comes with knowledge that is not obsolete. He has to open. The Prophet ﷺ has given it.

How will that knowledge be given out? It is through reflections. You can direct a mirror any way you like. Similarly, the eyes of people will be reflecting that knowledge to anyone they want from Sayyidinā Mahdī ؏ to the eyes of his caliphas and from the caliphas to his deputies and from the deputies to the different spiritual leaders. From leaders that knowledge is moving very quickly.

Today sometimes they show movies that they put for you a new knowledge a lot of knowledge through a lot of reflections or by inserting a chip in your body which contains a lot of knowledges. Did you see that? No, come I will show you.

He said that "The Prophet ﷺ was ordered to open only from that Name. *wa ummirū bi tilka al-ayāt* - He was ordered to reveal those verses of Holy Qur'ān in that capacity in that position and in that level. But in the level of the 99 Names that are above the level of Sayyidinā Jibrīl ؏, the Prophet ﷺ was ordered not to open that to the Ummah, and was ordered not to reveal it. Therefore he spoke according to what our hearts can take.

If that knowledge would be opened, our hearts would not be able to take it and they could break—everyone would faint and there will be no more life; neither on earth nor in the universe. A little bit will be opened in time of Mahdī ؏ but all of it will be opened in Paradise."

And he said "In that night the third knowledge that Allah gave to the Prophet ﷺ in that Ascension Allah showed him all *Awliyā'ullāh* that Allah had created. All of them 124,000 in every time."

It means anyone that goes, passes; another comes and sits in his place. So 124,000 living always.

مِنَ الْمُؤْمِنِينَ رِجَالٌ صَدَقُوا مَا عَاهَدُوا اللَّهَ عَلَيْهِ فَمِنْهُم مَّن قَضَى نَحْبَهُ وَمِنْهُم مَّن يَنتَظِرُ وَمَا بَدَّلُوا تَبْدِيلًا

mina al-mu'minīna rijālun ṣadaqū mā 'āhadū Allāha 'alayh fa-minhum man qaḍā naḥbahu wa-minhum man yantaẓiru wa-mā baddalū tabdīlā

Among the believers are men that have kept their covenant with Allah. Some have passed and some are waiting. (Sūrat al-Aḥzāb, 33:23)

Those who passed are replaced by another. Might be one is dying and another coming in every moment. Allah showed Sayyidinā Muhammad ﷺ all these *Awliyā'*. They are the assistants to the Prophet ﷺ. *'Awn ar-Rasūl* ﷺ. I order that they will be able to assist and support the Prophet ﷺ he called him in order to give him *al-quwatta al-qudsiyy*a, the sanctified power or the holy power that is from the *azaliyya abadiyya* - from pre-eternal to post-eternal. It is a power that has to be dressed on the Prophet ﷺ and from the Prophet ﷺ has to be dressed on the saints that are in this presence. "These are your assistants. Dress them from that sanctified power. If you don't dress them they cannot carry that work. They have to carry that power."

"When he gave him that permission to use that power, Prophet ﷺ dressed every *Walī* by himself and then in that Divine Presence was dressed with the holy power of that *Walī* and that is why we see different levels of *Walī*. We see many different *Walī*. You cannot say that the only *Walī* is your shaykh. But there are a lot of *Walīs* around. You only focus on your shaykh - that is your duty to focus. That is where we are connected and that is where our duty lies. And when he dressed him with what Allah gave him, and he dressed the *Awliyā'ullāh*, then Allah opened to him the meaning of:

وَلَقَدْ كَرَّمْنَا بَنِي آدَمَ

Wa laqad karamnaa Bani Ādam.

We have honored the Children of Ādam. (Sūrat al-Isrā', 17:70)

So when that verse was revealed Prophet ﷺ was brought inside to be shown with what Allah has honored them. So *Awliyā'ullāh* were astonished and stunned with what they saw there. They saw the real honor that Allah had given to human beings and who is going to appear under that verse and manifestation of holy Qur'ān. They could not say anything. Then after that third level and Prophet ﷺ dressed the *Awliyā'ullāh* and Prophet ﷺ took the *Awliyā'ullāh* into that ocean and then the Prophet ﷺ took all the atoms and offspring of human beings, took them clean and then you are as on the Day of Promises, clean.

يُولَدُ الإِنسَانُ عَلَى الفِطْرَةِ، فَأَبَوَاهُ يُهَوِّدَانِهِ أَوْ يُنَصِّرَانِهِ أَوْ يُمَجِّسَانِهِ.

yūladu al-insānu ʿalā al-fiṭrah, fa-abawāhu yuhawwidānihi aw yunaṣṣirānihi aw yumajjisānihi

Man is born upon *fiṭra* (innocence), but it is his parents who make him a Jew, a Christian or a Magian. (Bukhārī, Muslim)

He showed them the purity that human beings that they are born on. And he showed them to Sayyidinā Muhammad ﷺ and said "They are clean. Would you like to keep them in trust?"

He said *naʿm Yā Rabbī.* And Allah gave them in trust to him ﷺ. That is why Allah gave the Prophet ﷺ *shafāʿa.* To intercede for the Ummah. And He gave them and what happened we leave for next time.

May Allāh ﷻ forgive us and may Allāh ﷻ bless us.

Wa min Allāhi 't-tawfīq, bi ḥurmati 'l-ḥabīb, bi ḥurmati 'l-Fātiḥa.

And with Allāh is success, for the honor of the Beloved, and by the sanctity of al-Fātiḥah, the opening chapter of the Qur'ān.

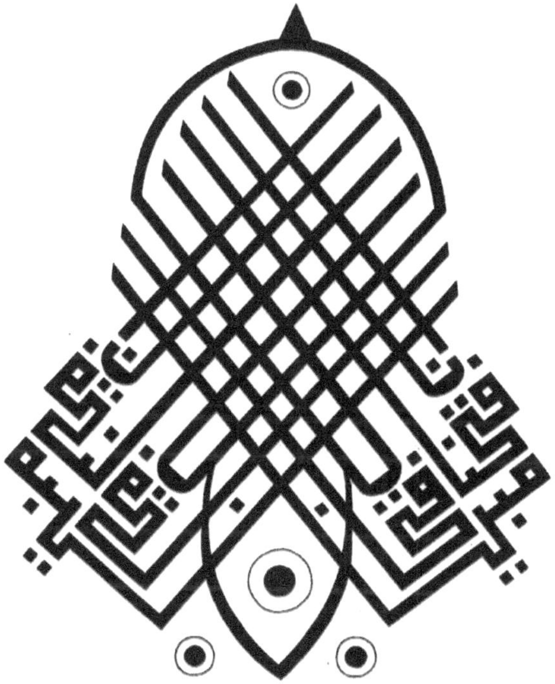

Secrets of Isrā' and Miʿrāj, Part 3

The third wisdom of Allah bringing Sayyidinā Muhammad ﷺ on al-Isrā' wal-Miʿrāj was to show him all the saints of the Ummah that are going to be guiding it and to give them that holy eternal power by which they are able to guide and to carry their responsibilities.

Allah ﷻ delivered all the Ummah; not just the Ummah of the Prophet ﷺ, but all the descendants of Sayyidinā Ādam ؑ clean and Sayyidinā Muhammad ﷺ took them as a trust, clean.

When Allah asked him ﷺ, "Do you accept to take all of Bani Ādam as a trust?" he was happy and he said, "Yes, *Yā Rabbī*." They were very clean, very transparent with no sins on them. Then as soon as he said, "yes" Allah ﷻ showed him what they are going to do in *dunyā* and what kind of bad behaviors and bad characteristics they had; how much they are going to make conspiracy and make tyranny and to kill one another and do things that Allah doesn't like and how they are going to be veiled with the darkness of those dark characteristics. When he ﷺ saw that, the Prophet ﷺ became afraid. He said *"Yā Rabbī,* that is too much. Send me some of your sincere ones to guide the Ummah after me, to give them and inherit from me some of my power to guide and teach human beings my way, the *ṣirāṭ al-mustaqīm*, the straight path."

Those who misbehaved in *dunyā* were from the group that when Allah ﷻ called the *dharrāt Bani Ādam* on the Day of Promises when we were still atoms and only in spirit and Allah called us and said, "Who am I?" and a group of them said, "You are our Lord and we are Your servants." And another group said, "You are what You are and we are what we are," and a third group said, "We are what we are."

The first group are Allah's ﷻ sincere ones, the ones who are going to be guides and teachers. The second group Allah took and sent them to the *Bahr az-zulmah*, the Ocean of Darkness because they needed to be cleaned and polished. He sent them there to fight their egos and to struggle. That was in the Day of Promises, before their appearance in *dunyā*. The *dunyā* is a small reflection of what happened there. 80,000 of Allah's Years they were thrown in that Ocean of Darkness. How many years is that? When we come to *dunyā* we don't recall any of that but that is existing. On Judgment Day we will be seeing how much wrong we have done and how much we have disobeyed and at that time we will regret.

Here in *dunyā* we are like someone under anesthesia. We cannot see what we did at that time. On Judgment Day all that will become manifest and we will see it. *Awliyā'ullāh* can see what happened at that time because they are pure. They are from the ones who said, "You are our Lord and we are your servants." Allah made them see.

As for the rest, they said, "We are we and you are what You are," meaning "You are the Lord, but we are the lords of our own selves." So Allah sent them back to that Ocean of Darkness, and after 80,000 more years brought them out and asked them a second time, "Who am I and who are you?" After that heavy training and intense struggle, some of them responded, "You are our Lord and we are Your servants..."

Yet others continued to say, "You are what You are and we are what we are," and Allah left them in that darkness for another 80,000 years.

Those in *dunyā* who are sincere and pious know that they are the ones who said on the Day of Promises, "You are our Lord and we are Your servants."

Those who have been taken out of that darkness, meaning they are struggling in *dunyā* between good and bad, are the ones who repented after they first refused to accept Allah's Lordship. After going through that tremendous struggle against their own selves they finally accepted to say, "You are our Lord and we are Your servants..."

Those who were stubborn and didn't accept Allah ﷻ in this life are the disbelievers and corrupted people, heretics and atheists; they rejected Allah at that time and saw only themselves.

Grandshaykh continued, saying that there are two types of unbelievers: unbelievers who disbelieve and stubborn unbelievers, *muʿānidīn*. Similarly there are corrupt *munāfiqs* [hypocrites] and stubborn *munāfiq*s.

Those who are not stubborn from that group will one day find guidance. That is why we find people who come to the right way and convert. They are not stubborn in disbelief. Once they know the truth they come quickly running to it.

So the Prophet ﷺ saw all this and said, "*Yā Rabbī*, this is too much, give me some supporters," and Allah gave him *Awliyā'ullāh.*

Now what Grandshaykh said next is very important. "Allah wants to show that as much as He gave Sayyidinā Muhammad ﷺ of power, he is still not able to reach everything, meaning 'you are still in need of Me at every moment. I am the Lord who can do everything perfectly. You cannot do everything without Me.' He wants to show him ﷺ that he cannot turn everyone to be a believer. 'Your power is limited to an extent. You can have everyone but I want to keep some whom you cannot affect, to show you I am the Creator, you are not the Creator.' Therefore He left some people misguided and they were enemies to the Prophet ﷺ like Abū Jahl and Abū Lahab. And what did Allah say? He said:

إِنَّكَ لَا تَهْدِي مَنْ أَحْبَبْتَ وَلَكِنَّ اللَّهَ يَهْدِي مَن يَشَاءُ وَهُوَ أَعْلَمُ بِالْمُهْتَدِينَ

innaka lā tahdī man ʿaḥbabta wa lākinna Allāha yahdī man yashā' wa-huwa ʿaʿlamu bil-muhtadīn

It is true thou wilt not be able to guide every one, whom thou lovest; but Allah guides those whom He will and He knows best those who receive guidance. (Sūrat al- Qaṣaṣ, 28:56)

So those people who are here and there who are sitting and studying and learning the hadith of the Prophet and Qur'ān, they must know that they are under protection and saved on the Day of Promises and they are under the guidance of *Awliyā'ullāh* who will guide them to the protection of Sayyidinā Muhammad ﷺ and his blessings. They are accepting Allah, accepting the Prophet ﷺ and accepting Islam, and although we are full of shortcomings we are under the *shafā'a* of the Prophet ﷺ.

وَرَحْمَتِي وَسِعَتْ كُلَّ شَيْءٍ فَسَأَكْتُبُهَا لِلَّذِينَ يَتَّقُونَ وَيُؤْتُونَ الزَّكَاةَ وَالَّذِينَ هُم بِآيَاتِنَا يُؤْمِنُونَ

wa-raḥmatī wasi'at kulla shay' fa-sa-aktubuhā li-lladhīna yattaqūna wa-yu'tūna al-zakāh

My mercy extends to all things. That (mercy) I shall ordain for those who do right, and practise regular charity, and those who believe in Our signs;- (Sūrat al-A'rāf, 7:156)

"My Mercy has encompassed everything and wrapped everything. I am going to write it for the people are accepting, who are devoted, who are giving what they can give and not holding what Allah gave them and giving in the way of Allah." As they give, Allah gives more. If you give Allah *'ibādah*, Allah gives more rewards. You fast more, He will give you more power. If you pray more, He gives you more blessings. If you are a generous person giving of what wealth Allah gave of *dunyā*, He will send more.

If you give all, as Sayyidinā Abū Bakr ؓ your *'īmān* will be strong. If you give half, as Sayyidinā 'Umar ؓ gave, you will get half of what Abū Bakr gave. The Prophet ﷺ said to him, "You have half the *'īmān* of Sayyidinā Abū Bakr."

There are people who give and their hands are trembling. Some give and regret what they gave. There are those who give and their hands tremble.

You pray two *rak'āts* … next time you pray two more *rak'āts*. That is better, you receive more. You fast one day Sunnah you receive more, and if you fast two days that is better.

One day they do good, one day bad, *thumma 'āmanū thumma kafarū*, "*then they believed, then they disbelieved*", but not under *thumma -azdādū kufran*, "*and they increased in disbelief*" but we are struggling. Always struggling. This is our shortcoming.

So when Allah showed the Prophet ﷺ this it was to show him, "My power is unlimited while your power is limited."

Awliyā'ullāh look at their students, those whom Allah ﷻ has assigned to be their followers. They can have followers even from the *mu'ānidīn*, stubborn ones, he will try to work on them. And he might have students from unbeliever who aren't stubborn, *mu'ānidīn*. And he might receive students from those who were thrown into *Baḥr al-ẓulmah* and then came back and acknowledge that Allah is the lord. And he might have students who are *munāfiqīn* and even stubborn *munāfiqīn* who are corrupt persons. Despite this, all of them fall under the *khiṭāb*, Allah's address:

قُلْ يَا عِبَادِيَ الَّذِينَ أَسْرَفُوا عَلَى أَنفُسِهِمْ لَا تَقْنَطُوا مِن رَّحْمَةِ اللَّهِ إِنَّ اللَّهَ يَغْفِرُ الذُّنُوبَ جَمِيعًا إِنَّهُ هُوَ الْغَفُورُ الرَّحِيمُ

qul yā 'ibādīya alladhīna asrafū 'alā anfusihim lā taqnaṭū min raḥmati Allāh 'inna Allāha yaghfiru al-dhunūba jamī'an

Say [O Muhammad]: "O my Servants who have transgressed against their souls! Despair not of the Mercy of Allah. for Allah forgives all sins: for He is Oft-Forgiving, Most Merciful." (Sūrat az-Zumar, 39:5)

So on the Day of Promises Allah gave a group to each *Walī* and at that time the heart of Prophet relaxed as Allah had given supporters to assist him in guiding people towards Allah ﷻ. And *Awliyā'ullāh* in *dunyā* are trying their best to guide people as much as they can. Some people are not able to be guided even though they are assigned to you when they are unable to guide them they refer them back to the Prophet ﷺ saying, "Ya Rasūlullah, we were unable to guide these." Then they fall under the hadith:

شَفَاعَتِي لِأَهْلِ الْكَبَائِرِ مِنْ أُمَّتِي

"shafā'atī li-'ahli al-kabā'ir min 'ummatī

My intercession is for the committers of grave sins from my Nation." (Sunan Abī Dāwūd, Jāmi' al-Tirmidhī, and Musnad Aḥmad)

And those who the Prophet ﷺ cannot clean and guide, that is an *'alāmah,* a sign, to teach everyone that even the Prophet ﷺ has a limit and Allah is the only One with no limits. That is to show *Awliyā'ullāh* that Sayyidinā Muhammad ﷺ with everything that Allah gave him is still within limits and Allah is the one with no limits that has treasures and oceans of mercy that He can give without question.

Grandshaykh said that "There is a special *Raḥmat* that Allah will open on the Day of Judgment to the Prophet ﷺ and that *Awliyā'* know about it but there is no permission to speak about it. That *Raḥmat* is to save the Ummat an-Nabī ﷺ completely from any hellfire or punishment."

He said,"These knowledges and this particular *Raḥmat* have been rooted and planted in the hearts of *Awliyā'ullāh.* There is no permission to talk about it and their tongues are frozen. That will not come until the time for the secret of Qur'ān appears and to manifest and *taṣrī*, run like a waterfall in the heart of everyone. At that time that *Raḥmat* will appear and the people will know about it. That is only when secret of Qur'ān will appear and that is happening soon, and what I am talking is like drizzle before the heavy rainstorm. The heavy rainstorm is coming. Prepare yourselves. It will come suddenly like a tornado that comes and appears on the horizon. It will take everything with it. Those who have a very well-based cement foundation are not affected by the tornado. But those who don't have a fixed base will be blown out with that tornado."

"Some people who are also preparing themselves for that big event, that storm, might come and they don't see it, but they are safe. That is similar to the situation of that lady who was in time of Sayyidinā Nūḥ ﷺ, though the storm and flood came and overtook the world she never experienced it because she was a believer."

And he said "O my students. I have good tidings for you." He was explaining the great level that Allah gave to Sayyidinā Muhammad ﷺ. And though He showed him that he is limited to some extent yet compared to *Awliyā'ullāh* and compared to all other prophets and compared to all other human beings what the Prophet ﷺ was given is beyond limits. Whatever Allah gave to all other human beings is not even a drop compared to the ocean He gave to the Prophet ﷺ. But even that ocean that Allah gave to him, compared to Allah's is in a limit.

He said that, "Don't think that after Allah called the Prophet ﷺ on Isrā' and Mi'rāj and opened to him the secret of the manifestation of the 99 Names and the Greatest Name *Ism Allāh al-'A'ẓam*, don't think after all that was manifested to him and all these secrets appeared to him, that the Prophet ﷺ came back to us. That is impossible—*dunyā* at that time cannot carry Sayyidinā Muhammad ﷺ. What appeared to us back from the Prophet was only a reflection of the full reality which stayed there, because *dunyā* cannot carry that power. It will break into pieces and go into rubble; this whole world. The Prophet ﷺ is like a huge voltage distributor—you cannot approach. They say "danger of death," you cannot approach.

Sayyidinā Muhammad ﷺ with all these manifestations of the Beautiful Names and Attributes this whole universe cannot carry him ﷺ and so Allah ﷻ kept the reality of Prophet ﷺ in His Divine Presence always giving, giving, and giving. And He sent only one reflection of that back to earth and the rest is with Allah in the Divine Presence. And we will explain what has been left there next time.

Wa min Allāhi 't-tawfīq, bi ḥurmati 'l-ḥabīb, bi ḥurmati 'l-Fātiḥah.

And with Allāh is success, for the honor of the Beloved, and by the sanctity of al-Fātiḥah, the opening chapter of the Qur'ān.

Awliyā' take from the Secrets of the Prophet ﷺ

Grandshaykh ق said: "One breath of a person doing *Dhikrullāh* (and how many breaths we did), is more heavier and more valuable to Allah than all the heavens and the earth. One breath of a person sitting in circle of *Dhikrullāh.*"

Imagine… don't imagine, but think, how much we have been rewarded for that. That is meditation and *taffakur*.

تَفَكُّرُ سَاعَةٍ خَيْرٌ مِنْ عِبَادَةِ سَبْعِينَ سَنَةٍ

> The Prophet said, "To reflect [on Allah's Beautiful Names and Attributes and to remember Him] for one hour is better rewarded more than seventy years in worship." (*Jam'ī al-Ṣaghīr* of al-Suyūṭī)

That doesn't mean you don't have to do worship but it means if you do one hour of *dhikr* then is it like 70 years of worship.

We are very pleased to come to the *tekke* today, this is where Allah likes most. Because it is not fancy, people are doing it from their love. From nothing they are trying to do something. Allah likes that; the Prophet ﷺ likes that and *Awliyā'ullāh* like that.

Al-Ḥamdu lillāh with the *baraka* of our brother, that gathering of *Dhikr* has been running. Try to bring more people with you. Try to convince them and you will get more and more *baraka*.

May Allah bless this event and bless this place and bless us in *dunyā* and *ākhirah* and make us to be with the Prophet ﷺ *dunyā* and *ākhirah.*

Wa min Allāhi 't-tawfīq, bi ḥurmati 'l-ḥabīb, bi ḥurmati 'l-Fātiḥa.

And with Allāh is success, for the honor of the Beloved, and by the sanctity of al-Fātiḥah, the opening chapter of the Qur'ān.

The Arrogance of Some 'Doctors'

Sometimes because of their short vision, people might give an analysis that diminishes the respect of people. That is why you have to be very careful in a situation you praise someone so much, he begins to thinks he knows everything and he can cover all areas. [adhan sounds and Mawlana stands up] Like those who become professors and doctors, they begin to think they understand every area. Not these doctors [points to the doctors in audience] but especially doctors in Islamic Shari'ah. They sometimes become jealous of medical doctors because medical doctors are the ones who are called 'doctors'. We have known this since we were children. We never called a scholar a doctor. I never heard that until recently, in the last 30 or 40 years. When we were in our twenties or younger we never heard someone called a doctor in Shariʿah.

Now they became jealous of medical doctors, so everyone wants to call himself a doctor. With all respect to their knowledge, for a scholar to be authentic at least he must have decent respect towards the Prophet ﷺ. At minimum he has to keep respect towards Sayyidinā Muhammad ﷺ so that when he speaks he knows what he is speaking about. But because they have put 'doctor' in front of their name they think they have the right to say anything they like.

Unfortunately,... [a picture falls from the wall.] This is a sign; another sign. In everything there is a sign. To be respected humbleness is essential. Not humble in your house or humble when you speak with someone, but to be humble knowing that your knowledge is insufficient compared to the knowledge of *Awliyā'ullāh;* insufficient compared to knowledge of the Ṣaḥābah, and insignificant compared to the knowledge of the Prophet ﷺ. They try to speak as if the Prophet ﷺ doesn't know what he is saying.

I was looking at an article in the Egyptian newspaper, "al-Ahram" on the international page where they spoke about *aṭ-Ṭibb an-Nabawī* ﷺ, the Prophetic Medicine. And if you look at the pictures of those speaking only one is wearing a turban. All the rest are wearing suits and ties. At least keep respect. If they want to say, "we are doctors," say, "we are doctors." In front of all their names, 'doctor', 'doctor',... except one who has 'shaykh' in front of his name, but the rest, all of whom have no turbans, have *dal*, 'd.' in front of their name—the abbreviation for 'doctor'.

Because they are doctors they think they know everything. Why? The Prophet ﷺ gave them his secrets, yet they say things in this article that they should feel ashamed to mention. They are going to feel ashamed on Judgment Day having said that the Prophet ﷺ doesn't know about Prophetic Medicine. They say, "The Prophet ﷺ doesn't know; why we must take what the Prophet ﷺ prescribed in his time?" They were saying he was testing it on himself, thinking it will work.

One topic was "*al-Qur'ān shifā'un li'ṣ-ṣudūr wa laysa li'l-abdān* —"The Qur'ān is cure for the hearts, and not for the bodies." The one saying this is a doctor, *ad-dawktar* among 1, 2, 3, 4, 5 doctors, where each one is writing a different article. Another one says, *al-ʿAṣr an-Nubuwwah lā yukāsu ʿalayh*—"What was done in the time of the Prophet ﷺ is not to be imitated in this time." This means "what the Prophet ﷺ did of medicine and what *ḥukamā*, wise people did, is not something you can build on today." They mean, "It was wrong, so don't build on it. Go according to technology today."

Another topic is "*At-tibb lays bi-himmat ar-rusul*—"Medicine is not responsibility of messengers."

The prophets and messengers came to guide human beings. Cannot the Prophet Sayyidinā Muhammad ﷺ, who went for Miʿrāj to the Divine Presence, tell someone how to be cured and he would be cured? Instead they say, "That is not the job of messengers." So these are the scholars of today, the scholars of the Ummah.

Another scholar here in "al-Qudsu 'l-ʿArabī" from another university is narrating the story of his love for his second wife saying:

al-ḥubbu junūn
wa al-junūnu funūn
wa al-ḥayātu shujūn,
wa li-llāhi fī khalqihi shuʿūn
Love is madness
And madness has many arts forms.
life is full of pain and suffering
And to Allah belong mysteries in His creation

This man is very famous, he is [even] called Shaykh al-Islam today. I don't have anything but respect for them, but don't bring Islam so low.

For Sayyidinā Muhammad ﷺ you don't want to accept things he did and in one article you reject what he said and in another you don't feel ashamed to speak about what you did in love. He might be very old and he is marrying someone very young. What effect on those who are very young if our *shuyukh* are doing something like that?

So these who call themselves doctors in Islam, they no longer have any wisdom. They have nothing except what they memorized and learned. They are not like the four Imāms: Imām Abū Ḥanīfah, Imām Mālik, Imām al-Shāfiʿī, or Imām Aḥmad ibn Ḥanbal, or other Imāms who came through history. They are no longer wise ones.

If they are wise at least give a good description of Prophetic Medicine. Don't say, "It is not worth anything to use today. There is perfection in everything that the Prophet ﷺ did. Did they not read in Sūrat an-Najm, that even if the Prophet ﷺ coughs it is revelation:

وَمَا يَنطِقُ عَنِ الْهَوَى إِنْ هُوَ إِلَّا وَحْيٌ يُوحَى

Wa mā yanṭiqu ʿani l-hawā in huwa illā waḥyun yūḥā

and neither does he speak out of his own desire: that [which he conveys to you] is but [a divine] inspiration with which he is being inspired

(Sūrat an-Najm, 53:3-4)

He never said anything that is from his own desires. It must be revelation.

Is that not correct Shaykh ʿAbd al-Sattār? [Yes *ḥaqqan.*] *ḥaqqan wa ṣidqan.* What they are saying in these articles is that all these medicines the Prophet ﷺ used to prescribe for people are not important, as it is not revelation. It is an experience that he tried but it didn't work out, it failed. It did not fail. They are telling the Ummah not to follow the Prophet ﷺ. That is the smallest meaning we can understand. Because in everything that the Prophet ﷺ said there is a secret. *Awliyā'ullāh* in every move they do there must be a secret. When you go to a *Walī* and ask, "What do I have to read?" he will tell you what to read for the purpose you are seeking.

I will tell you a story. Grandshaykh ق said, "*Ahlu l-ʿazā'im ahlu ṭ-ṭarīqah.* The people of the *ṭarīqah* are those who try to hold very tight on the *ʿAzīmah*; the highest level of Shariʿah law. They do not go with the easiest permitted way. The easy way, *rukhaṣ al-Sharīʿah* is permitted, no doubt, but the highest way is better. Therefore they keep the highest way.

For example according to the easy way, when you go to sleep you don't need to have *wuḍū*, ablution. But *Awliyā'ullāh* don't accept that. They say we must sleep on *wuḍū* and further, we must pray two *rakʿāts* of *Taḥiyyatu l-Wuḍū'* after making it. Furthermore, if someone from *Ahlu l-ʿazā'im* wakes up at night they must make a fresh *wuḍū,* even in cold places. So even if they use the bathroom five times in the night, each time they must make *wuḍū* and pray *Sunnat al-wuḍū* five times. That is the difference between *Ahlu l-ʿazā'im* vs. *Ahl al-rukhaṣ*. He said *al-Walī min Ahlu l-ʿazā'im,* a saint must be from the People of firm resolve in strictness of the Sharīʿah. They must take the hardest level on themselves but with students they may prescribe an easier way, *alā qadr al-istiʿdād*, "according to their levels of preparedness, Allah will open to them ٱلْمَقَامُ ٱلْفَرْدَانِي *al-Maqām al-Fardānī,* the Unique Station.

For every *Walī* there is a unique station, and above all of them you reach Sulṭān al-Awliyā' the Ghawth, who is on the highest unique station. In his <u>*al-Futūḥāt al-Makkiyyah*</u> Ibn ʿArabī described the Holy Prophet ﷺ as the single unique golden brick in a huge brick building and on the other side facing him is the is the silver brick, who is the Sulṭān al-Awliyā'. That means that Sulṭān al-Awliyā' is always facing Sayyidinā Muhammad ﷺ and receiving from him to dispatch to all other *Walīs*. And don't say there are only *Walī* in Naqshbandi. There 124,000 *Walī*. This one sitting beside you is a *Walī* [points to Shaykh Abdus Sattar Khan]. Whoever in Chicago goes to him, Allah accepts his *duʿā'*.

So anyone who is in the circle of *al-Maqām al-Fardānī* is going to be in the circle of the Prophet ﷺ. Now I am quoting a story Grandshaykh told. In his village in his area of Dagestan there was a rich businessman. Mawlana Grandshaykh was young at that time. That rich man wanted to go for hajj. So to reach Mecca, first they must walk with camels until they reach the sea. From there they take a ship and go to

Jeddah and then travel by land from Jeddah to Mecca. He was accompanying another person who was one of *Awliyā'ullāh*, a saint. So he took that *Walī* with him and told him, "You are my companion. I will spend everything on you, you come with me."

That *Walī* had reached the *al-Maqām al-Fardānī*, one of the unique stations. When you accompany a *Walī*, don't think it is going to be easy. It is better not to accompany one because your going and coming are not going to be easy. That *Walī* wants to be sure your hajj is accepted. For that reason, Grandshaykh used to say, "There are three things you have to ask your shaykh. One of them is when you want to travel for hajj—you have to ask your shaykh whether he gives permission or not."

That is because every hajj is not the same. It is not on every hajj that Allah sends His Mercy or His Divine Manifestation on the people at Arafat. As the Prophet ﷺ said, "Hajj is Arafat." Therefore, when you stand on Arafat that is the hajj, even if you could not complete the remaining *manāsik*, rituals. In that case, your hajj will not be perfect but you will be considered a *hajji*, and the people will call you by that title.

Awliyā'ullāh look at al-Lawḥ al-Maḥfūẓ, the Preserved Tablets, to determine if Allah is sending the manifestations of his Beautiful Names and Attributes on Arafat in that year. If not, they tell you "Don't go this year. Go next year." However, if you have never done hajj, then you must go, because it is an obligation. Only when you begin to go multiple times do you ask if there is permission because the first time is obligatory, so if you are able to go in that year, you must go.

Similarly, when you want to marry, you must ask the shaykh. It might be that you are in love with someone but that one might not be the one written for you. Thirdly, when you want to migrate from one place to another you must ask your shaykh. Without asking your shaykh you cannot do these three things.

So that rich man went to that *Walī* and said, "I want you to accompany me on hajj." The *Walī* said, "yes", so he took him, and they set out. On the way they took a boat. Then, like today, if you have something valuable, money or a passport, you try to keep it hidden. So that rich man who sponsored the shaykh was keeping his money hidden.

That shaykh was from the Naqshbandiyya from the *silsilah* of Grandshaykh. There are 7007 Naqshbandī shaykhs in any era. Not each one is carrying the secret from the main line. There might be one main shaykh and there are five or ten to whom he gives some secrets, to do work here and there. So that *Walī* who was accompanying him asked him, "Where are you putting your money?" He said, "I am putting it on my chest tied under my clothes. I don't want it to be lost." So, he said, "give it to me; I will take care of it." But that man didn't want to give it to that *Walī*.

We all make mistakes at times. If a *Walī* asks you something don't say "no". Allah might save you from many difficulties you are unaware of. The *Walī* said, "Give it to me; I will keep it safe for you," but the man said, "No, I am putting in a safe place."

So the *Walī* said, "As you like." Then they boarded the boat, which was one of the big boats that used to come to Jeddah, 90 years ago. Someone on the boat had brought a monkey along. He was bringing that monkey to Jeddah; it might be he wanted to live there and raise monkeys, Allah knows. So out of nowhere that monkey came and jumped on the man and stole the money from where he was hiding it and then ran all the way up to the top of the mast of the boat. No one could reach there. Then the monkey opened the wallet, and in it there were 1000 golden coins. He took one golden coin and threw it to the man. Then he took the next golden coin and threw it into the sea. One to the man; one to the sea; one to the man; one to the sea. That man was crying seeing that the money was disappearing. One to him, one to the sea until it was all finished. The sea took 500 golden coins and the man took 500.

That man was furious. The *Walī* said, "Why are you angry?" The man said, "Didn't you see what happened?" He said, "Ok, what happened is good. But look nothing will happen without Allah's Will. And don't talk too much or else or I will stay away from you." Then the man became worried because he knows he is a *Walī*.

As they were speaking like that, and while the man was still angry the *Walī* was reciting some *awrād*, teaching it to the man's wife, who was accompanying them. He heard that and asked his wife, "What are you learning?" When she told him, he said, "Can I read it as well?" Now just at the moment he was arguing with the shaykh the woman was taking ablution and suddenly she slipped and fell into the sea.

See here, how when you want to accompany a shaykh it will be difficult, full of tests. Therefore it is said, "Being near the shaykh is like being near fire."

So what happened next?

The lady disappeared into the sea. They stopped the boat and they looked and looked but they didn't find her. The man was crying; he had lost his wife and he had lost his money. He began shouting, "What kind of shaykh are you? What kind of *Walī* are you? Why did I bring you?"

You might wonder why I brought this story now. I mentioned how these doctors today don't understand Prophetic Medicine. They said, "no" to Prophetic Medicine. They say, "why do you eat this or that?" They don't know the wisdoms behind it because they are no longer wise. Scholars were wiser in the past. Scholars such as 'Alī al-Qārī sought out the very smallest details in order to praise the Prophet ﷺ in the highest way. Today they are trying to find the very smallest detail to put down the Prophet ﷺ.

What happened next? That businessman *kafara*, not in the meaning that he denying Allah's existence but in the way we intend in Arabic, that he got fed up with the shaykh. He didn't want to see him anymore.

The shaykh didn't speak a word and the boat sailed on. They reached the port and the people began coming out. Suddenly the man saw his wife, by the boat, on the dock. ...

He was so happy when he saw his wife, that he looked at her and said, "I am so happy to see you. How did you get here? You fell into the sea; what happened?" She said, "Ask the Shaykh."

Now he understood he had made a great mistake. Why did she tell him "ask the Shaykh"? It means she saw something special coming from that *Walī*. "Ask the *Walī*, ask the Shaykh!" He came to the Shaykh and said, "*Yā Sayyidī*!" Now he is calling him "*Sayyidī*!" while before he was rejecting him. He said, "I am still angry because I lost the money, but I am overjoyed to see my wife back."

Don't underestimate the power of *Awliyā'ullāh*. Don't say, "Why are we not seeing such miracles anymore?" This is the century of ignorance. That is what the Prophet ﷺ said. There will come a time "when ignorance covers the earth. At that time Allah will send one of my grandchildren to bring out the true knowledge." There are *Awliyā'ullāh* existing today, but their tongues are frozen. They cannot speak out. If they speak it comes out scrambled. Allah changes their words. If they want to say, "I saw Sayyidinā Mahdī ؈ and he is here in this room and he is ordering his deputies to be here and listen to the *ṣuḥbah*" that *Walī*'s words will become scrambled so that what he is saying seems like reciting Qur'ān or reciting a hadith. He might say that but the people will hear something completely differently. That is why in the same association the people hear the shaykh differently. Each hears in a different code and at a different wavelength—that is why each hears something different than the other.

So that *Walī* said, "O my brother. I learned from my Shaykh and he learned from his Shaykh and he learned from his Shaykh all the way to the Prophet ﷺ that if anyone wants to travel from one place to another by boat or camel, that there are a lot of created beings in these streets and ways. They might be heavenly beings or they might be earthly. There are a lot of animals; some might be domestic and others might be wild. And there are many tyrants. If you recite '*Bismillāhi r-raḥmāni r-raḥīm, dhālika taqdīru 'l-'azīzi l-ḥakīm*' Allah ﷻ will take care of you, even if the boat is sinking and all are about to drown, Allah will send special angels to take you to shore."

That is why Grandshaykh and Mawlana Shaykh said, "When you travel on a boat or plane and recite بِسْمِ ٱللَّهِ ٱلرَّحْمَٰنِ ٱلرَّحِيمِ ذَٰلِكَ تَقْدِيرُ ٱلْعَزِيزِ ٱلْحَكِيمِ '*Bismillāhi r-raḥmāni r-raḥīm, dhālika taqdīru 'l-'azīzi l-ḥakīm*' and Allah will send angels to protect you.

On that *wird,* recitation, there are special angels who are responsible for anyone who recites it.

The shaykh said, "I taught that *wird* to her to recite and she was reciting it every day. When she fell she saw an angel come and take her from the sea."

And she said, *Ṣadaqa ash-shaykh,* "the shaykh spoke the truth," The Shaykh said, "If I had not been with you, your wife would be dead now. That is the first assistance I did for you. The second one was that you are coming for hajj and you owed Allah money because you didn't pay your *zakat.* So in order for your hajj to be accepted you had to pay the *zakat* you owed. You didn't pay it voluntarily so we sent that monkey to take that money and we sent Allah's Right to the ocean and gave whatever balance remained to you."

"That is the second thing that made your hajj to be accepted."

I brought up that story by Mawlana's permission, answering those who wrote that article on *Ṭibb an-Nabawī,* Prophetic Medicine. These people are blind from being saints. In the past *ʿulamā' al-ummah* were true scholars and *Awliyā'ullāh* at the same time, and Allah gave them secrets. Today they are "doctor, doctor, doctor." That is arrogance! Take that 'doctorship' and throw it away. Why do you want to put in front of your name *dāl,* for "doctor"? Why do you want to say "doctor"? You are telling the people you are a doctor. You are trying to find a way to please the newspaper because they brought that question to you in order to say the Prophet ﷺ didn't know. Why? Do you want to cause non-Muslims not to look at the Prophet ﷺ as elevated? They want to diminish the status of the Prophet ﷺ. These are Muslims and non-Muslims read that. When a non-Muslim reads that what will he or she say? "How do you say your Prophet went for Miʿrāj and he cannot prescribe a medicine?"

Why do they want to stir up the mud? If you are blind don't make the Ummah blind.

There are secrets in every Word of Allah and in every one of Allah's Beautiful Names and Attributes and in every word that the Prophet ﷺ said in his life from the beginning of his life when his mother gave birth to him up to when he passed away. He was asking for his Ummah. If Sayyidinā ʿĪsā ﵇ can talk at birth cannot Sayyidinā Muhammad ﷺ talk on his birthday?

About Sayyidinā ʿĪsā ﵇, Allah ﷻ said:

فَأَشَارَتْ إِلَيْهِ قَالُوا كَيْفَ نُكَلِّمُ مَن كَانَ فِي الْمَهْدِ صَبِيًّا قَالَ إِنِّي عَبْدُ اللَّهِ آتَانِيَ الْكِتَابَ وَجَعَلَنِي نَبِيًّا وَجَعَلَنِي مُبَارَكًا أَيْنَ مَا كُنتُ وَأَوْصَانِي بِالصَّلَاةِ وَالزَّكَاةِ مَا دُمْتُ حَيًّا وَالسَّلَامُ عَلَيَّ يَوْمَ وُلِدتُّ وَيَوْمَ أَمُوتُ وَيَوْمَ أُبْعَثُ حَيًّا

Fa-ashārat ilayhi qālū kayfa nukallimu man kāna fī al-mahdi ṣabiyyan Qāla innī ʿabdu Allāh, ātānīya al-kitāba wa-jaʿalanī nabiyyan Wa-jaʿalanī mubārakan ayna mā kuntu Wa-awṣānī bi-ṣ-ṣalāti wa-z-zakāti mā dumtu ḥayyān Wa-s-salāmu ʿalayya yawma wulidtu wa-yawma amūtu wa-yawma ubʿathu ḥayyān.

Thereupon she pointed to him. They exclaimed: "How can we talk to one who [as yet] is a little boy in the cradle?" He said: "I am indeed a servant of Allah. He has given me revelation and made me a prophet; and [has endowed me with] piety towards my mother; and He has not made me haughty or bereft of grace. "Hence, peace was upon me on the day when I was born, and [will be upon me] on the day of my death, and on the day when I shall be raised to life [again]!" (Sūrah Maryam, 19:29-30)

Ātānīya al-kitāba – "He gave me the Book, al-Injīl." Allah had not yet given him *nubuwwah*, for he was still a baby in the cradle. First he said, “I am ʿAbdullāh.” He didn’t say, “I am a *Nabī*.” He said, “I am a servant.” You cannot be a prophet before you first become a servant. When you reach that level only then can you qualify for prophethood. By tongue we all say we are *ʿabd* but we still haven’t reached the level of servanthood. He said, “*I am a servant of Allah and He gave me the Book*,” before he had yet received the book. You have to have a book before you become a prophet—*wa-jaʿalanī nabiyyan, "Then He made me a prophet. Then He made me blessed wherever I am and He commanded me to pray and commanded me to give charity as long as I am alive."*

Why did the Prophet ﷺ go for Miʿrāj? Sayyidinā ʿĪsā ؑ is in the first heaven. He was raised up and he is there, waiting permission to return to this world. Sayyidinā Muhammad ﷺ went to:

فَكَانَ قَابَ قَوْسَيْنِ أَوْ أَدْنَى

fa-kāna qāba qawsayni aw adnā

And he was at the station of two bow's length or nearer. (Sūrat an-Najm, 53:9)

Sayyidinā ʿĪsā ؑ was curing the sick and raising the dead. If Sayyidinā Muhammad ﷺ said eat “this food and you will be cured” then you will be cured. We are not listening to these stupid people and what they are saying—with all my respect to what they study.

Look today: every sincere Muslim is wearing the shoes or sandals of the Prophet ﷺ to show it is honor for us to raise up the shoes of the Prophet ﷺ on our heads. *Awliyāʾullāh* ask their followers to be dust on the shoes of the Prophet ﷺ. And if you go into what scholars have said about the Prophet ﷺ, you know that he had one pair of shoes and four *khuffs*. If you look at the explanations of scholars regarding his shoes, and what *baraka* his shoes carry, will not what he says about medicine be full of *baraka*? I am not saying "Do not go to doctors." Go to them, but don't come against the Prophet ﷺ with such articles.

Know that in every *wird* or *adab* you mention there is a secret. *Awliyā'ullāh* give you these to recite because through recitation they want to raise you up to the *Maqām al-Fardānī*, the Unique Station. Raising you to that level is not simple and is not easy. *Awliyā'ullāh* are not playing with us.

He said, "Whoever likes to go to Paradise it is simple - follow the five obligations: *Shahadatu an la ilaha illa-Allah anna Muhammad Rasūlullāh, wa iqamus-salaat wa ita'uz-zakaat, wa sawmu Ramadan wa hajju'l-bayt*. But if you want to be with the Prophet ﷺ in

فِي مَقْعَدِ صِدْقٍ عِندَ مَلِيكٍ مُّقْتَدِرٍ

maqʿadi ṣidqin ʿinda malīkin muqtadir

In an Assembly of Truth, in the Presence of a Sovereign Omnipotent."

(Sūrat al-Qamar, 54:55)

There are other procedures you have to follow.

So Grandshaykh said that if you do your obligations that is ok. But that doesn't mean you are not still a wild animal. Because human beings are known as a "talking animals," *ḥayawānun nāṭiq*. You cannot say, "Why is he is calling us talking animals?" You can be wild or you can be domestic. He said, "*Awliyā'ullāh* look at these doctors, who only do the five obligations without attaining the *Maqām al-Iḥsān* —trying to perfect their behavior. They are looking only from a very narrow perspective, to keep the minimum obligations, not looking at the *ʿAzīmah,* most stringent level, but following the *rukhṣa*, the most relaxed rulings. They are like wild animals that have been released in a jungle. They go everywhere.

And he said, "Those who are *Awliyā'ullāh* and their students who are following a *Walī*, their description is like a mountain and what you find on the mountain. Yes, on the mountain you find wild animals."

All these doctors, doctors, doctors who think they are the peacocks of the Ummah are stepping on the mountain thinking they can crush it. But who can harm a mountain? If a million people step on a mountain they will not affect it. *Awliyā'ullāh* are mountains and their followers are rocks on these mountains. It is very difficult to remove these rocks. These people can mingle among the *murīds* but they cannot reach their levels. *Awliyā'ullāh* are always ascending higher and higher.

He said, *lā tabaddal wa lā tughayyir* - like oceans "there is no change and no alteration to mountains." Look how quiet they are. They are like oceans. Look in Chicago here, where do all the sewers go? To Lake Michigan. And yet the lake stays sweet and we are speaking of only a lake. Does it become dirty? No. What then do you think about the ocean? It never gets dirty. Even if all the sewers of whole world go into it, it remains clean, *ṭahūr*. You can clean with it and take showers with it.

Awliyā'ullāh are like oceans. They eat the sins of human beings and their waste. They clean them and send them back clean. They can reach the Prophet ﷺ.

He said,"You are connected with an ocean. You are connected with a *Sulṭān* who connects you with *Sulṭān as-Salāṭīn,* Sayyidinā Muhammad ﷺ."

May Allah keep us always with the Prophet ﷺ

Wa min Allāhi 't-tawfīq, bi ḥurmati 'l-ḥabīb, bi ḥurmati 'l-Fātiḥah.

And with Allāh is success, for the honor of the Beloved, and by the sanctity of al-Fātiḥah, the opening chapter of the Qur'ān.

Treating a patient is not *dunyā*, you are giving him Prophetic Medicine to cure the patient, in order for him or her to worship more. That is not *dunyā*. They have built their argument against Prophetic Medicine on one hadith in which the Prophet ﷺ said, "There is no food that doesn't have within it both illness and cure, except rice. Rice is all cure. In all others there is both remedy and illness." (cited by Al-Sakhāwī and graded very weak or forged).

What is the majority of scientific research done by doctors today? They are using plants and different sources to develop medicines. Yet when the Prophet ﷺ said:

عَنْ أَبِي هُرَيْرَةَ، قَالَ: قَالَ رَسُولُ اللَّهِ ﷺ : فِي الْحَبَّةِ السَّوْدَاءِ شِفَاءٌ مِنْ كُلِّ دَاءٍ إِلَّا السَّامَ. قَالَ ابْنُ شِهَابٍ: وَالسَّامُ الْمَوْتُ.

> "In the black seed there is healing for every disease, except death." Ibn Shihāb (al-Zuhrī, the second narrator) explained: "*al-Sām*" means death.

These Muslim 'doctors' even came against *ḥabbati 'l-baraka.*

When the Prophet ﷺ says, "Paradise is under the feet of the mothers" it means because they teach their children, for it is said, "Whoever teaches me a word I become a slave to him." So children must be as 'slaves' to their mothers, in the sense of seeking to always serve them, not more than that.

In the name of modernity, the children want to go here and there. Today they want to be independent: "We want to live by ourselves." This means there is something missing in the family. For example, if you take one lamp out of a chandelier, it looks odd. The family today looks like that—there is a bulb missing.

People run to America for what? [*dunyā*] Not only *dunyā* but for 'civilization' as well. Ask this doctor, he has a 401K. What happened to it? [It was wiped out in stock market crash]

This one is a professor, another good example. Pakistanis, Arabs, all of us, are stupid. We send our daughters to study and they become doctors or lawyers after studying. Yet at the end where do they go? They stay at home. It is better to send them to Pakistan. What do they do there? The same, they sit at home. So save the headache. I am not the one to say, "don't educate your children." But make sure that when they get married they take good care of the children. Let them save their children.

Wa min Allāhi 't-tawfīq, bi ḥurmati 'l-ḥabīb, bi ḥurmati 'l-Fātiḥah.

And with Allāh is success, for the honor of the Beloved, and by the sanctity of al-Fātiḥah, the opening chapter of the Qur'ān.

Allah Created the Judgment to Show the Greatness of Prophet Muhammad ﷺ

Do *Anbiyā*, prophets, get afraid? They might get afraid. Sayyidinā Mūsā was afraid from Firaʿun. If prophets are afraid, what about us? When Sayyidinā Shuʿayb went to Sayyidinā Mūsā, he said to him:

$$قَالَ لَا تَخَفْ نَجَوْتَ مِنَ ٱلْقَوْمِ ٱلظَّالِمِينَ$$

qāla lā takhaf, najāwta mina 'l-qawmi 'ẓ-ẓālimīn
He said, 'Do not be afraid. You have been saved from the wrongdoing people.' (Sūrat al-Qaṣaṣ, 28:25)

It means, "Don't be afraid! You are now safe in my territory." Are we safe from Shayṭān? No. Therefore we have to fear, and not take everything for granted. I had to cut his Qurʾān recitation because we got afraid. Why did we get afraid? Maybe there was one police car that showed up for guiding traffic, and everyone got scared and ran up, so I had to cut him off. Why then, when the alarm bell is ringing from Heavens through the Holy Qurʾān, are we not afraid? We pass through the verses like *murūr al-kirām*, as if it doesn't mean anything.

I think that we are in a problem, we are in trouble if we are not going to clean ourselves, to throw away bad behavior. Everyone knows what his or her weakness is. The common illness for everyone is the main trunk of the Tree of Sins or Bad Behaviors. Now if the trunk dies, the branches will die. That trunk is anger, pride and arrogance. Forget about generosity and forget about *ʿilm*, knowledge.

In the narration of Abū Hurayrah in *Saḥīḥ Muslim*, you see what the Prophet ﷺ said to the martyr, "You are not a martyr, you are a liar;" to the *ʿalim*, "You are not an *ʿalim*, you did it for yourself (for your ego), so you are a liar;" and for the generous one who has money, *lā tumannimu bi-mālika*, "Don't try to show off by saying about yourself, 'O! I gave, I gave, I gave!'" You don't need to. Allah will give the whole universe!

The Prophet ﷺ is al-Qāsim, "The One Who Divides." No one divides except the Prophet ﷺ. That is why it is forbidden to call your son "al-Qāsim" or "Abū 'l-Qāsim," because it is only for the Prophet ﷺ.[4] Don't show us your generosity with your money as it might be that a poor person gives one small coin that is better than the millions you are giving.

---

[4] The people used to call out: "O Abū 'l-Qāsim!" The Messenger of Allah would turn towards them. Then they said: "O Messenger of Allah, we only mean so-and-so." So the Messenger of Allah said: "Name yourselves by my name, but do not call yourselves by my kunya (Abū 'l-Qāsim)." (*Saḥīḥ al-Bukhārī*, *Saḥīḥ Muslim*.)

So the most important thing is to leave showing off being generous or not, being an *ʿalim* or not and being a martyr or not. The problem is a common problem in every patient [that comes to the shaykh], which is in every human being: arrogance and anger. Arrogance brings hatred and jealousy and anger brings arrogance and arrogance brings the rest of all the bad manners. So don't be arrogant! It means that if someone says to you something, say "yes," accept and go along with his opinion. Don't put your ego there because then the form of Shaytan will appear.

I was explaining about illnesses that comes in the body. For every illness in the body, both physical and spiritual illness, Allah allowed Shaytan to enter the heart. There is a small clot in the heart and you can see it; that is where Shaytan goes in and comes out. That was only removed from the heart of the Prophet ﷺ, who said, "I am the only one in the universe that I ride on my Shaytan and on my ego." The Prophet ﷺ was the only one who *ruwwaḍa*, 'trained' his ego to accept what he wants; it means Shaytan cannot approach. But for us, that is our main problem. Everyone! Think to yourselves and don't come and say, "Pray for me!" We are all asking Allah ﷻ, but you might not get what you seek. Allah will not prohibit you from getting it, but He might delay what you are asking for.

There are two kinds of illness: normal physical illness and the illness of the soul. That soul illness is more difficult to treat, as it occurs when Shaytan enters the human being. There are holes throughout the body; every cell has a hole and each person's body contains trillions of cells. Every cell has a characteristic such that not every shaytan can enter it, to go in and come out. Every Shaytan knows his specific entrance and every entrance in the body is different. When Shaytan enters, he's like a cat. Do you know what the cat does? Do you have cat at home? When she wants to mate, sometimes she sprays everywhere! So when Shaytan enters into a cell and goes out, he will spray his negative energy and that is when people get sick. So, the source of every illness is Shaytan's spray; he sprays and goes out, and that is because of what actions you are doing, not realizing that Allah might not be happy with it.

As we mentioned one comes on Judgment Day as a martyr and Allah says to him, "You are a liar." Another comes as an *ʿalim* and Allah says, "You are a liar." A generous person comes and Allah say, "You are a liar! You did it from arrogance, only to show off, not for Me!"

What is needed from us is to act only for Allah ﷻ with no arrogance in whatever we do. That is why the Prophet ﷺ said--and this hadith is not scary but very, very merciful--he ﷺ said:

انما بعثت لاتمم مكارم الاخلاق

innamā buʿithtu li-utammima makārim al-akhlāq

> I have been sent to perfect the best of conduct (your behavior and character). (Bazzār)

He said, "*Innamā* Allah ﷻ sent me especially..." "*Innamā*" means "to confirm and affirm that Allah has sent me for one purpose: to complete the good characters in human beings." That means, before death, you will know where you will go after this *dunyā,* without your good characters being completed. Impossible! This is a confirmation from Prophet ﷺ, "I affirm and confirm to you that Allah has sent me to perfect your manners." If we are not perfected in *dunyā*... Prophet ﷺ will perfect you but you might not see it because you are veiled, but you will see it as soon as you leave *dunyā*! That is why the Prophet's ﷺ *shafā'ah*, intercession, removes all sins. He will intercede and will have already completed us.

Now it is true we have to mention *aḥadīth* and verses of Holy Qur'ān that put fear of Allah ﷻ in us, but in which way? Fear of losing His Love, fear of not seeing Him in Paradise, fear in anything that makes Him not happy with us. If this whole *dunyā* does sins day and night, Allah ﷻ will never be affected! Does it affect Allah ﷻ? No. If something doesn't affect Him, what is He going to do with you? Your negativity did not have any effect on Him? *Awliyā'ullāh* say that this is where intercession comes in. Allah ﷻ can and will send anyone to Paradise without judgment!

فَمَن يَعْمَلْ مِثْقَالَ ذَرَّةٍ خَيْرًا يَرَهُ وَمَن يَعْمَلْ مِثْقَالَ ذَرَّةٍ شَرًّا يَرَهُ

faman ya'mal mithqāla dharratin khayran yarahu
wa-man ya'mal mithqāla dharratin sharran yarahu

Whosoever has done an atom's weight of good shall see it, and whosoever has done an atom's weight of evil shall see it. (Sūrah az-Zalzalah, 99:7-8)

Why does He say that? Why, can Allah not send everyone to Paradise? Why does He have to say, "No, I have to judge them?" Do you know why? To show us the Greatness of Sayyidinā Muhammad ﷺ! He doesn't want except for the Prophet ﷺ to do it. Although Allah ﷻ can do it—not only can He do it, but He will do it—He wants us to know that because of His Prophet ﷺ He accepted it *'uluww sha'nu 'n-Nabī* ﷺ, the loftiness of the rank of the Prophet ﷺ to give the Prophet ﷺ a high level of prestige.

This is what it means, "Look at the Prophet ﷺ, because that is your door!" Why should Allah ﷻ judge us on something He doesn't even look at? He prohibited us to look at something bad, so how will Allah seek to look at something bad? Allah doesn't like to see bad. Does He judge bad? He is not seeing it and He doesn't want to see it! He can send everyone to Paradise, but Allah says in the Holy Qur'ān, "*Yā* Muhammad! *Yā Rasūlallāh*! I now finished My Judgment: those for Heaven for Heaven and those for punishment for punishment; now do what you want! Do what you want! I am giving you permission." This is what it means as it shows the Greatness of Sayyidinā Muhammad ﷺ; a greatness that cannot be described.

So on one hand Allah ﷻ shows us "punishment," "punishment," "punishment," "great punishment," "heavy punishment," "He is going to make people to drink the juice of Hellfire," as in some *aḥadīth* from the Prophet ﷺ describing *ʿusāratu ahli jahannam*, Allah will juice the whole Hellfire and give to people to drink, after which their stomach will go into pieces from the huge temperature and from the dirtiness of that juice! Why did Allah ﷻ say that? To say that Muhammad ﷺ is coming to take you to Paradise, *taʿzhīmu 'n-Nabī*, to show the Greatness of the Prophet ﷺ and to make all prophets come to him, as when they see that *shafāʿah* is in his hands all of them with all their nations will come to him!

Do you think the Prophet ﷺ will reject them? No. What will he do? I heard from Grandshaykh, ق, that *Awliyā'ullāh* say even on Judgment Day when people are running for safety and when there is no jealousy amongst them, still, people will be jealous from one another. Why? Because they are going to see *Ummat an-Nabī* ﷺ sent to Paradise with no account! So what did Grandshaykh say, ق? *SubhaanAllah,* look how deep *Awliyā'ullāh* can go! He said, "The Prophet ﷺ will make *shafāʿah* on Judgment Day, *yata-shaffaʿu li-sā'iri 'l-umam awwalan,* he will intercede for the nations of all other prophets and send them to Paradise first. Then he will intercede for his *ummah* and send them at the end after all those nations that went before." Why? He said, "He doesn't want the nations of all other prophets to have jealousy of *Ummat an-Nabī* ﷺ, because with the *shafāʿah* of the Prophet ﷺ, Allah will put them in *Jannat al-Firdaws al-Aʿlā*, the Highest Paradise. So they will not see their levels."

Therefore, in order that the other nations will not envy *Ummat an-Nabī* ﷺ, first He will send them to the lower Paradises where they will be happy. After that, He will send *Ummat an-Nabī* to a Paradise where they cannot be seen. Allah will open a 'door' for them (we say a 'door,' but it's not a door). Allah will open something for them where they go directly and there, they can see Allah ﷻ! The other *umam* (nations) cannot unless they are *mu'mins* among them--that is different.

As the Prophet ﷺ said, "I have been sent to perfect your characters," and even in Paradise he knows that other nations or our nation will get jealous of each other. That is why you don't see the Paradise of your brother or your brother doesn't see your Paradise because there is no jealousy there, as it's not allowed. So the Prophet ﷺ will perfect us completely before we reach there!

May Allah ﷻ keep us under the Prophet's arms, under his feet, under his sandals, at his threshold, *In shā' Allāh.* We are asking, "*Yā Sayyidī, yā Rasūlallāh! Yā Raḥmatan li 'l-ʿAlamīn! Yā Shafiʿyyi 'l-Mudhnibīn!* We are coming to you, to your door, to your threshold and we are asking and requesting and begging:

يَا مَنْ يُغِيثُ الوَرَى بَعْدَ مَا قَنَطُوا

yā man yughīthu 'l-warā ba'da mā qanatū

"O You *who brings relief to all creation after they have despaired ..."*

Allah will give support, *yā Rasūlallāh*! Present us to Allah clean every night, don't let us carry this dirtiness on ourselves, on our souls, on our ego."

Wa min Allāhi 't-tawfīq, bi ḥurmati 'l-ḥabīb, bi ḥurmati 'l-Fātiḥah.

And with Allāh is success, for the honor of the Beloved, and by the sanctity of al-Fātiḥah, the opening chapter of the Qur'ān.

١٣٥٤

Only Prophet ﷺ Can Carry the Greatness of Qur'ān

What did Allah ﷻ say about the Prophet ﷺ in the Holy Qur'ān? He said:

لَوْ أَنزَلْنَا هَٰذَا الْقُرْآنَ عَلَىٰ جَبَلٍ لَّرَأَيْتَهُ خَاشِعًا مُّتَصَدِّعًا مِّنْ خَشْيَةِ اللَّهِ وَتِلْكَ الْأَمْثَالُ نَضْرِبُهَا لِلنَّاسِ لَعَلَّهُمْ يَتَفَكَّرُونَ

law anzalnā hādhā 'l-Qur'āna ʿalā jabalin la-ra'aytahu khāshiʿan mutaṣaddiʿan min khashyati 'llāh, wa-tilka 'l-amthāl naḍribuhā li-n-nāsi laʿallahum yatafakkarūn.

Had We sent down this Qur'ān on a mountain, verily, you would have seen it humble itself and cleave asunder for fear of Allah! Such are the similitudes which We propound to men, that they may reflect. (Sūrat al-Ḥashr, 59:21)

It means not one single mountain, not one, can carry the greatness of Holy Qur'ān. If the Holy Qur'ān had descended in this universe, and would be hanging in this universe, this whole universe would shatter. A mountain compared to *ʿaẓamatullāh*, to Allah's Greatness, is nothing! But as soon as the Holy Qur'ān reached the atmosphere of this universe, it did not shatter. Why? This will give you a meaning that *al-qalb Muḥammadī* will never shatter! The Qur'ān was revealed to the Prophet's ﷺ heart, and it did not shatter. It means Prophet's ﷺ heart will never shatter. That is why he was able to go to Miʿrāj, it has that greatness of power, heavenly power. He reached *Qāba Qawsayni aw Adnā.* "Two bows' length or nearer." If the Holy Qur'ān comes in this universe, it will shatter, but Sayyidinā Muḥammad's ﷺ heart did not shatter! (Mawlana stands and sits.)

See the greatness of Prophet ﷺ that his heart was able to carry that revelation and Sayyidinā Mūsā ﵇ was not able to. And when Sayyidinā Khiḍr ﵇ said, *"You will never be able to have patience with me!"* Sayyidinā Mūsā ﵇ said:

قَالَ سَتَجِدُنِي إِن شَاءَ اللَّهُ صَابِرًا

Qāla satajidunī in shā'Allāhu ṣābiran

You will find me, if Allah wants, among the patient. (Sūrat al-Kahf, 18:70)

He knew he was not patient, that's why he said, *In shā'Allāh.* Allah didn't wish it, therefore he was not able to stay with Sayyidinā al-Khiḍr ﵇, although Sayyidinā Mūsā's ﵇ rank is much higher than the rank of Sayyidinā al-Khiḍr ﵇; there is no resemblance between their ranks. Of course, who is Khiḍr ﵇ in front of Sayyidinā Mūsā ﵇? But Allah wanted to show that, "Only one of My servants can stand in front of Me, *yā* Mūsā ﵇, don't ask to see Me. Seeing Me is only for Sayyidinā Muhammad ﷺ!" That is why Allah will be seen in heavens, but not in all heavens.

Only in the one in which Sayyidinā Muhammad ﷺ is present. So there is a deep teaching here: "No one can carry. So don't come and approach Me if you don't have a connection." Where there is a connection, the flow of knowledge will come. Without a connection, there will be no flow of knowledge.

Wa min Allāhi 't-tawfīq, bi ḥurmati 'l-ḥabīb, bi ḥurmati 'l-Fātiḥah.

And with Allāh is success, for the honor of the Beloved, and by the sanctity of al-Fātiḥah, the opening chapter of the Qur'ān.

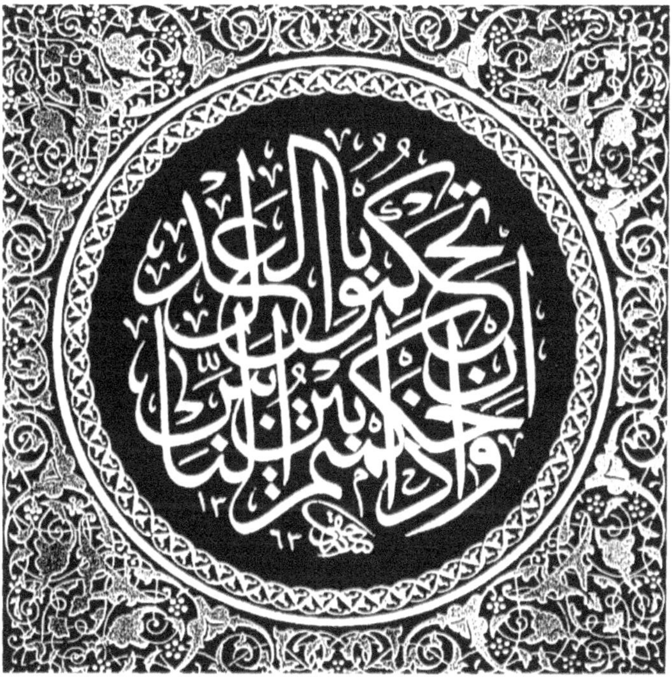
وإذا حكمتم بين الناس أن تحكموا بالعدل

The Four Levels of *Dhikr* and the Heart of Sayyidinā ʿAlī

We are seeking the *shafāʿah*, intercession of Sayyidinā Muḥammad ﷺ. We are beloved to Allāh ﷻ and beloved to the Prophet ﷺ. You are those who love the Prophet ﷺ and you are those whom Allāh honored, and us, along with you, to be among the ummah of Sayyidinā Muḥammad ﷺ, who made this a "forgiven ummah."

First I want to mention that in December I traveled to Indonesia, Singapore and Malaysia. One day there was a light you could see far from the shore, where buildings of American and European companies had fallen down after they built a little bit; in fact, anything they built there fell down. They tried to open a bar and so on, but there is a *maqām* of a *walī*, Shaykh Ismāʿīl. Whether it is day or night, you can only get there by boat; it is fifteen or twenty minutes from shore. They first came to the island for barakah perhaps 200 years ago, and a lot of Hindus come to Shaykh Ismāʿīl's tomb, like at Sayyidinā Jalāl ad-Dīn ar-Rūmī's tomb, where diverse people claim, "He is our master."

The story is that we were in Malacca and we were invited to the house of a person I have known for a long time. He invited us to his house; he expected about seventy or eighty people, but more than 400 people came to his house, which is huge. I saw two pictures on the kitchen wall and thought they looked familiar.

I asked him, "Whose picture is this first one? I know who it is."

He said, "This is Mawlānā Shaykh Nāẓim," and he was laughing. I said, "This other picture is familiar to me although I never saw that person, but he is very familiar, as if I know him."

He said, "O, I think this is someone you know. He is my shaykh, and Shaykh Nāẓim is also my shaykh."

I said, "Who is that? I have seen him many times, I know him."

He said, "Do you know Shaykh Ṭāhir al-Qādrī?"

I said, "Yes, I know him."

He said, "This is his father." He took bayʿah with him a long time ago and his name is Ghulām ar-Rasūl. He said, "Dr. Ṭāhir al-Qādrī was here and I hosted him in my home."

Look at how Allāh ﷻ has put things together so that people can understand there is no distance for Him! So, after this introduction, I would like to mention that I am a simple person, like you; you might be better than me. I have to say, "*Astaghfirullāh*," because no one is higher or lower, as the Prophet ﷺ said, "human beings are equal like the teeth of a comb."

Human beings are the most respected creation of Allah ﷻ. Allah ﷻ said:

وَلَقَدْ كَرَّمْنَا بَنِي آدَمَ

wa-laqad karramnā banī Ādam.

And indeed We have honored the children of Ādam (Sūrat al-Isrā', 17:70)

With what did Allah ﷻ honor them? He honored them by creating them as *'abd, 'ibādullāh*, "Servants for Him." Prophet ﷺ said, "The best time I like is when Allah calls me 'Abdullāh." So Allah created human beings, as it is mentioned in many *ahadith*, from *Baḥr al-Qudrah*. And in *Baḥr al-Qudrah* what Allah created first was the Light of Prophet ﷺ. He put that Light in *Baḥr al-Qudrah* and it was turning, and turning, and as it was turning Creations were coming from *Baḥr al-Qudrah*. That means it was mixed with the Light of Prophet ﷺ. That Light that was in *Baḥr al-Qudrah*, Allah put it in the forehead of Sayyidinā Adam ﷺ and asked angels to make *sajdah*. Why Allah ordered them to make *sajdah*? We know and all `ulama know as they speak about it, that it was *Sajdat al-iḥtirām wa laysa sajdat al-'ibādah*, "a *sajdah* of respect not a *sajdah* of worshipness,"

They made *Sajdat al-iḥtirām*, giving respect and praising, and the angels are ordered to keep their *sajdah* non-stop from the day they have been created until Allāh knows when. That order is not only o the angels that were already created, but also those who will be created in the future. Also, Sayyidinā Muḥammad ﷺ will make the first *sajdah* on the Day of Judgment, which means as soon as he comes forth he goes into *sajdah*. This tells us how important *sajdah* is. Therefore, whenever you finish your prayers, do one *sajdah*.

He goes into *sajdah* and begins to make a *du'ā'* that never came to him before; that is a ḥadīth.

What kind of *du'ā*s are these? These are keys of Paradise. Every one of us has a special *du'ā'* on his head that is a special code, or a key to his place in Paradise. So the Prophet ﷺ was reading all these *du'ā*s that are special codes to let everyone go to Paradise! Out of respect he could not raise his head, and then the Voice came, "*Yā Muḥammad*! Raise your head and ask, you will be granted." The Prophet ﷺ said, "*Yā Rabbī*! I need my ummah, I cannot go without them!" Allāh said, "Take one third of them, with no account, to Paradise."

So where is Ṣirāṭ al-Mustaqīm? With the *shafā'ah* of the Prophet ﷺ, they will go straight to Paradise; they won't need to walk. They will say, "*Bismi llāhi r-Raḥmāni r-Raḥīm*," and they will be in their place in Paradise. Then the Prophet ﷺ went into *sajdah* again and Allāh ﷻ opened for him *du'ā*s that had never opened before, and said, "Raise your head and ask, for you will be granted!" Then Allāh ﷻ said, "Take half of the rest." Who is Ṣirāṭ al-Mustaqīm? It is the Prophet ﷺ! It is not *shirk*; rather, it is *shafā'ah*, intercession, a divine code by which you reach your goal.

The Prophet ﷺ went into *sajdah* another time, and began to make *du'ā'* he never made before, not in the first time nor in the second time. And it might go through your mind, "What kind of *du'ā'*?" The Prophet ﷺ, Ṣaḥābah and *Awliyā' Allāh* recite all kinds of *du'ās* which are recorded, and people read them daily. So it means that *du'ā*s other than these are being opened to the Prophet ﷺ. It cannot be any *du'ā'* that is already found in Arabic, such as *Ḥizb al-barr*, *Ḥizb al-baḥr*, Muḥiyyidīn ibn 'Arabī's *du'ā'*, … and thousands of others. But the Prophet ﷺ said, "*Du'ā'* that has never been said before," which means letters put together in such a way as never said before, like the letters at the beginning of sūrahs: *ḥā' mīm kāf; ḥā' yā' 'ayn ṣād,* and so on.

We must realize the greatness of the Prophet ﷺ, that with these *du'ā*s Allāh will be pleased with what he is reading and will free the ummah, saying "Go!" and again, "Go!" And then, at the last one, Allāh ﷻ will ask, "What do you want?" The Prophet ﷺ will answer, "I want the rest," and Allāh will say, "Take them all except one, the worst one."

How do many Muslims say, "*Lā ilāha illā llāh Muḥammadun rasūlu llāh*," and yet they do the worst things? And Allāh will keep the worst of them, and we hope we are not that one, we hope everyone enters Allāh's *maghfirah* and goes to Paradise! Allāh ﷻ keeps the worst one and says, "Who gave *shafā'ah* to the Prophet ﷺ? Who gave him this *raḥmah* on his ummah? I gave it to him, and My raḥmah is bigger than his. Take all your people and go to Paradise!" Corrected transliteration

Regarding the meaning of the name, "al-Muṣṭafā," you have, for example, two or three cups and you choose one and say, "This is al-Muṣṭafā, the Chosen One," but to compare him ﷺ to others is not honoring 'Aẓamat an-Nabī ﷺ ! Did Allāh ﷻ bring the whole ummah and all human beings and choose one from among them? No. That doesn't honor that, *lā yalīqu bi-'Aẓamat an-Nabī* ﷺ ; that is not related to Prophet's ﷺ greatness! To say, "He is al-Muṣṭafā," means nothing in all Creation—human beings, angels, universes and all other Creations—cannot be compared to the greatness of that one whom Allāh ﷻ dressed with His Beautiful Names and Attributes and named him to be different than everyone else! That is why Imām Muḥammad al-Būṣīrī ؓ said:

مُحَمَّدٌ بَشَرٌ

وَلَيْسَ كَالْبَشَرِ

Muḥammadun basharun
wa-laysa kal-bashar,

Muhammad ﷺ is a human being
but not like other human beings;

بَلْ هُوَ يَاقُوتٌ
وَالنَّاسُ كَالْحَجَرِ

bal huwa yāqūtun
wa-n-nāsu kal-ḥajar
Muhammad ﷺ is a gem
and the rest of mankind are pebbles."

It means Muhammad ﷺ is not like me and you. The Prophet ﷺ has no shadow! If someone has no shadow it means that one is subtle, he has no form, and the power of spirituality is overtaking his body. That is why I was amazed when, here in London, I visited a person who has a Holy Hair of the Prophet ﷺ—and I have seen many but this one is extra special. Last time I came told him, "Bring the Holy Hair and let us make *ziyārah* to it." Some time before that, I had asked to him give me half of the Holy Hair. He was so generous, he said, "Take as much as you like."

During this visit, he shone a flashlight on it. I was so amazed to see that the Holy Hair had grown back to its normal size! It was incredible! So I told Mawlānā Shaykh Nāẓim and he said, "Don't you know that the Holy Hair of the Prophet ﷺ is alive? Of course it is going to grow back to its normal size when it was with the Prophet ﷺ !"

So we looked at that Holy Hair, which was supported by a small rock, and when we shone the flashlight on it, the rock had a shadow and the Holy Hair had no shadow! That was utterly amazing. Whatever we say to describe the Prophet, there is no way to truly describe his greatness!! So what is t hat Shaykh going to benefit from all this effort (to unite Muslims)?

Why did Sayyidinā Abū Bakr ؓ always put the Prophet ﷺ in front of him? Because his love to him was so strong. So the Prophet is everything for *Awliyā' Allāh*—they don't care what they are called, "doctor" or "shaykh." Even Mawlānā Shaykh writes after his name, "*al-khādim al-faqīr al-ḥaqīr*," which means, "the servant of the poor lowly beggar." They are seeking to open more *masājid* here and there around the world. Their thought is not to have a title, nor to have a big car, because what difference does it make if you drive a big car or a small car? That show of humility will open the door. That is what Islām is: to show humility and humbleness and to build relationships with different mosques.

To make *Ṣilat ar-Raḥim*, relationship between members of the Muslim community, is preferred because we are brothers in spirit and our father is the Prophet ﷺ, and we all love him. He is the Seal of Messengers ﷺ and he was created before all, even before Sayyidinā Ādam ﷺ. Therefore it is important to make relationships between different mosques.

Unfortunately, you see some groups distributing flyers about suicide bombing. We never saw that in the Holy Qur'ān. In Islām there is nothing like that. You are ambassadors of Islām and therefore your job is to bring Muslim youth to love of Allāh ﷻ and love of the Prophet ﷺ, for them not to be on the streets in gangs making all kinds of problems. Teach them to live a normal kind of life, to study. Our life is going to all different places. I was like you; I studied in Christian schools, then in the American University of Beirut, then in a Belgian university. The benefit is to show that we Muslims are normal people.

Was-salāmu ʿalaykum wa raḥmatullāh.

[*Duʿā'*]

Wa min Allāhi 't-tawfīq, bi ḥurmati 'l-ḥabīb, bi ḥurmati 'l-Fātiḥa.

And with Allāh is success, for the honor of the Beloved, and by the sanctity of al-Fātiḥah, the opening chapter of the Qur'ān.

To Kiss the Holy Threshold of Prophet ﷺ

One day I decided to visit al-Madīnah al-Munawwarah, as I was living in Jeddah most of the time. so every Thursday and Friday I prayed there. I received a call from my shaykh, Shaykh Muḥammad Nāẓim al-Ḥaqqānī ق. He said, "Where are you going?" I answered, "*Yā sayyidī*! If there is permission, I am going to visit the Prophet ﷺ." He said, "Kiss his threshold for me."

When someone says something like that to you, especially your shaykh, your mind begins to think, "How am I going to do that with all those barriers and guards? It is impossible."

There is a problem many of us face today and the answer comes with this story, as well as the true meaning of spirituality. Spirituality is not *ʿamal*, something you have to do, but it is something in addition to giving charity, fasting, praying and making Ḥajj. It is the way to reach *Maqām al-Iḥsān* as mentioned in the ḥadīth of Sayyidinā ʿUmar ؓ, that to reach the state of *Iḥsān*, Moral Excellence, you have to fulfill the Five Pillars of Islām, then accept the six Pillars of *Īmān* and then follow the principles of how to reach the state of *Iḥsān*.

That is very complex and difficult to do and if you say, "I will go to that station by myself," you will only turn in circles. You must have a guide to reach that spiritual station, and if you seek one you will find one, because the saints are brothers and all of them love each other. I am not speaking about false saints, but about real saints that give their lives for their students.

So that time I went and I was driving about 120 miles per hour in order to reach quickly, because Mawlānā said, "Go and kiss the threshold of the Prophet ﷺ," so I knew there must be an opening. I reached there quickly by the *barakah* of the Prophet ﷺ and then had to shower and go to that holy place that Allāh has made *qiṭʿatun mina 'l-jannah*, a piece of Paradise! At al-Muwājahah, the holy place of Paradise (it is heavy on my heart to say "grave"), one tries to stay as long as possible and one does not want to go out! When we visit the Prophet ﷺ, it is *adab* to stand as much as we can in his presence, not even making *duʿā'*, but only standing there trying to connect our heart with his heart in a way that:

تَفَكُّرُ سَاعَةٍ خَيْرٌ مِنْ عِبَادَةِ سَبْعِينَ سَنَةً

Tafakkuru sāʿatin khayrun min ʿibādati sabʿīna sanah.

To remember Allāh ﷻ (contemplate or meditate) for one hour is better than seventy years of worship.

That is for one hour when you are contemplating by yourself, so what do you think it is when you are in the holy presence of the Prophet ﷺ? When passing there everyone might stand five minutes, seven minutes, ten minutes and then go. Some might stand longer and longer; it depends on how much they are in that connection. So with the guidance of our *shuyūkh*, we have visited the Prophet ﷺ with Mawlānā Shaykh Nāẓim many times, may Allāh give him long life. Back in the time when there were no barriers, I saw Mawlānā Shaykh stand there and make *duʿā'* for 90 minutes! It was really more like a conversation. You feel you don't see that as you need a lot to reach that level of *mushāhadah*, witnessing, but you can feel the holy presence.

Mawlānā Shaykh Nāẓim ق stood there for one-and-a-half hours and then he moved to the place of Abū Bakr aṣ-Ṣiddīq ؓ and stood another half hour, and then to Sayyidinā ʿUmar ؓ another half hour, and then to Bāb Jibrīl, *maḥbiṭ al-waḥiy* (where Sayyidinā Jibrīl ؑ came with *waḥiy* to the Prophet ﷺ), and then we went back to the *maqām* of Sayyidah Fāṭimah az-Zahrā' ؓ. That is the location which Grandshaykh ق said the angels moved her holy body to the end of the Rawḍa, to the place where Sayyidinā ʿĪsā ؑ is to be buried. That is why *Awliyā' Allāh* see Sayyidah Fāṭimah ؑ there. Mawlānā spent 45 minutes there and then went to Bāb at-Tawbah (now closed), where he made a special *duʿā'* and *sajdah*.

You must take the opportunity when it is presented, and whatever was in my heart I was making sure to take that opportunity! Normally, many guards tell you to move, and I don't stand at the closest area; I normally stand further away, near the wall. However, that night, although there were many guards, one of them with a red beard was the head guard and he didn't approach me nor allow any guard to come to me. It was strange, because you cannot stand there one hour or one-and-a-half hours as normally they will tell you to move even after five minutes.

So I finished and went to kiss the big pillar in the back as no one will see you there, then one of the head guards approached me and I said to myself, "It is finished now." He came to me and said, "Do you want to kiss the threshold of the Prophet ﷺ?" I said "yes!" and he took me to the door of the Prophet ﷺ and I was able to kiss the holy threshold. At that time everything disappeared: there were no guards and I saw nothing but the threshold of the Prophet ﷺ! I kissed it and stood up, and then everything returned to normal.

That guard said, "Give my *salāms* to Shaykh Nāẓim." He never knew Mawlānā Shaykh Nāẓim, and Shaykh Nāẓim never called him and he never called Shaykh Nāẓim!

I left and went to Madrasat ash-Shūnā, where Mawlānā Shaykh Nāẓim usually goes. There I heard footsteps running behind me and I said to myself, "O, they are coming!" I turned and saw one of the guards approaching and he was holding a very beautiful decorated Qur'ān that he gave to me and said, "O Hishām! This is a gift from my father for Shaykh Nāẓim." I thanked him and didn't say anything, nor did I ask him anything as that is *tark al-adab*, outside of good conduct. Ṭarīqah is not to ask anything, but rather to *asmaʿū wa-aʿū*, listen and act on what you heard. So I was so deep into what had happened, it was as if I was lost. You cannot understand it and I don't understand it even today. You cannot use your mind in such situations.

ثُمَّ ٱرْجِعِ ٱلْبَصَرَ كَرَّتَيْنِ يَنقَلِبْ إِلَيْكَ ٱلْبَصَرُ خَاسِئًا وَهُوَ حَسِيرٌ

Thumma rji'i l-baṣara karratayni yanqalib ilayka l-baṣaru khāsiyan wa-huwa ḥasīr.

Then look again and yet again; your sight will return to you weak and made dim. (Sūrat al-Mulk, 67:4)

Look at one star, twice even! *Yanqalib ilayka l-baṣaru khāsiyan wa-huwa ḥasīr*—your sight returns back defeated from one star, so what do you think about 80 billion stars that are in our galaxy? What do we know by the mind in our head? We know nothing, but by the mind in our heart we know everything. What did Allāh say to the Prophet ﷺ and the Prophet ﷺ said to us?

مَا وَسِعَنِي أَرْضِي وَلَا سَمَائِي وَلَكِنْ وَسِعَنِي قَلْبُ عَبْدِي الْمُؤْمِن

Mā wasi'anī arḍī wa-lā samā'ī wa-lākin wasi'anī qalbu 'abdī al-mu'min.

Neither My Heavens nor My Earth contain Me, but the heart of My believing servant contains Me. (Ḥadīth Qudsī, *al-Iḥyā'* of Imām al-Ghazālī)

It means, "The believer's heart contained My Light, My Attributes, the understanding of the universe!" Do you think *Awliyā' Allāh* don't have *the* power to pass beyond this universe? The Prophet ﷺ went beyond this universe, beyond the stars! He ﷺ passed through 80 billion stars in our galaxy and then he passed 60 billion galaxies and even further, to *Qāba Qawsayni aw Adnā*—what might be one centimeter or one millimeter from the Divine Presence!

To Follow in the Prophet's Footsteps ﷺ

Allāh ﷻ said to the prophets, and especially to His saints:

قُلْ إِن كُنتُمْ تُحِبُّونَ ٱللَّهَ فَٱتَّبِعُونِى يُحْبِبْكُمُ ٱللَّهُ وَيَغْفِرْ لَكُمْ ذُنُوبَكُمْ ۗ وَٱللَّهُ غَفُورٌ رَّحِيمٌ

Qul in kuntum tuḥibbūna Allāha fa-ttabi'ūnī yuḥbibkumullāhu wa-yaghfir lakum dhunūbakum wa-Allāhu Ghafūrun Raḥīm.

Say (O Muḥammad), "If you (really) love Allah, then follow me! Allah will love you and forgive your sins, and Allah is Oft-Forgiving, Most Merciful." (Sūrat Āli 'Imrān, 3:31)

This is *khāṣṣ*, a special understanding for them. Do *Awliyā' Allāh* follow the Prophet ﷺ or not? We might struggle to follow, but they do not—they spiritually gave up their lives for the Prophet ﷺ. That means to follow the Prophet ﷺ in every step. If he went for Mi'rāj, they go for Mi'rāj, or else they are not *Awliyā'*. A *walī* must follow in the footsteps of the Prophet ﷺ! Does a *walī* love Allāh ﷻ or not? Yes, that is a condition to be a *walī*. That means they are following in the footsteps of the Prophet ﷺ and going in Mi'rāj, and that is why they can guide—because they are following, learning, and giving!

Sayyidunā 'Abd al-Qādir al-Jīlānī ق said in his *Fath ar-Rabbānī*, "*Yā ghulām*, O child!" His students were great scholars who sat facing him, the Ghawth. He said, "*Yā ghulām*! You are still a child as you didn't reach maturity yet." That is dangerous, because if we are not mature, how are we going to obey or be responsible?

You have to understand when he says, "*Yā Ghulām!*" There is a secret there because he is the Ghawth. I never said that before, although we were going through that book in Ramaḍān every morning, but they are saying it now to open this secret.

So it means you aren't responsible—the *Awliyā' Allāh* are responsible. If you take the hand of your guide, he is responsible to guide you, and if not, he is the one responsible. There is danger *fī kitābat al-'ilmi wa-ḥifẓihi bi-ghayri 'amal*, in writing and memorizing knowledge without acting on it. That is why it is dangerous. Many, many scholars spend their lives writing presentations, but they are not practicing what they learned.

He said, "*'Aysh yanf'ak.*" This is not literary Arabic—it's slang. They put, "I like that as it is important." What is it going to benefit you if you are not doing it and not practicing it? It means, "You donkey!" Spirituality is *'amal*—practice. Even if you practice one *'amal* a day, it is better than memorizing thousands!

And he quoted a ḥadīth of the Prophet ﷺ that I like to mention: *Yaqūlu Allāh 'azza wa-jall li'l-anbiyā' wa'l-'ulamā'*, Allāh says on Judgment Day to the prophets and scholars—meaning the pious people: "O! If you thought yourselves *antum kuntum ru'āt khalqī*, that you are the ones authorized to be shepherds for the nations—what have you done with your flocks? What have you shown them and what have you taught them? You are responsible and you are liable!"

That is why all prophets on Judgment Day—where do they run? Towards Sayyidunā Muḥammad ﷺ. What are they going to answer? So if *Anbiyā'* run to the Prophet ﷺ, where is the *'ālim* on that Day? Is there any more *'ālim* then, when even *Anbiyā'* are shaking there?

Where are the *'ulamā'* who sit on chairs in *dunyā* giving fatwas, as if they are the biggest peacocks? They have to run to the Prophet ﷺ, they cannot go directly to Allāh ﷻ. And if they are not accepting, then they will go directly to Hell!

Today we see too many kings sitting on their chairs like roosters on their chickens. We also think of ourselves as kings. Ask two people with similar understanding—will you find that? No, you won't, because each has his own opinion.

إِذَا كُنْتُمْ ثَلَاثَةً فِي سَفَرٍ فَأَمِّرُوا أَحَدَكُمْ

The Prophet ﷺ said: "If you are three, put one as *amīr*, leader."

But if you do that now, they will fight one hour to see who is *amīr*! That is not spirituality. Spirituality is *taslīmiyya*—to submit.

Allāh ﷻ says to them: *Antum kuntum khazānat kunūzī*, "You were the trustees or the guardians of My treasures!"

Because all the treasures are in the hands of kings. *Hal waṣaltum al-fuqarā'*? "Did you make relations with the poor?"

When Sayyidunā 'Umar ؓ became the *khalīfah*, he was crying. His wife asked him, "Why are you crying? You became *khalīfah*." He said, "Now I have to cry, because if anyone is hungry, I am responsible."

He used to carry sacks of food on his back and distribute to the poor people. Today they are kings and queens, holding the treasures of the world, raising the price of oil and sucking the blood of people! Who raised the price of petroleum in order to build their Gulf nations into prostitution? Go and see there. They built their nations by raising the price of petroleum as a monopoly, while the poor become poorer and the rich become richer.

And that is a ḥadīth of the Prophet ﷺ quoted by Sayyidunā 'Abd al-Qādir al-Jīlānī ق and mentioned in the book *Kanz al-'Ummāl*: "Did you take care of the poor and did you take care of the *aytām*—orphans?"

How much food is sent to orphans which you find the next day being sold on the black market?

Allāh ﷻ will ask them: "Did you take from the money that is written on you as My right and give it to poor people?"

So where do we stand now—are we *ghulām* or not? We are *ghulām* now, because we are responsible, but since we are *ghulām*, we are not responsible! It is not me saying this—it is Sayyidunā 'Abd al-Qādir al-Jīlānī ق saying it. He will take responsibility for them.

One *walī* is enough to take everyone and not only put them in Paradise but raise them to *maq'ad ṣidqin 'inda malīkin muqtadir, "a seat of truth near the Sovereign, the Omnipotent."* (Sūrat al-Qamar, 54:55) Be happy! You think the Prophet ﷺ can be alone in Paradise? He has to have people with him—so be happy, smile! That is *Maqām at-Tashrīf*.

The Difference between an *'Alim* and a *Walī*

When the Prophet ﷺ went in Ascension he saw Sayyīdinā Mūsā ﷺ, who always likes to ask questions. He even asked Allah ﷻ:

قَالَ رَبِّ أَرِنِي أَنظُرْ إِلَيْكَ

Qāla rabbī ārinī anẓur ilayk.

He said, "O my Lord! Show Yourself to me that I may look upon You." (Sūrat al-ʿArāf, 7:143)

It is so easy for him! As for Prophet Muhammad ﷺ he never had any question, he only listens and obeys. He listened to Sayyīdinā Jibrīl ﷺ. The only time he had a question was in the Ascension, when he left the Seven Heavens and he was ascending further, he asked Sayyīdinā Jibrīl ﷺ, "Are you not coming with me?" to accompany him as a friend. Sayyīdinā Jibrīl ﷺ said, "I cannot."

Therefore the Prophet ﷺ moved to the Divine Presence alone. He was in *Maqām at-Tawḥīd*, the Station of Divine Oneness. Today "*tawḥīd*" is all they speak about! Is Prophet ﷺ going to be exclusively with this group that came recently? What about the Muslims who came before, were they not on *tawḥīd*?

Returning to our story: when Sayyīdinā Mūsā ﷺ met Rasoolullah ﷺ in the Ascension he said, "*Yā Sayyidī, yā Rasūlullāh*! Can I ask this question, as this comes to my heart all the time. You said, *'ulamā ummatī ka-anbīyā Banī Isrā'īl*, "(Genuine) scholars are inheritors of the Prophet ﷺ."[5] Could it be their knowledge is like our knowledge? Can you give me the answer, *yā Rasūlullāh*, as to how these people are going to inherit from prophets?"

The Prophet ﷺ called one through the souls, *fi 'l-arwāḥ*, as Allah ﷻ said, "*Alastu bi rabbikum qālū balā*," so the Prophet ﷺ can bring any soul he wants from the past and future. He brought forth the soul of one who was to come in the future, after his time, and he said, "That is one."

Sayyīdinā Mūsā ﷺ asked, "What is your name?"

That one said, "Muḥammad bin Muḥammad bin Muḥammad bin Muḥammad bin Muḥammad bin Muḥammad bin Muḥammad al-Ghazālī," seven times, and if he was able to say it a hundred times he would have, but he felt shy in front of the Prophet ﷺ.

Sayyīdinā Mūsā ﷺ said, "What is this? I thought you were an inheritor of the Prophet ﷺ? Why did you say, 'Muḥammad bin Muḥammad bin Muḥammad bin Muḥammad bin Muḥammad bin Muḥammad bin al-Ghazālī'?"

5 Inheritors are not like prophets, but they have knowledge like prophets.

He answered, "If I can say 'Muḥammad' until Judgment Day, it will not stop!"[6]

So he said, "*Yā* Mūsā! Why do you object when I say 'Muḥammad bin Muḥammad bin Muḥammad bin Muḥammad bin Muḥammad bin Muḥammad bin al-Ghazālī'? Why didn't you object to your own actions when Allāh asked you *'what is in your hand'* and you gave all the classifications you are going to use in your lifetime?"

Sayyīdinā Mūsā ﷺ said, "Because that is the place of honor for me to be with the Prophet ﷺ in *Maqām at-Tashrīf!*"

So that is the difference between an *'ālim* and a *walī*: how to imitate the Prophet ﷺ and practice his sunnah. Practice is important!

In the ḥadīth of Sayyīdinā 'Umar ؓ, the Prophet ﷺ described *Maqām al-Iḥsān*, then Sayyīdinā Jibrīl asked, "Tell me about the Hour, *yā Rasūlullāh*."

Prophet ﷺ said, "The one asked doesn't know more than the one who is asking." That is humbleness; Prophet ﷺ hid his knowledge.

Then Sayyīdinā Jibrīl asked, "Then tell me of its signs."

Prophet ﷺ narrated the signs, including, "The naked, barefooted Bedouins will compete in (building) high buildings."

Now in the deserts of Gulf countries they are competing to erect the tallest building in the world. Are we seeing that or not? There is no more time, O Muslims! Allah shook the Earth three weeks ago and He can shake the Earth whenever He wants to! That was the U.S. stock market crash. That day of judgment is coming, so don't let it cheat us!

Sayyīdinā 'Abd al-Qādir al-Jilānī ق also says in this book, "On the Judgment Day a caller will call out, 'Where are the oppressors? Let them come!'"

We are afraid to be oppressors to ourselves! Are we oppressors or not? We don't know for sure, and even he who doesn't know is struggling. If we are not oppressors to ourselves, it means we don't make sins. Do we make sins? Say 'yes' and ask forgiveness, as that is better than saying 'no'. Did we commit hidden *shirk* or not? Anything related to ourselves is hidden *shirk,* such as pride, arrogance, self-praise, etc.

Sayyīdinā 'Abd al-Qādir al-Jilānī ق then writes, *Ayna 'awwām aẓ-ẓulama? Ayna man yarā min qalaman*? "The oppressors used pens to judge people and send them to prison although they are innocent." *Ẓalama* is one who will benefit from anyone, even if they kill people, like in the Mafia, which is everywhere today. Today you are afraid not to pay a traffic ticket because they might put you in jail, but what happened to corporation CEOs that sucked billions of dollars from the common

---

[6] As much as you say the name of the Prophet ﷺ, Allah sends angels to say *salāms* on you.

people? Are they oppressors or not? Did anyone put them in jail? All those who manipulated the stock market for their gain and harmed so many people will be questioned on Judgment Day, because they made rich people richer and poor people poorer.

Sayyīdinā ʿAbd al-Qādir al-Jilānī ق continues, "Where is anyone from those who possess a pen? Come here to witness on them, gather them and put them in a casket of fire!"

May Allāh ﷻ forgive us and may Allāh ﷻ bless us.

Wa-min Allāhi 't-tawfīq, bi-ḥurmati 'l-Ḥabīb, bi-ḥurmati 'l-Fātiḥah.

And success is from Allah. By the sanctity of the Beloved, by the sanctity of al-Fātiḥah.

الشيخ
١٤١٤

The Immense Station of Servanthood of Prophet Muhammad ﷺ

As-salāmu ʿalaykum wa raḥmatullāhi wa barakātuh

Alhamdulillah that Allah ﷻ has honored us to be from the Ummah of the Beloved and we thank Him for His great bounty on us to make us of his ummah. in His Godship to us, Allah ﷻ is in the Station of Pride and Greatness, and we say, "*Ash-hadu an lā ilāha illa-Llāh, wa ash-hadu anna Muḥammadan Rasūlullāh. Allāhu Akbar, Allāhu Akbar, Allāhu Akbar!*

وَلِلَّهِ ٱلْعِزَّةُ وَلِرَسُولِهِ وَلِلْمُؤْمِنِينَ وَلَٰكِنَّ ٱلْمُنَافِقِينَ لَا يَعْلَمُونَ

Wa li'llāhi 'l-ʿizzatu wa li-rasūlihi wa li-'l-mu'minīn, wa lākinna 'l-munāfiqīna lā yaʿlamūn

And honor belongs to Allah, and to His Messenger, and to the believers—but the hypocrites do not understand. (Sūrat al-Munāfiqūn, 63:8)

O Muslim brothers and sisters! Allah ﷻ has brought us together from far places. First of all, I want to say: may Allah have mercy on our great shaykh, Mawlānā Abāh Anom, and we are proud that Shaykh Wafīullāh has taken the oath from his shaykh, Mawlānā Abāh Anom, and has his intention to take this *ṭarīqah* as far as he can. May Allah ﷻ give him more power to do that.

I knew him fifteen years ago when there was *tawṣiyyah* (advice) given on a TV broadcast talk show with Shaykh Wafīuddīn, and it was, *al-ḥamdu lillāh*, successful. Allah ﷻ wanted us to coordinate more and more and to come to each other. He is like my son; I respect him and I respect his knowledge.

إِنَّمَا بُعِثْتُ لِأُتَمِّمَ مَكَارِمَ ٱلْأَخْلَاقِ

Innamā buʿithtu li-utimmu makārima 'l-akhlāq

I was sent not except to perfect the best of conduct. (Bukhārī in al-Adab al-Mufrad)

No one in this universe knows the reality of Sayyidunā Muḥammad ﷺ, his greatness and his nearness to the Divine Presence — not even the angels! Allah ﷻ raised him:

وَرَفَعْنَا لَكَ ذِكْرَكَ

Wa rafaʿnā laka dhikrak

And We have elevated your remembrance! (Sūrat ash-Sharḥ, 94:4)

Allah ﷻ raised him and raised his remembrance. When He says "*dhikrak*," it means: "It is not just your name, *yā* Muḥammad, but it is a name to be praised!"

إِنَّ ٱللَّهَ وَمَلَائِكَتَهُ يُصَلُّونَ عَلَى ٱلنَّبِيِّ ۚ يَا أَيُّهَا ٱلَّذِينَ آمَنُوا صَلُّوا عَلَيْهِ وَسَلِّمُوا تَسْلِيمًا

Inna 'llāha wa-malā'ikatahu yuṣallūna 'ala 'n-nabī yā ayyuhā 'lladhīna āmanū ṣallū 'alayhi wa-sallimū taslīmā

Verily, Allah and His angels send blessings upon the Prophet. O you who believe! Send blessings upon him and greet him with peace. (Sūrat al-Aḥzāb, 33:56)

The angels saw the Prophet ﷺ as they made *ṣalawāt* to him, and since Allah ﷻ ordered them to send *ṣalawāt* upon an-Nabī ﷺ, they are always singing it. Their *ṣalawāt* is not like ours, because they are *ma'ṣūmīn*—free from sin—and their praise is pure! They send theirs directly to the Prophet ﷺ, but our *ṣalawāt* is incomplete.

Through the *nūr* (light) that Allah ﷻ sent to the Prophet ﷺ, He raised his character:

وَإِنَّكَ لَعَلَىٰ خُلُقٍ عَظِيمٍ

Wa innaka la'alā khuluqin 'aẓīm

Verily, you (O Muḥammad) are of the most exalted character. (Sūrat al-Qalam, 68:4)

Allah ﷻ was telling the Prophet ﷺ: "I have perfected your character to be the most perfect character in this universe."

We say the Prophet ﷺ was sent to bring Islam. Allah ﷻ said:

إِنَّ الدِّينَ عِندَ ٱللَّهِ ٱلْإِسْلَامُ

Inna 'd-dīna 'inda 'llāhi 'l-Islām

Indeed, the religion in Allah's view is Islam (submission to His Will). (Sūrat Āli 'Imrān, 3:19)

Arsalahu bi 'r-risālah, risālat al-Islām. The Prophet ﷺ said: "I have been sent with my *risālah* (message) to complete the best of character." Therefore, Islam is *akhlāq* (virtuous character). This statement: "*The religion in Allah's view is Islam*" is equivalent to:

Innamā bu'ithtu li-utammima makārima 'l-akhlāq

"I have been sent to perfect the best of conduct"

Because Islam is *akhlāq*, and *akhlāq* is Islam. *'Aẓam al-akhlāq*—the best of character—is when a person throws away his bad character. For example, if this is a dirty picture and I choose not to look at it and throw it away, that is the best character. If I look at it, that is the worst character. Islam wants you to throw the bad character from your heart.

In a *majālis* (spiritual gatherings) such as this one, people are coming together not for business *n*or for *dunyā*, but for *Ākhirah*. This purifies their hearts from the love of *dunya* and fills them with the love of Allah ﷻ and Sayyidunā Muḥammad ﷺ, which is what Allah loves!

We return to: "I have surely been sent with my *baʿthah* (mission and power) to complete the best of conduct."

The Prophet ﷺ did not say "to teach" (*li-uʿallima*) but "to complete" (*li-utammima*). This means the Prophet ﷺ will not let one of his ummah leave this *dunya* without perfecting him. Even at the moment of someone's last breath, the Prophet ﷺ will be there to complete *makārima 'l-akhlāq* on the dying person as he says: *Ash-hadu an lā ilāha illa-Llāh, wa ash-hadu anna Muḥammadan Rasūlullāh*

It is important to note the difference between *li-utammima* and *li-uʿallima. Li-utammima* means the Prophet ﷺ is responsible for the Ummah to be perfected before they leave this world. He carried this burden on his shoulders, always saying: "My ummah! My ummah!"

Allah ﷻ said:

وَوَضَعْنَا عَنكَ وِزْرَكَ

Wa waḍaʿnā ʿanka wizrak

And We removed from you your burden. (Sūrat ash-Sharḥ, 94:2)

It means, "We removed the burdens from your back and We are giving you the ability to perfect your ummah; We are giving you *sajdah*." This means: "We have removed the heavy burden of this ummah's sins that were burdening your back, *yā Muḥammad.*"

[Audience: *Yā Muḥammad! Allāhumma ṣalli ʿalā Muḥammad. Ṣallū ʿala 'n-Nabī* ﷺ*!*]

"Why are you worried? Did We not open your chest?" Allah ﷻ said:

أَلَمْ نَشْرَحْ لَكَ صَدْرَكَ

Alam nashraḥ laka ṣadrak

Have We not expanded for you your breast? (Sūrat ash-Sharḥ, 94:1)

He didn't say "*Alam nashraḥ laka ṣadrak*" and limit it. That means it is not possible for *inshirāḥ ṣadra an-Nabī* ﷺ to have a limit, because Allah ﷻ expanded the chest of Sayyidunā Muḥammad ﷺ at the level of His own greatness!

قلب العبد بيتُ الرب

Qalb al-*ʿabd baytu 'r-Rabb*

The heart of the slave is the House of the Lord. (Iḥyā' 'Ulūm al-Dīn of al-Ghazālī)

قلب المؤمن عرش الله

Qalb al-mu'min 'Arshullāh

The heart of the believer is the Throne of Allah. (Mu'jam al-Kabīr of al-Ṭabarānī)

Here, *al-'abd* refers to Sayyidunā Muḥammad ﷺ—*al-'abd al-ḥaqīqī*, the true servant responsible before Allah. On the Day of Judgment, he will be in *Maqām as-Sujūd* in the Divine Presence, in *sajdah*, and Allah will open to him *du'ās* never revealed before.

He said: "I will make that *du'ā*, and then Allah ﷻ will say: '*Yā Muḥammad*! Raise your head. I will give this to you."

So if you are a real *'abd*, make *sajdah. Maqām al-'Ubūdiyyah,* the Station of Worshipping, is in *sajdah*, which is the perfect symbol of servanthood. To be a true *'abd* is to be always in *sujūd*. The angels are proof of this level of *'ubūdiyyah*:

وَإِذْ قُلْنَا لِلْمَلَائِكَةِ اسْجُدُوا لِآدَمَ فَسَجَدُوا إِلَّا إِبْلِيسَ

Wa idh qulnā li 'l-malā'ikati 'sjudū li Ādama fa-sajadū illā Iblīs

And when We said to the angels, "Prostrate yourselves before Ādam," they all prostrated themselves, except Iblīs. (Sūrat al-Baqarah, 2:34)

Allah ﷻ ordered the angels to make *sajdah* to the *nūr* of Sayyidunā Muḥammad ﷺ, which was present in the form of Sayyidunā Ādam ﷺ. This was a *sajdah* of *ihtirām*—respect—not worship.

When you prostrate before Allah's servant, the angels make *sajdah* with you, since Allah ordered them to do so. This applies to the ummah: When the ummah makes *sajdah*, the angels also make *sajdah*.

Some who possess divine knowledge say: When you make *sajdah*, the two angels on your right and left also prostrate with you. Then Allah ﷻ replaces them with two new angels. With every *sajdah*, Allah gives you two more angels! On the Day of Judgment, when you rise from your grave, you will see all these angels with you—your reward for making *sujūd* in your prayers.

Those angels will prostrate to Allah ﷻ until the Day of Judgment and will never raise their heads!

The Qur'ānic evidence is: "*When Allah said to the angels, 'Make sajdah to Ādam,' they all prostrated except Iblīs.*"

This *sajdah* was not to Ādam ﷺ, but in reverence to Sayyidunā Muḥammad ﷺ. You will not find any verse in the Qur'ān that says: *"Raise your heads, O angels."* No—there is not one such verse. So they remain in *sujūd* until the Day of Judgment.

Allah ﷻ addressed His Beloved Prophet ﷺ with the title *'abd* (servant):

سُبْحَانَ ٱلَّذِي أَسْرَىٰ بِعَبْدِهِ لَيْلًا مِّنَ ٱلْمَسْجِدِ ٱلْحَرَامِ إِلَى ٱلْمَسْجِدِ ٱلْأَقْصَى ٱلَّذِي بَارَكْنَا حَوْلَهُۥ لِنُرِيَهُۥ مِنْ ءَايَاتِنَآ ۚ إِنَّهُۥ هُوَ ٱلسَّمِيعُ ٱلْبَصِيرُ

Subḥāna 'lladhī asrā bi-'abdihi laylan mina 'l-masjidi 'l-ḥarām ilā 'l-masjidi 'l-aqṣā alladhī bāraknā ḥawlahu li-nuriyahu min āyātinā innahu huwa 's-Samī'u 'l-Baṣīr

Glory be to He Who transported His servant by night from the Inviolable House of Worship (at Mecca) to the Remote House of Worship (at Jerusalem), the environs of which We had blessed so that We might show him some of Our signs. Verily, He Alone is All-Hearing, All-Seeing. (Sūrat al-Isrā', 17:1)

He is the only true servant to Allah ﷻ with all his characteristics. The Prophet ﷺ spent his entire life in *sajdah*; he is in *sajdah* in his grave, and he will be in *sajdah* on Judgment Day until Allah says: *Irfa' rā'sak — "Raise your head."*

Then he will make *du'ā,* and Allah will open to him a *du'ā* never opened before.

What is the meaning of "a *du'ā* that was never opened before"? Even with thousands of *du'ās* in books like *Dalā'il al-Khayrāt*, the Prophet ﷺ speaks of something entirely new—perhaps in a divine language, or with secret letters like *alif, lām, mīm* from the Qur'ān.

**عَنْ أَنَسِ بْنِ مَالِكٍ رَضِيَ اللهُ عَنْهُ مَرْفُوعًا: أَخْبَرَ النَّبِيُّ صَلَّى اللهُ عَلَيْهِ وَسَلَّمَ: أَنَّهُ يَأْتِي فَيَسْجُدُ لِرَبِّهِ وَيَحْمَدُهُ [لَا يَبْدَأُ بِالشَّفَاعَةِ أَوَّلًا]، ثُمَّ يُقَالُ لَهُ: ارْفَعْ رَأْسَكَ، وَقُلْ يُسْمَعْ، وَسَلْ تُعطَ، وَاشْفَعْ تُشَفَّعْ.

Allah says to the Prophet ﷺ: *Irfa' rā'sak* — "Raise your head and ask, I will give to you."

The Prophet ﷺ replies: *"Yā Rabbī!* I want what You gave me—I want my ummah."

Allah responds: *"Yā* Muḥammad! Take one-third of them and send them to Paradise without account (*bi-ghayri ḥisāb*)." (Ḥadīth in *al-Adab al-Mufrad* by al-Bukhārī)

Then the Prophet ﷺ goes into *sajdah* again, and Allah opens to him another *du'ā*. He asks again, and Allah says: "Take another third."

Then the Prophet ﷺ goes into *sajdah* a third time and asks for the rest. Allah says: *"Take all except one—he is the worst of human beings."*

What does this one do that others don't? Even with all the sins Muslims commit, they are under the *sajdah* of the Prophet ﷺ. So what is this unimaginable sin?

Allah knows, but He wants to show His *raḥmah*, so He says:

وَمَآ أَرْسَلْنَٰكَ إِلَّا رَحْمَةً لِّلْعَٰلَمِينَ

Wa mā arsalnāka illā raḥmatan li-'l-'ālamīn

(O Muḥammad!) We have sent you not except as a Mercy for all the Worlds. (Sūrat al-Anbiyā', 21:107)

Even with all his *sajdah*, that one still cannot enter Paradise. But the Prophet ﷺ insists: "I want that one too." Allah says: "I gave them all to you except this one—he is Mine. But with My *Raḥmah*, I am sending him with you." Through Allah's *Raḥmah*, even that one enters Paradise.

This *majlis*, a gathering for the praise of the Prophet ﷺ, is a *majlis raḥmah wa maghfira*—a gathering of mercy and forgiveness, and a gathering of good-hearted people.

وَفَوْقَ كُلِّ ذِي عِلْمٍ عَلِيمٌ

Wa fawqa kulli dhī 'ilmin 'alīm

Above every knower is a (higher) knower. (Sūrat Yūsuf, 12:76)

Above every angel there is an angel, and above every professor there is a professor.

That means: *be humble*, because when you make yourself humble, you become everything. The Prophet ﷺ said:

مَنْ تَوَاضَعَ لِلَّهِ رَفَعَهُ

Man tawāḍa'a li-llāhi rafa'ahu

Whoever shows humility for Allah, He will raise him. (*Saḥīḥ Muslim*)

Shaykh Wafīuddīn is showing humility to us by inviting us all here. We are not worth anything, and we only hope to be on the threshold of *'atāb an-Nabī* ﷺ. May Allāh ﷻ grant him more and more knowledge, grant you more and more knowledge, and forgive us all.

Wa min Allāhi 't-tawfīq, wa-salām 'alaykum wa raḥmatullāhi wa barakātuh

And from Allah is all success. Peace be upon you, and the mercy of Allah and His blessings.

نور على نور

Passing of the World through the Eye of the Needle

When the Prophet ﷺ went in the night of Ascension, Laylat al-Isrā' wa'l-Miʿrāj, and was approaching his Lord, he reached a place where Archangel Jibrīl (the Holy Spirit) said, "I cannot go any further. This is my limit." The Prophet ﷺ proceeded to leave our time and penetrate into Allah's 'time.' He went through five stations or levels. When they asked him about those levels, he said:

> There are five hundred of Allah's years between each station of Paradise, (as-Suyuti, Ibn Kathir, lbn Qayyim.)

And Allah said:

... يَوْمٍ كَانَ مِقْدَارُهُ أَلْفَ سَنَةٍ مِّمَّا تَعُدُّونَ

a Day the length whereof will be [like] a thousand years of your reckoning (Sūratu 's-Sajdah, 32:5)

In human time, the Prophet's ﷺ journey took him five times five hundred times three hundred and fifty times one thousand years!

Was he going through empty space? Was there no creation there, only a void? There are creations, and he was penetrating through their time. In one night, he was the Prophet for all these stations. How long did he live there? With every creation through which he passed, he lived a complete life. To us, in one second he penetrated everything. But Allah stretched that second and made it so immense as to enable him to live 500 of Allah's years. In a short time, he lived through a very long time.

God can make the camel go through the eye of a needle without making the universe smaller and without making the eye of the needle larger (C.f. Sūratu 'l-Aʿarāf, 7:40) How will you understand that? And how to explain it?

Power of the Shaykh

One day two disciples of Sayyidinā ʿUbaydullāh al-Aḥrār, one of the saints of the Golden Chain, were making ablution at the river-shore. One of them was saying, "*Subḥānallāh*, God is great, and our shaykh is great! Allah has said in his Holy Book that He can make the camel go through the eye of a needle without making the universe smaller and without making the eye of the needle larger. And our shaykh has this power! He can do this." The other one was not yet a good disciple. He mumbled, "For Allah, fine, we can understand; but for our shaykh...?" As soon as he said this, he slipped into the river and found himself in a completely deserted place. He started walking until he reached a village and asked where he was. He was told that he was seven months away from his original spot. At that time there were no cars or other such means of transportation. Who put him there?

That was the power of the shaykh. The disciple had been thrown there: be careful not to be thrown! In the village, he found a blacksmith. He asked for some food and the blacksmith said, 'Yes, but you have to work for me.' He used him for one year and found him a very trustworthy person, so he gave him his daughter in marriage.

Don't make any mistake with your shaykh! If they say that he can make this earth pass through the eye of a needle, say "Yes!" What are you going to lose? Nothing. Why say "no" then? If he says, "This is black," say "it is black"; "this is white," say "it is white." What is going to happen? Nothing. You will be raised. It is better than to stay in your level. Better to be in higher levels than in lower. So say, "Yes, *Na'am! Ṣadaqta yā Sayyidī*," as Sayyidinā Abī Bakr al-Ṣiddīq ؓ kept saying to the Prophet (peace be upon him), "Yes! You have said the truth, O Prophet!" But no; they want you to fight your shaykh. They want you to say that they are wrong and you are right. Right about what? You are full of ego, you are sitting in your own waste, and you dare ask, "From where is that bad smell coming?"

Do not dare to speak about your shaykh. Whatever the shaykh does or says, say, *Āmannā wa Ṣadaqnā* "we believe and we bear witness to the truth." This will give you more power. But it is hard for someone to say 'Yes, you are right,' for the ego whispers to you to say, "No, he is wrong and you know better than him. His age is eighty and your age is thirty: you know better! How can you say yes?"

When Shaykh 'Ubaydullāh saw that his disciple understood and accepted, he appeared to him and told him: "Your doubt cost you seven years and five children! I am bringing all of your family back so that people will believe." In one second, he found himself back in the water into which he had slipped seven years before, but only one second of his life had elapsed. He came back home and saw his family and five children running towards him.

After seven years, he found himself with five children. He was reflecting after all that time how he got there, and said, "*Subḥānallāh*, all this because I made a mistake with my shaykh."

The shaykh can reach anywhere in space and time without impediment. If you give him complete trust and complete faith, your faith will effect the miracle. If you don't have faith, and if you have any doubt, it will not lead to the best result. Complete faith in the shaykh will get you whatever you like.

The Last Seven Breaths

"When you are giving away your seven last breaths, Allah can elongate them," our shaykh said, "up to 137 years. He will never send you away from this world except with complete and perfected worship." In our eyes your last breath may take one second, but in the eyes of saints and the Prophet ﷺ and Allah, it can go up to 137 years of complete and perfect worship.

We were asking whether the Prophet ﷺ was travelling through empty spaces or spaces full of creation. When he was moving with the speed that traverses 500 years of Allah's reckoning, he covered immense space. When the Prophet ﷺ was passing through those spaces, Allah at that time brought their creation into being. The Prophet ﷺ, therefore, was the key for that creation. The Prophet's ﷺ passing through time and space is like the code that effects creation within it. Such is the creation of this earth from nothing to "Be!" and it was.

Allah is so great that no one can reach His greatness, even the Prophet Muhammad (peace be upon him). Allah is great above everything. This is to clarify the understanding of what I am going to say next. For the Prophet was manifesting the Attributes of God for this creation. Such is the wisdom with which Allah sent him to His presence.

قُلْ يَا عِبَادِيَ الَّذِينَ أَسْرَفُوا عَلَى أَنْفُسِهِمْ لَا تَقْنَطُوا مِن رَحْمَةِ اللَّهِ، إِنَّ اللَّهَ يَغْفِرُ الذُّنُوبَ جَمِيعًا، إِنَّهُ هُوَ الْغَفُورُ الرَّحِيمُ.

Say, *"O My servants who have transgressed against themselves, do not despair of the mercy of Allah."* (Sūrat Az-Zumar, 39:53)

Allah said, "Say: O My servants!" He did not say, "Say: O Allah's servants!" He is talking to the Prophet. Yet later in the verse, He speaks of Himself in the third person: "Do not despair of the mercy of Allah." Why did He not use the third person for "My servants" also? And why did He not say, "Do not despair of My mercy?" This means, "O Prophet, these are your servants. Tell them not to be disappointed in Allah's Mercy." There are two subjects, one here, one there. The sense is, therefore, "O Prophet, tell your servants not to despair of Allah's Mercy." If Allah wanted to refer these servants to Himself, He would say to the Prophet, "O Prophet, tell My servants not to despair of My Mercy." We are, therefore, servants of the Prophet.

A saint came to Madinah one day. Everyone was praying towards *qiblah.* He was praying in the direction of the grave of the Prophet ﷺ. They came to him and said, "You have to pray towards the Ka'bah, are you praying to the Prophet ﷺ?" He said, "Of course I am praying towards the direction of the Prophet ﷺ!" He continued: "If not for the Prophet ﷺ how would I know about the Ka'bah! The Prophet ﷺ will pray towards the Ka'bah, and I shall pray towards him! It will reach. But if I myself pray towards Ka'bah, where will it reach?"

It means "I am directing myself towards the one whom I know. He will direct himself towards his Lord."

Earth, Moon and Sun

The moon represents, in Sufi teachings, the saint who is always facing the Prophet ﷺ never swerving from his presence. The sun is the Seal of Prophets, and the Seal of Saints is the moon. They always face each other. Without the Seal of Prophets, there are no reflections on this earth. And without the Seal of Saints, there are no reflections on earth. Reflections follow a route from God to the Prophet ﷺ, as the Prophet ﷺ is the mirror of God, the Other Face of God, similarly lights reflect from the Prophet ﷺ to the Seal of Saints.

What is 'the Other Face'? Just as we can see only one side of the moon, the bright side, while the other side is dark, similarly we can only see the manifestation of God: that is the Prophet ﷺ. What we see of God's manifestation is the Prophet ﷺ! No one can see God Himself.

The side that is reflecting God's light towards us, then, is the Prophet ﷺ . But even that reflected light cannot shine upon us directly: no one can behold it. It is reflected yet another time, therefore, to the other mirror which is the Seal of Saints. Having descended from God to the mirror of the Prophet ﷺ, the light of God then goes from the Prophet ﷺ to the mirror of the Seal of Saints.

The five poles, *quṭbs*, or great saints, are responsible for providing the knowledge and carrying the burden of ī, intercession. The Prophet ﷺ is "distributing" himself into them as into five points or powers. Every power represents a part of him in every century. This is the secret of the meaning of:

وَاعْلَمُوا أَنَّ فِيكُمْ رَسُولَ اللَّهِ

It must be known to you that the Prophet is among you at all times.
(Sūratu 'l-Ḥujurāt, 49:7)

It is in this sense also that the Prophet ﷺ said in hadith, "I have one hour with my Lord and one hour with creation," and, "I have one side facing my Lord, and one side facing creation."

Records of human history begin, at the earliest, seven thousand years ago. But they have discovered some bones now, and they now say that human beings existed millions of years ago. If so, where are the records of their civilization? Were they so dumb as not to leave a scrap of their passage over millions of years, when only in one hundred years we are capable of such a civilization as ours? Allah has brought people and removed them.

When we read Sūratu 'l-Fatiha, we recite:

Owner of the Day of Judgment

We have to know which judgment. Does Allah have only one Day of Judgment? That is the common understanding. Allah's Words mean continuity! They are never stopping. As His creation never stops, so it is with His Day of Judgment. Every second there is a Day of Judgment. Every moment, Allah is creating and He is judging. This is God's Greatness: He creates on one side and He judges on the other-unceasingly.

When Sayyidina Muḥammad ﷺ asked Archangel Jibrīl, "O Jibrīl, do you know when Allah sent Adam?" Archangel Jibrīl ؑ said, "Which Adam ؑ are you talking about?" Khiḍr said, "Is there any Adam other than this Adam?" Archangel Jibrīl ؑ said, "I know of 124,000 Adams." They came, they had their creation, they had their Judgment Day, and they left. The Adam you are referring to is the last Adam - Before him, 123,999 Adams came. This is what I know: "I saw their creation and I saw their judgment. I asked my Lord one day and said, 'O my Lord, can you show me Your creation since the beginning, and can you show me where it ends?' And Allah opened to me an ocean of which there is no beginning and of which there is no end! An ocean like a desert, all full of grains like sand, and each grain of sand was in itself a complete universe such as the one you see, made of heaven and earth, suns and stars as far as the eye can see. What you consider a universe is a grain of sand in relation to the ocean of Allah's creation!"

"A green bird alights there every day and his food is one grain of sand of that creation. As soon as the bird puts one grain of sand in his mouth, Allah creates a creation by saying 'Be!' and it will be. This whole universe is but a grain of sand to this green bird, which he takes into his mouth. That bird is the Prophet Muhammad ﷺ, and every grain of sand he puts in his mouth is a complete creation with its beginning, its end, and its judgment day. What then are you asking me about?"

No one knows the secret of *Māliki yawmi 'd-dīn,* "*Owner of the Day of Judgment.*" Allah is continuously creating and continuously taking back everything back to its origin. In relation to what we know and think, we are still babies. Our knowledge is nothing compared to the knowledge of saints of the Golden Chain, or to the knowledge of the Prophet ﷺ, or to the knowledge of God.

May Allah open for us the way to our hearts and give us from the wisdom of this knowledge, and bless us.

Islamic Calendar and Holy Days

The Islamic calendar is lunar-based, with twelve months of 29 or 30 days. A lunar year is shorter than a solar year, so Muslim holy days cycle back in the Gregorian (Western) calendar. This is how Ramaḍān is celebrated at different times of the year, as the annual Islamic calendar is ten days shorter than the Gregorian calendar.

Four Islamic months are sacred: Muḥarram, Rajab, Dhūl-Q'adah and Dhūl-Ḥijjah. Holy months include "God's Month" (Rajab), "Prophet's Month" (Sha'bān) and the "Month of the People" (Ramaḍān), in which pious acts are rewarded more generously.

Months of the Islamic Calendar

1) Muḥarram
2) Ṣafar
3) Rabī' al-Awwal (Rabī' I)
4) Rabī' al-Thāniyah (Rabī' II)
5) Jumāda al- Awwal (Jumādi I)
6) Jumāda al-Thāniyah (Jumādi II)
7) Rajab
8) Sha'bān
9) Ramaḍān
10) Shawwāl
11) Dhū'l-Q'adah
12) Dhū'l-Ḥijjah

Important Dates

al-Hijra

The 1st of Muḥarram marks the beginning of the Islamic New Year, chosen because it is the anniversary of Prophet Muḥammad's ﷺ historic *Hijra* (migration) from Mecca to Madinah, where he established the first, preeminent Muslim community in which he introduced unprecedented social reforms, including civil law, human and women's rights, religious tolerance, taxation to serve the community, and military ethics.

'Ashura

On 10th of Muḥarram, 'Ashūrā commemorates many sacred events, such as Noah's ark coming to rest, the birth of Abraham, and the building of the Ka'bah in Mecca. 'Ashūrā is a major holy day, marked with two days of fasting, on the 9th/10th or on 10th/11th based on a holy tradition (*ḥadīth*) of Sayyīdinā Muḥammad ﷺ.

Mawlid

Mawlid al-Nabī ﷺ, 12th Rabī' al-Awwal, commemorates Prophet Muḥammad's ﷺ birth in 570. Mawlid is celebrated globally throughout this month in huge communal gatherings in which a famous poem "Qasīdat al-Burdah" is recited, accompanied by drummers, illustrious poetry recitals, religious singing, eloquent sermons, gift giving, feasts, and feeding the poor. Most Muslim nations observe Mawlid as a national holiday.

Laylat al-Isrā' wal-Mi'rāj

Literally, "the Night Journey and Ascension," the 27th of Rajab is when Sayyīdinā Muḥammad ﷺ physically traveled from Mecca to Jerusalem, ascended in all the levels of Heaven from a rock in the Dome of the Rock, and returned to Mecca—while his bed was still warm. In the Night Journey, Islam's five daily prayers were ordained by God. Sayyīdinā Muḥammad ﷺ also prayed with prophets Abraham, Moses, and Jesus in Jerusalem's al-Aqsā Mosque, along with all the other prophets and messengers of God, signifying that Muslims, Christians, and Jews worship and serve one god. This holy event designated Jerusalem as the third holiest site in Islam, after Mecca and Madinah.

Laylat al-Bara'ah (Niṣf Sha'bān)

The "Night of Freedom from Fire" occurs on 15th Sha'bān. On this night God's Mercy is great; hence, the night is spent reciting Holy Qur'an and special prayers, as well as visiting the deceased.

Ramadan

Many regard Ramaḍān, the ninth month of the Islamic calendar, the holiest month of the year. Muslims observe a strict fast and participate in pious activities such as charitable giving and peace making. It is a time of intense spiritual renewal for those who observe it. Fasting is meant to instill social awareness of the needy, and to promote gratitude for God's endless favors. The fast is typically broken in a communal setting, and hence Ramaḍān is a highly social month. At night, a special Ramaḍān prayer known as "*Tarāwīḥ*" is offered in congregation, in which one-thirtieth of the Holy Qur'an is recited by the *imām* (prayer leader); thus the entire holy book of six thousand verses is recited in this month.

Eid ['Īd] al-Fiṭr

"Festival of Fast-Breaking" marks the end of Ramaḍān and is celebrated the first three days of Shawwāl. It is a time for charity and celebration with family and friends for completing a month of blessings and joy. In the Last Days of Ramaḍān, each Muslim family gives "Zakāt al-Fiṭr"(charity of fast-breaking) which consists of cash and/or food, to help the poor. On the first early morning of Eid, Muslims observe a special congregational prayer, such as Christmas/Easter Mass or the High Holy Days. After Eid prayer is a time to visit family and friends, and give gifts and money (especially to children). Many specialty foods and sweets are prepared solely for Eid days. In most Muslim countries, the entire three days of Eid is a national holiday.

Yawm al-ʿArafah

"Day of ʿArafah," 9 Dhū'l-Ḥijjah, occurs just before the celebration of Eid al-Adḥā. Pilgrims on Hajj assemble for the "standing" on the plain of ʿArafah, located outside Mecca, where they contemplate the Day of Standing (Resurrection Day). Muslims elsewhere in the world fast this day, and gather at a local mosque for prayers. Thus, those who cannot perform Hajj that year still honor the sacrifice of Abraham.

Eid [ʿĪd] al-Aḍḥā

The "Feast of Sacrifice," celebrated from the 10th-13th Dhū'l-Ḥijjah, marks Prophet Abraham's willingness to sacrifice his son Ismāʿīl on God's order. To honor this event, Muslims perform Hajj, the pilgrimage to Mecca that is incumbent on every mature Muslim once in their life if they have the means. Celebrations begin with an animal sacrifice to commemorate Sayyīdinā Abraham's sacrifice. In Islam, he is known as *Khalīlullāh*, "God's friend." Many consider him the first Muslim and a premiere role model, for his obedience to God and willingness to sacrifice his only child without even questioning the command.

Glossary

ʿabd (pl. *ʿibād*): lit. slave; servant.

ʿAbdAllāh: Lit., "servant of God"

Abū Bakr aṣ-Ṣiddīq: the closest Companion of Prophet Muḥammad; the Prophet's father-in-law, who shared the *Hijrah* with him. After the Prophet's death, he was elected the first caliph (successor); known as one of the most saintly Companions.

Abū Yazīd/Bayāzīd Bistāmī: A great ninth century *walī* and a master of the Naqshbandi Golden Chain.

adab: good manners, proper etiquette.

adhān: call to prayer.

Ākhirah: the Hereafter; afterlife.

al-: Arabic definite article, "the".

ʿalāmīn: world; universes.

Alḥamdūlillāh: praise God.

ʿAlī ibn Abī Ṭālib: first cousin of Prophet Muḥammad, married to his daughter Fāṭimah; the fourth caliph.

alif: first letter of Arabic alphabet.

ʿAlīm, al-: the Knower, a divine attribute

Allāh: proper name for God in Arabic.

Allāhu Akbar: God is Greater.

ʿāmal: good deed (pl. *ʿamāl*).

amīr (pl., *umarā*): chief, leader, head of a nation or people.

anā: first person singular pronoun

anbīyā: prophets (sing. *nabī*).

ʿaql: intellect, reason; from the root *ʿaqila*: lit., "to fetter."

ʿArafah, ʿArafat: a plain near Mecca where pilgrims gather for the principal rite of Hajj.

ʿarif: knower, Gnostic; one who has reached spiritual knowledge of his Lord.

ʿĀrifūnʿ bil-Lāh: knowers of God.

Ar-Raḥīm: The Mercy-Giving, Merciful, Munificent, one of Allāh's ninety-nine Holy Names.

Ar-Raḥmān: The Most Merciful, Compassionate, Beneficent; the most repeated of Allāh's Holy Names.

ʿarsh, al-: the Divine Throne.

aṣl: root, origin, basis.

astāghfirullāh: lit. "I seek Allāh's forgiveness."

Awlīyāullāh: saints of Allāh (sing. *walī*).

āyah (pl. *ayāt*): a verse of the Holy Qur'ān.

Āyat al-Kursī: "Verse of the Throne,"

a well-known supplication from the Qur'ān (2:255).

ʿAzraʾīl: the Archangel of Death.

Badīʿ al-: The Innovator; a Divine Name.

Banī Ādam: Children of Adam; humanity.

Bayt al-Maqdis: the Sacred Mosque in Jerusalem, built at the site where Solomon's Temple was later erected.

Bayt al-Mā'mūr: much-frequented house; this refers to the Kaʿbah of the Heavens, which is the prototype of the Kaʿbah on Earth, circumambulated by the angels.

bayaʿ: pledge; in the context of this book, the pledge of initiation of a disciple (*murīd*) to a shaykh.

Bismillāhi'r-Raḥmāni'r-Raḥīm: "In the name of the All-Merciful, the All-Compassionate"; introductory verse to all chapters of the Qur'ān, except the ninth.

Dajjāl: the False Messiah (Anti-Christ) will appear at the end-time of this world, to deceive Mankind with false divinity.

dalālah: evidence.

dhāt: self / selfhood.

dhawq (pl. *adhwāq*): tasting; technical term referring to the experiential aspect of gnosis.

dhikr: remembrance, mention of God in His Holy Names or phrases of glorification.

dīyā: light.

Diwān al-Awlīyā: the nightly gathering of saints with Prophet Muḥammad in the spiritual realm.

duʿā: supplication.

dunyā: world; worldly life.

ʿEid: festival; the two major celebrations of Islam are ʿEid al-Fitr, after Ramaḍān; and ʿEid al-Adha, the Festival of Sacrifice during the time of Hajj, which commemorates the sacrifice of Prophet Abraham.

fard: obligatory worship.

Fātiḥah: Sūratu 'l-Fātiḥah; the opening chapter of the Qur'ān.

Ghafūr, al-: The Forgiver; one of the Holy Names of God.

Ghawth: lit. "Helper"; the highest rank of all saints.

ghaybuʿ l-muṭlaq, al-: the Absolute Unknown; known only to God.

ghusl: full shower/bath obligated by a state of ritual impurity, performed before worship.

Grandshaykh: generally, a *walī* of great stature. In this text, refers to Mawlānā ʿAbdAllāh ad-Daghestāni (d. 1973), Mawlānā Shaykh Nazim's master.

hāʿ: the Arabic letter ه

ḥadīth Nabawī (pl., *aḥadīth*): prophetic tradition whose meaning and linguistic expression are those of Prophet Muḥammad.

Ḥadīth Qudsī: divine saying whose meaning directly reflects the meaning God intended but whose linguistic expression is not divine speech as in the Qur'ān.

ḥadr: present

Hajj: the sacred pilgrimage of Islam obligatory on every mature Muslim once in their life.

ḥalāl: permitted, lawful according to Islamic *Sharīʿah.*

Ḥaqīqah, al-: reality of existence; ultimate truth.

ḥaqq: truth

Ḥaqq, al-: the Divine Reality, one of the 99 Divine Names.

ḥarām: forbidden, unlawful.

ḥasanāt: good deeds.

hāshā: God forbid.

ḥarf: (pl. *ḥurūf*) letter; Arabic root "edge."

Ḥawā: Eve.

ḥaywān: animal.

Hijrah: emigration.

ḥikmah: wisdom.

ḥujjah: proof.

hūwa: the pronoun "he,"made up of the Arabic letters *hāʿ* and *wāw*.

ʿibādu ʾl-Lāh: servants of God.

ʿifrīt: a type of *jinn*, huge and powerful.

iḥsān: doing good, "It is to worship God as though you see Him; for if you are not seeing Him, He sees you."

ikhlāṣ, al-: sincere devotion.

ilāh: (pl. *āliha*): idols or gods.

ilāhīyya: divinity.

ilhām: divine inspiration sent to *awlīyāullāh*.

ʿilm: knowledge, science.

ʿIlmu ʾl-Awrāq: Knowledge of Papers.

ʿIlmu ʾl-Adhwāq: Knowledge of Taste.

ʿIlmu ʾl-Hurūf: Science of Letters.

ʿilmu ʾl-kalām: scholastic theology.

ʿilmun ladunnī: divinely inspired knowledge.

Īmān: faith, belief.

imām: leader of congregational prayer; an advanced scholar followed by a large community.

insān: humanity; pupil of the eye.

insānu ʾl-kāmil, al-: the Perfect Man, *i.e.,* Prophet Muḥammad.

irādatullāh: the Will of God.

irshād: spiritual guidance.

ism: name.

isma-Llāh: name of God.

isrāʿ: night journey; used here in reference to the night journey of Prophet Muḥammad.

Isrāʿfīl: Archangel Rafael, in charge of blowing the Final Trumpet.

jalāl: majesty.

jamāl: beauty.

jamaʿa: group, congregation.

Jannah: Paradise.

jihād: to struggle in God's Path.

Jibrīl: Jibrīl, Archangel of revelation.

Jinn: a species of living beings created from fire, invisible to most humans. *Jinns* can be Muslim or non-Muslim.

Jumuʿah: Friday congregational prayer, held in a large mosque.

Kaʿbah: the first House of God, located in Mecca, Saudi Arabia to which pilgrimage is made and to which Muslims face in prayer.

kāfir: unbeliever.

Kalāmullāh al-Qadīm: lit., Allāh's Ancient Words, *viz.* the Holy Qur'ān.

kalīmat at-tawḥīd: lā ilāha illa-Llāh: "There is no god but Al-Lāh (the God)."

karāmat: miracles.

khalīfah: deputy.

Khāliq, al-: the Creator, one of 99 Divine Names.

khalq: Creation.

khāniqah: designated smaller place for worship other than a mosque; *zāwiyah.*

khuluq: conduct, manners.

Kirāmun Kātabīn: honored Scribe angels.

lā: no; not; not existent; the particle of negation.

lā ilāha illa-Llāh Muḥammadun Rasūlullāh: There is no deity except Allāh, Muḥammad is the Messenger of Allāh.

lām: Arabic letter ل.

al-Lawḥ al-Maḥfūẓ: the Preserved Tablets.

Laylat al-Isrā' wa 'l-Mi'rāj: the Night Journey and Ascension of Prophet Muḥammad to Jerusalem and to the Seven Heavens.

Madīnātu 'l-Munawwara: the Illuminated city; city of Prophet Muḥammad; Madinah.

mahr: dowry, given by the groom to the bride.

malakūt: Divine Kingdom.

Malik, al-: the Sovereign, a Divine Name.

Mālik: Archangel of Hell.

maqām: spiritual station; tomb of a prophet, messenger or saint.

ma'rifah: gnosis.

Māshā'Allāh: as Allāh Wills.

Mawlānā: lit. "Our master" or "our patron,"referring to an esteemed person.

maẓhar: place of disclosure.

miḥrāb: prayer niche.

Mikā'īl: Michael, Archangel of rain.

mīzān: the scale that weighs our deeds on Judgment Day.

mīm: Arabic letter م.

minbar: pulpit.

Miracles: of saints, known as *karamāt*; of prophets, known as *mu'jizāt* (lit., "That which renders powerless or helpless").

Mi'rāj: the ascension of Prophet Muḥammad from Jerusalem to the Seven Heavens.

Muḥammadun rasūlu 'l-Lāh: Muḥammad is the Messenger of God.

mulk, al-: the World of dominion.

Mu'min, al-: Guardian of Faith, one of the 99 Names of God.

mu'min: a believer.

munājāt: invocation to God in a very intimate form.

Munkir: one of the angels of the grave.

murīd: disciple, student, follower.

murshid: spiritual guide; *pir*.

mushāhadah: direct witnessing.

mushrik (pl. *mushrikūn*): idolater; polytheist.

muwwāḥid (pl. *muwāḥḥidūn*): those who affirm God's Oneness.

nabī: a prophet of God.

nafs: lower self, ego.

Nakīr: the other angel of the grave (with Munkir).

nūr: light.

Nūḥ: the prophet Noah.

Nūr, an-: "The Source of Light"; a Divine Name.

Qādir, al-: "The Powerful"; a Divine Name.

qalam, al-: the Pen.

qiblah: direction, specifically, the direction faced by Muslims during prayer and other worship, towards the Sacred House in Mecca.

Quddūs, al-: "The Holy One"; a Divine Name.

qurb: nearness

quṭb (pl. *aqṭāb*): axis or pole. Among the poles are:

Quṭbu 'l-Bilād: Pole of the Lands.

Quṭbu 'l-Irshād: Pole of Guidance.

Quṭbu 'l-Aqṭāb: Pole of Poles.

Quṭbu 'l-A'ẓam: Highest Pole.

Quṭbu 'l-Mutaṣarrif: Pole of Affairs.

al-quṭbīyyatu 'l-kubrā: the highest station of poleship.

Rabb, ar-: the Lord.

Raḥīm, ar-: "The Most Compassionate"; a Divine Name.

Raḥmān, ar-: "The All-Merciful"; a Divine Name.

raḥmā: mercy.

raka'at: one full set of prescribed motions in prayer. Each prayer consists of a one or more *raka'ats.*

Ramaḍān: the ninth month of the Islamic calendar; month of fasting.

Rasūl: a messenger of God.

Rasūlullāh: the Messenger of God, Muḥammad ﷺ.

Ra'ūf, ar-: "The Most Kind"; a Divine Name.

Razzāq, ar-: "The Provider"; a Divine Name.

rawḥānīyyah: spirituality; spiritual essence of something.

Riḍwān: Archangel of Paradise.

rizq: provision; sustenance.

rūḥ: spirit. *Ar-Rūḥ* is the name of a great angel.

rukū': bowing posture of the prayer.

ṣadaqah: voluntary charity.

Ṣaḥābah (sing., *ṣaḥābī*): Companions of the Prophet; the first Muslims.

ṣaḥīḥ: authentic; term certifying validity of a *ḥadīth* of the Prophet.

ṣāim: fasting person (pl. *ṣāimūn*)

sajda (pl. *sujūd*): prostration.

ṣalāt: ritual prayer, one of the five obligatory pillars of Islam. Also, to invoke blessing on the Prophet.

Ṣalāt an-Najāt: prayer of salvation, offered in the late hours of night.

ṣalawāt (sing. *ṣalāt*): invoking blessings and peace upon the Prophet.

salām: peace.

Salām, as-: "The Peaceful"; a Divine Name. *As-salāmu 'alaykum:* "Peace be upon you," the Islamic greeting.

Ṣamad, aṣ-: Self-Sufficient, upon whom creatures depend.

ṣawm, ṣiyām: fasting.

sayyi'āt: bad deeds; sins.

sayyid: leader; also, a descendant of Prophet Muḥammad.

Sayyīdinā: our master (fem. *sayyidunā; sayyidatunā*: our mistress).

shahādah: lit. testimony; the testimony of Islamic faith: *lā ilāha illa 'l-Lāh wa Muḥammadun rasūlu 'l-Lāh*, "There is no god but Allāh, the One God, and Muḥammad is the Messenger of God."

Shāh Naqshband: Muḥammad Bahauddin Shah Naqshband, a great eighth century *walī,* and the founder of the Naqshbandi Ṭarīqah.

shaykh: lit. "old Man," a religious guide, teacher; master of spiritual discipline.

shifā': cure.

shirk: polytheism, idolatry, ascribing partners to God

ṣiffāt: attributes; term referring to Divine Attributes.

Silsilat adh-dhahabīyya: "Golden Chain"of spiritual authority in Islam

sohbet (Arabic, *suḥbah*): association: the assembly or discourse of a shaykh.

subḥānAllāh: glory be to God.

sulṭān/sulṭānah: ruler, monarch.

Sulṭān al-Awlīyā: lit., "King of the *awlīyā*; the highest-ranking saint.

Sūnnah: Practices of Prophet Muḥammad in actions and words; what he did, said, recommended, or approved of in his Companions.

sūrah: a chapter of the Qur'ān; picture, image.

Sūratu 'l-Ikhlāṣ: Chapter 114 of Holy Qur'ān; the Chapter of Sincerity.

ṭabīb: doctor.

tābi'īn: the Successors, one generation after the Prophet's Companions.

tafsīr: to explain, expound, explicate, or interpret; technical term for commentary or exegesis of the Holy Qur'ān.

tajallī (pl. *tajallīyāt*): theophanies, God's self-disclosures, Divine Self-manifestation.

takbīr: lit. "Allāhu Akbar,"God is Great.

tarawīḥ: the special nightly prayers of Ramaḍān.

ṭarīqat/ṭarīqah: lit., way, road or path. An Islamic order or path of discipline and devotion under a guide or shaykh; Sufism.

taṣbīḥ: recitation glorifying or praising God.

tawāḍa': humbleness.

ṭawāf: the rite of circumambulating the Ka'bah while glorifying God during Hajj and 'Umra.

tawḥīd: unity; universal or primordial Islam, submission to God, as the sole Master of destiny and ultimate Reality.

Tawrāt: Torah

tayammum: Alternate ritual ablution performed in the absence of water.

ʿubūdīyyah: state of worshipfulness; servanthood.

ʿulamā (sing. *ʿālim*): scholars.

ʿulūmu ʾl-awwalīna wa ʾl-ākhirīn: Knowledge of the "Firsts" and the "Lasts" refers to the knowledge God poured into the heart of Prophet Muḥammad during his Holy Ascension to the Divine Presence.

ʿulūm al-Islāmī: Islamic religious sciences.

Ummāh: faith community, nation.

ʿUmar ibn al-Khaṭṭāb: an eminent Companion of Prophet Muḥammad and second caliph of Islam.

ʿumra: the minor pilgrimage to Mecca, performed at any time of the year.

ʿUthmān ibn ʿAffān: eminent Companion of the Prophet; his son-in-law and third caliph of Islam, renowned for compiling the Qur'ān.

walad: a child.

waladī: my child.

walāyah: proximity or closeness; sainthood.

walī (pl. *awlīyā*): saint, or "he who assists"; guardian; protector.

wasīlah: a means; holy station of Prophet Muḥammad as God's intermediary to grant supplications.

wāw: Arabic letter و

wujūd, al-: existence; "to find," "the act of finding," and "being found."

Yʿaqūb: Jacob; the prophet.

yamīn: the right hand; previously meant "oath."

Yawm al-ʿahdi waʾl-mīthāq: Day of Oath and Covenant, a heavenly event before this Life, when all souls of humanity were present to God, and He took from each the promise to accept His Sovereignty as Lord.

yawm al-qiyāmah: Day of Judgment.

Yūsuf: Joseph; the prophet.

zāwiyah: designated smaller place for worship other than a mosque; also *khāniqah.*

zīyāra: visitation to the grave of a prophet, a prophet's companion or a saint.

www.ingramcontent.com/pod-product-compliance
Lightning Source LLC
Chambersburg PA
CBHW030521080526
44586CB00011B/276
* 9 7 8 1 9 3 8 0 5 8 4 4 8 *